Tamm's Textbook

Warm-ups, online activities & homework shorts for use with Strayer's Ways of the World†

4th edition for the AP* Course (2019)
(Cover: Avid Readers)

Coursepak Series B   Independently made

David Tamm

*Advanced Placement program and AP are registered trademarks of the College Board, which was not involved in the production of, and does not endorse, this product.

†*Ways of the World: A Global History with Sources* 4th edition is written by Robert W. Strayer and Eric W. Nelson, and published by Bedford, Freeman & Worth. These parties were not involved in the production of, and do not endorse, this product.

Copyright © 2019

CONTENTS

This resource book is organized in the following way to integrate with *Ways of the World: A Global History+ 4th edition*:

Bell-ringers, warm ups, free-writes, Internet assignments, homework shorts and reviews by chapter

Addenda: Crash Course, Test Correction Forms, Movie Review Forms & More

LICENSING

Teachers are fully licensed by the copyright holder to copy individual worksheets out of this book in whatever quantity is needed for classroom use. Students may also order a full workbook as a consumable to write in throughout the year. These materials may not be distributed online in any form or shared with other teachers without expressed written permission.

"When given as a full workbook, this material improves content coherency, student enjoyment, parent appreciation, and teacher satisfaction."

-State of Florida Certified Teacher

"Sublimely usable."

"Great as weekly assignments"

"Spend one hour's pay, save 300 hours' planning time!"

"Rocket into the frontier of utility!"

"Textbooks are expensive. With this workbook, you get your money's worth!"

"They read the book, which is the main issue many have."

"Perfect if there's a substitute"

"Very progressive."

Suggested Year Plan

Most schools begin in late August or early September, leaving ~30 weeks to get through the book if you want any time for review before the exam. Some books, however, such as Stearns and Bentley, have more than ~30 chapters, making it hard to do 'a chapter a week' and still have time for review at the end. With 23 chapters, however, the Strayer text more than fits the bill scheduling-wise, especially if you want to enjoy the semblance of military-style class structure. What follows is the book's contents, and a blast from the past of how the AP World History course was ordered when it was young.

Strayer 4th ed. (2019)
Weekly Breakdown

McNeill's *A World History* (1967)
A Flashback

	Strayer	McNeill
Chapter 1	First People, First Farmers	In the Beginning
Chapter 2	First Civilizations	Diffusion of Civilization: First Phase
Chapter 3	State and Empire	Cosmopolitanism in the Middle East
Chapter 4	Culture and Religion	Definition of Indian Civilization
Chapter 5	Society and Inequality	Definition of Greek Civilization
Chapter 6	Commonalities and Variations	Definition of Chinese Civilization
Chapter 7	Commerce and Culture	Changes in the Barbarian World
Chapter 8	China and the World	Flowering of Greek Civilization
Chapter 9	The Worlds of Islam	Spread of Hellenistic Civilization
Chapter 10	The Worlds of Christendom	Flowering of Indian Civilization
Chapter 11	Pastoral Peoples	Barbarian Invasions and Civilized Response
Chapter 12	The Worlds of the 15th Century	Rise of Islam
Chapter 13	Political Transformations	China, India and Europe A.D. 600-1000
Chapter 14	Economic Transformations	Turkish and Mongol Conquests
Chapter 15	Cultural Transformations	Medieval Europe and Japan 1000-1500
Chapter 16	Atlantic Revolutions	Fringes of the Civilized World to 1500
Chapter 17	Revolutions of Industrialization	The Great Discoveries and Consequences
Chapter 18	Colonial Encounters in the East	Europe's Self-Transformation 1500-1648
Chapter 19	Empires in Collision	Europe's Outliers: Russia and America
Chapter 20	War and Revolution 1900-1950	Realm of Islam and Subject Communities
Chapter 21	Changing Global Landscape 1950-P	The Far East 1500-1750
Chapter 22	Technology, Economy, and Society	The Old Regime in Europe 1648-1789
Chapter 23	Demography, Culture, Environment	Asian Reactions to the Old Regime
Chapter 24	--	Industry's Transformation of the West
Chapter 25	--	Non-Western World since 1850
Chapter 26	--	Western World since 1917

Procedural Notes

Chapter 1: First Peoples, First Farmers

1 hr. means one class period
+Standalone means no technology required

Big History (1 pg., 15 min.): In class standalone+ warm-up. Introduce Big History, which some schools and textbooks refer to more than others, by having students look for the essential subject of each particular 'event' in the story of cosmic and social evolution.

Generations (1 pg., 15 min.): In class standalone warm-up. Get students to think in terms of generational movement through time with this quick warm-up.

Prehistoric Art Show (1 pg., 40 min.): Requires Internet connection for the image searches. If there is no internet, you can pull up the images on the screen and students can have 2-5 min to make their own 'interpretation of it. Talk about honoring the animal, good luck in childbirth and family, and *why* prehistoric people were compelled to make this art.

Chapter 2: First Civilizations

Mansplainin' World History? (1 pg., 15 min.): In class standalone warm-up. Introduce the historical discussion on sexual inequality and patriarchy by looking at the trend toward neutralizing traditionally male and Christian historical terminology such as 'mankind' vs 'humankind' and B.C. / A.D. vs. BCE / CE.

His-Story (1 pg., 15 min.): Jigsaw with textbook required. Each student gets a letter, either handed to them or that they pick out of a hat. They then 'do their part' of the jigsaw by going to the index and counting up all the male and female names under their letter. Be sure to emphasize they must be careful to not mistake some of the more exotic names for other kinds of nouns, which has certainly happened. Mozi is a Chinese male name, for example, but it might be confused for the name of a landform etc. Students then report and tabulate up on the board how many were in their their letter, and we total it up. The skew will be clear.

Ancient Law (1 pg., 20 min.) In class standalone. Students look at Hammurabi's code and compare it to the Mosaic code. Why do people obey? Out of fear of getting caught, out of a sense of community standards of legality, or because a higher ethical principle or lesson is internalized by them, and which code reflects which perspective?

Pyramid! (1 pg., 45 min.): In class on screen or at home online. Video Search: **David Macaulay Pyramid**. This World History video classic can be watched in a short way, by only watching the four or so animated segments, or in a long way by just letting it go. Well worth it either way. The answer form can be answered in full by the animated segments, however, in the interests of time. The Great Pyramid of Khufu is built by the Egyptians.

Chapter 3: State and Empire

The Oracle (2 pg., 20 min.): In class standalone warm-up or at home. Students practice lifting specific parts of 11 different short passages about instances the Oracle of Delphi was visited by enterprising people interested in getting a handle on future events. Concept of the self-fulfilling prophecy is looked at through the stories.

Greek Terms Used in English (3 pgs., 30 min.): In class standalone warm-up or at home. This is a good one for students to see a bit of the Hellenic language's effect on English words used all the time, by using inductive reasoning to discern the meaning of common Greek terms, prefixes and suffixes, from two examples.

Latin Terms in English (2 pgs., 20 min.): In class standalone warm-up or at home. With this, students will mark Latin terms they have used or already know about, which is hopefully a few at least, and try to make connections with ones that are new to them.

Emperors' Matrix (1 pg., 15 min.): This could be done in class by guessing, online as an assignment (in which case it would take a bit longer) or sent home for homework. Students take the most famous emperors, some of which are required for the curriculum and some not, but all with their place in the overall story of imperial rise, Pax Romana, decline, Christian rebirth, and continued decline and collapse.

Conrad-Demarest Model (1 pg., 15 min.): In class as a discussion or at home with a look toward discussing it. Allows students to compare Roman, Han and Gupta empires and their decline, according to the Conrad-Demarest model's 'symptoms'.

The Cycle of Empire (1 pg., 25 min.): In class on screen or at home on computer. If you do this one in class on screen as a warm up and discussion, then the teacher should go to the *Wikipedia* page on Thomas Cole, to the Cycle of Empire painting series by him. Save the paintings in order to your desktop, then present them one by one. They are Romantic era paintings by an American painter, and you can remind students how in early America the Neo-Classical style of Washington DC and the Founders was easing into the Romantic era, and that these paintings have classical rise and collapse as their theme.

Chapter 4: Culture and Religion

The Tao of Pooh (1 pg., 20 min.): In class standalone warm-up or at home online. If you do this one In class, you can show the Slideshare called *The Tao of Winnie the Pooh* and/or one of the short *Tao of Pooh* analysis videos, but preview them for the right one. You can also do an image search for *Tao of Pooh,* locate the yellow or multicolored character traits chart, and put it up on the screen. Students can do these at home too.

Secret Knowledge: Metaphors (1 pg., 20 min.): In class standalone warm-up or at home. There are threads between cultures and languages that speak of certain life-moments or situations that are common for people to go through no matter what country you live in. This explores the meaning in metaphors and proverbs, what used to be called 'peasant wisdom.' A lot we get from a Latin origin, then they change slightly in diffusion so like the Latin based languages, they appear in slightly different forms and stories depending on the country.

Who Mourns for Adonais? (1 pg., 1 hr.): In class all period or at home. It is **Season 2, Episode 2**, available on *Netflix* and *Hulu Plus*, among other places. In this *Star Trek* episode, written to reflect the 1960s notion that human progress through the historical timeline means we 'outgrow' some of the myths and legends of the past, the crew visits a planet where they encounter the Greek god Apollo. He is happy to see them and informs them that the Olympian gods were real! They were great and tall and could change form, and they came to Earth 3,000 years ago from that place the earthlings had just now 'grown up' enough to have come and found themselves. Interesting concept, good scifi (and would explain a lot too) ☺. In the episode, Apollo gets to be a bully because he wants his old status back. He wants the crew to be 'his people,' the Hellenes, again. But things don't turn out his way, and in the end, he comes to understand that the humans had indeed 'progressed beyond' needing the Olympians (who are a metaphor for our stories, myths and legends). Or have we?

Hellenic Philosophy: The Beginning of Reason (2 pgs., 30 min.): In class standalone warm-up or at home. Introduce philosophy, thought, and its effect on culture and science with these eight snippets followed by a short reading comprehension and extension response.

Hellenic Philosophy: Socrates (2 pgs., 30 min.): In class standalone warm-up or at home. Similar to the previous warm-up, and extending from it, this one focuses on the role of Socrates in beginning what used to be called the 'Great Conversation,' and extending the conversation from the physical to the ethical. Since Plato, Aristotle and Alexander, as well as the Hellenistic schools (except the Epicureans), the Neo-Platonists, Scholasticism and every school clear through to modern empirical science all find roots in Socrates, it is good to establish him as the 'first poster' in the biggest thread that's ever been posted.

Weeks and Days (1 pg., 20 min.): In class standalone warm-up or at home. Since our culture still uses the Greco-Roman days of the week and months of the year, this is a good introduction to the effects of Greco-Roman culture on our own. A whimsical warm up to see cultural diffusion in action.

Chapter 5: Society and Inequality

A Socialist Emperor? (1 pg., 20 min.): In class standalone warm-up. Introduce individualism vs. communitarianism and the dynamic between them with a warm up concerning Wang Mang, a proto-socialist. Explore the benefits and dangers of the philosophy, still with us and still hotly debated, by giving students the emperor's decision-making powers over 'who gets what' in a community, then learning a few lessons from it.

Roman City! (1 pg., 45 min.): In class on screen or at home online. Video Search: **David Macaulay Roman City**. This World History video classic can be watched in a short way, by only watching the four or so animated segments, or in a long way by just letting it go. Well worth it either way. The answer form can be answered in full by the animated segments, however, in the interests of time. A Roman city is built in conquered Gaul.

Arranged Marriages – Pro and Con (1 pg., 15 min.): In this chapter on India's caste system, the issue of arranged marriages comes up, which seems anathema to students in the modern West. However, there was a rationale for it. A nice discussion can be had on why people and families submit to arranged marriages, instead of 'love' between two people that springs from their knowing each other more and more. In this short assignment, students can reflect on why people get married, and if they are in psych, the Maslow hierarchy of needs will be familiar to them. What levels does marriage fulfill?

Media: Roman Places (2 pgs., 30 min.): On computer in school or at home. This image-based assignment is meant for students to do in about half a class period, but it may take more depending on log in times etc. with the computer. It has some Roman and Christianity questions and summaries.

Chapter 6: Commonalities and Variations: Africa, the Americas and Oceania

African Terms in English (1 pg., 15 min.): In class standalone warm-up or at home. English has a variety of African language terms as well- from the Niger-Congo, Nilotic and Khoisan families. Now in this warm-up, students can be introduced to terms we use from these languages. Good one to introduce the chapter with.

Great Clips: Lalibela / Mansa Musa (1 pg., 20 min.): In class on screen or at home online. These two segments *Video Search*: <u>CNN Millennium 12th century</u> (it is about 17:15 min. into the full episode for the first one), then *Video Search*: <u>CNN Millennium 14th century</u> (it is about 8:15 min. in) focus on East Africa and West Africa. First we head to Axum. We see a syncretic Christianity there, partly due to Lalibela's political designs and partly because it was absolutely disconnected from Europe. With a caveat. It is possible the legend of Prester John, which inspired explorers in the approaching era to go forth and find the 'lost Christian kingdom,' just as Columbus was- also- motivated by finding 'Eden,' is based on Axum/Ethiopia, a real life 'lost kingdom.' Next it's to Africa's gold-salt trade in Mali (Ch. 7), to see the Timbuktu, Mansa Musa's adoption of Islam, and the Hajj he took.

America Before Columbus (2 pgs., 30 min.): In school on the screen (teacher-guided), or with each student on their own computer, or at home. This basic warm-up to Pre-Columbian Mesoamerica and North America is located at http://antarcticaedu.com/20hst.htm. See the ceremonial centers, look at the cultural continuities.

Chapter 7: Commerce and Culture, 600-1450

Silk Road Trip (1 pg., 30 min.): In class on screen (teacher led), in class on individual computers, or at home on computer. This URL, located at http://Antarcticaedu.com/12hstsilk.htm, has a full tour from east to west along the world's longest road(s). Students note the peoples along the route and see their lifestyle, back then and today.

Diseases in History (2 pgs., 15 min.): In class standalone warm-up or at home. This can be done in conjunction with viewing the Crash Course World History Diseases episode, or with a lesson on the diffusion of things on the Silk Road.

Revenge of Phase 1? (1 pg., 15 min.): In class standalone warm-up or at home. This can be done in conjunction with viewing the Crash Course World History Diseases episode as well, or with a lesson on the diffusion of things on the Silk Road as well, but it hits closer to home because these are current day statistics.

Chapter 8: China and the World

Dynasties of China (1 pg., 20 min.). In class standalone or at home with textbook. Students name the dynasties of Chinese history from Xia to the present, and place them on a timeline. They also identify the philosophies that emerged from the Warring States period.

Chinese Provinces (1 pg. 20 min.) In class standalone. Using a translation guide provided on the sheet, students figure out what the names of China's provinces actually mean. They are often flowery, and it is a good time to talk about figurative language and how imagery is used in the names. Compared with the names of U.S. states, many of which are Indian names, China's provinces tend to be named after natural features of the landscape. Ideally, you can do an image search for "Map of Chinese Provinces Blank" and students can use some time to label them.

Chapter 9: The Worlds of Islam

Arabic Terms in English (2 pgs., 20 min.): In class standalone warm-up or at home. Introduce the Arab world with words adopted in English from Arabic, some of which may come as a surprise. Then talk about the Bedouins...

Largest Empires in History (1 pg., 15 min.): In class standalone warm-up or at home. Do this one on the day you are talking about the expansion of the Islamic Caliphate. It does some bringing-in of various empires in various chapters and compares their size and timeframe on a single graph. You could have students use different colors for each, with or without labeling, or all the same colors with labeling.

The Hajj (1 pg., 30 min.) – In class on the screen or at home. This is a multimedia response form for a video. There are many documentaries on the Hajj and Mecca, but this one is special because it is pre-9/11 and perhaps less political than others, and it is "the first time" an outside news agency from America was allowed in the Great Mosque. Everything is explained by the American news reporter, an American who is a convert to Islam, giving him access to Mecca. Video Search: _Hajj ABC News_.

Star Names (1 pg., 15 min.): In class standalone warm-up or at home. Naming bright stars was a multicultural enterprise. Greek, Roman and Arab names were adapted into English, so we can trace the etymology a bit by looking into those languages.

Islam-Related Terms (1 pg., 15 min.) In class standalone warm-up or at home. Students match the terms.

Chapter 10: The Worlds of Christendom

Cyrillic Alphabet (1 pg., 30 min.): In class with internet or an image of the Russian alphabet on a screen. Or at home. Students research what Cyrillic characters look like, write them, and transliterate cities and names from Cyrillic to English. They also have a bit of fun writing their own name in Cyrillic.

Medieval Philosophy (1 pg., 25 min.): In class standalone warm-up or at home. Get a glimpse into the Medieval mind by looking at the basic notions of Agustine, Late Antiquity's foremost philosopher, the post-collapse philosopher Boethius, the Silk Road philosopher Avicenna, St. Anselm of Canterbury who wrote in the time of William the Conqueror, the qadi Averroes, Moses Maimonides the Jewish intellectual from Alexandria, and finally Thomas Aquinas the Scholastic philosopher. As the last three of these are 1) Muslim, 2) Jewish and 3) Christian, Rabbi Jonathan Sacks of Great Britain argued in _The Dignity of Difference_ (1998) that they provide an example for us of intercultural exchange and mutual respect. In fact, Video Search: _Rabbi Jonathan Sacks Richard Dawkins debate_ for perhaps the most cogent debate to watch in looking at theism vs. atheism.

Slavic Terms Used in English (1 pg., 15 min.): In class standalone warm-up or at home. English has a variety of Slavic language terms as well. Students can be introduced to the Russian history part of this chapter by familiarizing themselves with some of them, while others they probably know, and since it is in a many answer multiple-choice format, it gives them an opportunity to deduce ones they don't, as in the Arab terms warm-up.

Central European Sights (1 pg., 15 min.): In class on screen or at home online. If done in class, the teacher should play three five minute clips: _Expedia Prague, Rick Steves Budapest_ and _Rick Steves Krakow_. In this chapter, Central Europe is touched on as a place where Christianity arrived in the 8th-11th centuries, via Cyril and Methodius, Adalbert, and others. The cultures built here over the next thousand years are reflected in the monuments in the historic cities of the region, and students can play scavenger hunt for a few minutes.

Cathedral! (1 pg., 45 min.): In class on screen or at home online. Video Search: **David Macaulay Cathedral**. This world history video classic can be watched in a short way by only watching the four or so animated segments, or in a long way by just letting it go. Well worth it either way. The answer form can be answered in full by the animated segments, however, in the interests of time. They build an Gothic cathedral in France.

Vikings (1 pg., 15 min.): In class with an atlas or a map on the screen. To accompany this one, a blank map of Europe with the Mediterranean on it, and with Iceland on it, should be printed out and copied on the back. Students will do a little geography and mapping of the routes the Vikings visited, labelling the impact they had in those places.

Comparisons: Byzantine and Latin Christendom (1 pg., 15 min.): In class standalone warm-up or homework. This vocab review (or introduction) can be used anytime during the chapter to reinforce some of the terminology and see how both Medieval civilizations had many of the same traits, but not all the same by any means.

Surnames (1 pg., 25 min.): In class with computer access for each student or at home online. What is a last name? What do our last names actually mean? What do they tell us about our origins? This is another one that is more to spark interest in connecting ourselves to the curriculum, but it also has value in that it can reveal what kinds of jobs our ancestors had, where they came from, and, through heraldry, what they believed was important.

Castle! (1 pg., 45 min.): In class on screen or at home online. Video Search: ***David Macaulay Castle***. This world history video classic can be watched in a short way by only watching the four or so animated segments, or in a long way by just letting it go. Well worth it either way. The answer form can be answered in full by the animated segments, however, in the interests of time. They build an Edwardian castle in Wales to secure the territory.

Castles Grand (1 pg., 30 min.): In class with computer access for each student or at home online. Medieval castles represent the most famous secular architecture of the time, from Windsor to the Crusader castles of the Levant. With this warm-up, students go to the URL: *http://antarcticaedu.com/19hstcastles.htm* for a rich tour through the famous ones, with nice images to accompany them. They look at some of the famous events that took place in and around them. The AP curriculum doesn't focus much on art or architecture, but if they are taking AP World, they aren't taking on-level World, in all probability. This is just a way to see something that isn't an analysis of labor systems but still holds value in the fields of political organization and technological change.

Chapter 11: Pastoral Peoples on the Global Stage

Central Asian Terms in English (1 pg., 15 min.): In class standalone warm-up or at home. English has a variety of Altaic (Turkic) and Mongol-language terms as well. But who would know that? Now in this warm-up, students can be introduced to the Nomadic Empires part of this chapter by familiarizing themselves with some of the Central Asian heritage as reflected in the English language, as with the Slavic and Arabic terms earlier.

Great Clips: Genghis Khan / Pax Mongolica (1 pg., 20 min.): In class on screen or at home online. This Courspak doesn't have multimedia answer forms for each CNN Millennium segment, only for segments that are particularly relevant to the curriculum, such as these two: *Video Search*: *CNN Millennium 13th century* (it is about 1 min. into the full episode for the first one), then *Video Search*: *CNN Millennium 13th century* (it is about 13 min. in). This program has always been highly recommended for the AP World History class since its inception, which was in 2001, two years after this series was first shown on CNN in 1999 to celebrate the "millennium". Finding the segments is easy- just move the cursor forward until you see the Earth zooming around to a new region.

Great Clips: Yuan Dynasty China / Tamerlane's Empire (1 pg., 20 min.): In class on screen or at home online. These two segments: *Video Search*: *CNN Millennium 13th century* (it is about 20 min. into the full episode for the first one), then *Video Search*: *CNN Millennium 14th century* (it is about 18 min. in) focus on China when the Mongols ruled it. The second clip is about the last great Central Asian empire, that of Timur. Their time in the sun having elapsed, these nomadic empires are about to be replaced by the rising power of the Gunpowder Empires.

Chapter 12: The Worlds of the 15th Century

Renaissance Literature (1 pg., 20 min.): In class (guessing), in school on a computer for each student, or at home. The site for this is http://hudsonfla.com/litrenaissance.htm - or any encyclopedia would work as well.

Zheng He's Treasure Ships / Renaissance Fashions / Russian Empire (1 pg., 30 min.): There are three segments this time. *Video Search*: *CNN Millennium 15th century* (the first is about 2 min. into the full episode), then: *CNN Millennium 15th century* (the second is right after the first, about 10:30 min. in), while for the third: *CNN Millennium 16th century* (about 15 min in). The focus of the first is Zheng He, who makes a major trip across the Indian Ocean, then is shut down by his own Ming government. Just as China ceases reaching out, Europe begins its awakening in the second clip, triggered in part by the return of Venetian and Genoese ships from the Levant and Egypt. Focus here is on the princely families of Italy and their sponsorship of art and fashion. The third looks at the Ivans (Eee-vahns) of Russia and the transition from Mongol Yoke to Muscovy to rising Russian Empire.

Great Clips: Mehmed II and the Ottomans / Akbar and the Mughals (1 pg., 20 min.): In class on screen or at home online. There are two segments. *Video Search*: *CNN Millennium 15th century* (the first is about 25 min. into the full episode). For the second, *Video Search*: *CNN Millennium 16th century* (about 28 min. in). The focus of the first is the Turkish victory over Byzantium in 1453, and the subsequent growth of Ottoman power throughout the rest of the century and through the 16th century. Discussion of Ottoman trade routes fits right in. The second looks at Babur's conquest of India and the establishment of Mughal rule, the culture shock of Muslim values governing a Hindu society, and the syncretic Divine Faith of Akbar. Nothing about Jahan and the Taj, however.

New Horizons Vocab Review (1 pg., 15 min.): In class standalone warm-up or at home. This wide-ranging chapter goes from China to Italy to Russia and does thematic twists and turns. It has a coherency, but like the Silk Road chapter, it is broad in its focus, which seems a bit of a contradiction in terms. This vocab review will help students keep straight the foci of the chapter.

Chapter 13: Political Transformations: Empires and Encounters

Explorers' Matrix (2 pg., 1 hr.): Can be done in school if students have individual computers, or at home. This thematic, cross-period 'warm-up' could be assigned as a way to open the chapter and have students do the work of disentangling all the names and significances. Handy chart to keep as well, for the next few chapters.

First Around the World? (1 pg., 1 hr.): On screen in class or at home online. The spirit of adventure that accompanied the sailors as they searched for silver and gold and new lands is apparent in this recreation of Magellan's voyage. *Video Search*: <u>Magellan Voyages of Discovery: Circumnavigation</u>. It features a modern-day British mountain climber narrating a trip around the world via the route of Magellan, alongside an actual descendent of Magellan himself. On a boat actually traveling around the world, they speak of the navigational difficulties, the hunger, the thirst, the scurvy, the death of Magellan along the way, the in-fighting, etc.

Crash Course World History #23: The Columbian Exchange (1 pg., 15 min.): In class on screen or at home online. Students look at John Green's vlog about the various benefits and harmful effects of the great movement of animals, plants, peoples and diseases across the continents, then at the bottom, chart out the book's (or Internet's) graphic on which critters, seeds, peeps and little nasties went where.

Chapter 14: Economic Transformations: Commerce and Consequence

Great Clips: Jamestown / Brazilian Slavery and Sugarcane (1 pg., 20 min.): In class on screen or at home online. There are two segments this time. *Video Search*: <u>CNN Millennium 17th century</u> (the first is about 8 min. into the full episode). *Video Search*: <u>CNN Millennium 17th century</u> (the second is right after the first, about 18 min. in). The focus of the first is the founding of the Jamestown colony on the shores of Virginia, and the opening of the North American continent to European migration and economic activity. The second clip is on what was happening in Brazil in the same century, focusing on the process of sugarcane growing and the harsh conditions endured by the African slaves who filled the planters' labor quotas.

Labor Systems (1 pg., 20 min.): In class standalone warm-up or at home. This labor systems matchup spans the curriculum from Egypt to the present day. Many of these systems have not been studied yet, but students can practice inferring and using context clues. A good discussion starter when looking at the ubiquity of systems of slavery and servitude, and yet careful to discern important contrasts (temporary vs. permanent, etc.).

Piracy on the Spanish Main (2 pgs., 45 min.): In class on screen or at home online. Video search for the History Channel documentary *True Caribbean Pirates*. Show the whole thing. It is a good documentary on what piracy was really like, so no Davy Jones' Locker or peg legs.

How to Pirate Sources (1pg., 45 min.). Requires Internet. This assignment takes a topic people like, pirates, and has students cite online sources. First, they learn a bit about some actual pirates, then research a particular one that interests them. The citations are the important part, at the end.

Inca Gold (or Silver) (1 pg., 25 min.). In class on screen or at home. Youtube *Ascent of Money Niall Ferguson Episode 1 Bullion to Bubbles*. Play the first 20 min. He visits Potosí in Bolivia, where the Spanish mined so much silver that they flooded the world market and caused inflation. Ask students about the dangers of hyperinflation.

Chapter 15: Cultural Transformations: Religion and Science

Christian Denominations (1 pg., 15 min.): In class standalone warm-up or at home. Use this quick one to introduce the chronology of the Reformation and get students to think about *why* there are so many different denominational churches in your community.

Henry VIII: The Tyrant King? (1 pg., 1 hr.): In class on screen or at home online. This documentary is good because it provides the rationale behind "off with her head" (if you can ever justify that) and shows Henry VIII, much vilified and certainly deservedly so... to a point... as a ruler confronted with a large number of serious issues to deal with all at the same time. Gives students a glimpse into the intrigue of the English court, to the point where some students have actually got really into the dynasties on their own because of it. *Video Search*: Henry VIII the Most Iconic King of English History.

A New Worldview (1 pg., 1 hr.): In class on screen or at home online. This History Channel program is called *The Universe,* and is its best episode, in that they have all the best astronomers on and the budget must have been a lot higher. It goes into the whole history of our worldview. Thus, this is definitely cross-periodization, with stops all the way from Ch. 10 to Ch. 38. The focus, however, is on the Scientific Revolution in Ch. 23.

Newton's Discovery (1 pg., 15 min.): In class on screen or at home online. This is an animated clip from Cosmos, the Neil Degrasse Tyson version. You may find it by video searching: *Cosmos Ep. 3: When Knowledge Conquered Fear*. Go directly to 17 min. in where Tyson is standing out in front of a London coffeehouse, and pause it, then when everyone is ready, play from there. The next 12 or so minutes are devoted to Isaac Newton.

The Age of Reason (1 pg., 20 min.): In class standalone warm-up or at home. This is a transition into the political change part of the chapter, when Absolutism is discussed on the way to the stirrings of the Enlightenment at chapter's conclusion. Students are encouraged to think about the purpose of government, and how the 'Quest for Order' at the beginning of civilization is really an ongoing thing, something that never really ends. The spectrum between order and freedom, and where communities of people choose to be, could be mentioned with this warm-up. At the end of it, students sketch a box, and on each side they place agents of influence over their behaviors and beliefs. This is to get some insight into Locke's 'Blank Slate' theory of environment-based human malleability.

Governing Strategies (1 pg., 15 min.): In class standalone warm-up or at home. This is a good one for talking about Absolutism's variety of faces. One such face is shown when there is a benevolent king and people feel glad and proud of their tradition, *their way* of having a monarch, but another occurs when there is a malevolent king and people become agitated against him, and he loses legitimacy, whereby *the stick* becomes the new way he enforces his legitimacy. For Enlightenment societies, the key is the consent of the governed, gained by entrance into the *social contract*. The state then loses legitimacy only when the citizens cease to believe in the contact, lose their common public sympathy, and pull out of it. Whether that is happening in the democracies of our day is something to think about, but there does seem to be a critical mass that when reached, fast-forwards social disintegration. Traditional societies come in one of two kinds: they may be tribal, governed by chieftains, probably without a constitution, and creedal, governed by religious or culture-based principles. In both cases, the law is handed down by a sovereign force, a chief, a king, or a god. *Nationalism* is a way for the state to have the loyalty of a specific group of people who feel part of the national community. Such people will not need to be conscripted into the military to fight for their community, they will do it voluntarily. While helpful, there need not be a written 'constitution', because people identify themselves as one with the community, and the constitution of the community resides inside them. A creed can and usually is part of the community, but it is within the context of the national community that people place their primary identity, and the creed is only one- albeit important- factor by which the community defines itself. The people themselves, and no extraneous cultural influence, form its core.

Word Project Builder (1 pg., 40 min.): With computer lab equipped with printer and MS Word. Copy the page, cut it into thirds and give each student one of the thirds. They all have the same directions. The students will practice making a Word document report on Renaissance-era events and happenings. If you don't have a printer, they can email it to the teacher.

Chapter 16: Atlantic Revolutions, Global Echoes

Absolutely Awesome! and Enlightenment Story (2 pgs., 30 min.): In class standalone warm-up or at home. This is a good way to contrast Absolutism and Enlightenment. First, students straighten out the names and places associated with Absolutism via word bank, then use another word bank to get a preview of the Enlightenment ideas and concepts, which are hinted on in this chapter at the very end, and will soon return in force.

American History Diagnostic Test (1 pg., 15 min.): In class on screen or at home online. Many of these questions will seem bizarre to your more adept students, for others they will be a thing to ponder. Your students may be agitated by the repetition, but tell them it will all make sense soon and to go with it. Then show them the 6 min. clip: *Mark Dice Fourth of July*. Tell them that now they know what they don't want to be when they grow up, and to pay extra special attention to this chapter.

In Congress, July 4, 1776 (2 pgs., 20 min.): In class standalone warm-up or at home. Small 'u' in United States? How could Jefferson have made such a huge basic grammar error at the very top of such an important document? In this warm-up, students can think about political change in the context of 1) American existence as colonies (to 1776), 2) As states which are sovereign and 'united' only by confederacy with each other (1776-1787), 3) As states which are truly united, and in acceptance of new political ties that bind, under Constitutional ratification (1787-on). Students can think about such ties as they read through the Declaration, and answer the questions as they go. It is part reading comp., part text analysis and part historical context.

Got Rights? Prove it! (2 pgs., 15 min.): In class standalone warm-up or at home. On one side is the Bill of Rights. On the other is a list of examples of violations of one or more of the amendments. While there isn't that much time in World History class for the classic documents, this brings Jefferson's shield of the citizen home to students' daily lives, and may be good for morale in that respect.

Phases of the French Revolution (1 pg., 20 min.): In class standalone or at home. This matching has 27 terms from a difficult part of this chapter, which can help reinforce chronology. Some terms might not be actual vocab words, and it might be a good idea to encourage students to identify those which are and those which are not.

Text Analysis: American Revolutionary Songs (2 pgs., 45 min.): In class on screen or at home online. If done in school, it would be best to download to desktop the following songs: *The Liberty Song, Yankee Doodle, The Revolutionary Alphabet, My Country Tis of Thee, The Star Spangled Banner, and America the Beautiful.* Good bets are to search them like this: <u>American Revolutionary Song: The Liberty Song</u>. <u>Yankee Doodle (American Patriotic Song)</u>, <u>American Revolution Song: The Revolutionary Alphabet</u>, <u>My Country Tis of Thee National Cathedral</u>, <u>Star Spangled Banner Jim Cornelison</u>, <u>America the Beautiful Neil Armstrong Memorial Service</u>. When ready, look at the lyrics with students first, then play the song. The questions will be answered in turn.

Text Analysis: European National Songs (2 pgs., 30 min.): In class on screen or at home online. If done in school, it would be best to download the following songs from Youtube: *God Save the Queen* (<u>God Save the Queen Royal Wedding</u>) This is one where Elizabeth II is in attendance, which is important, because when the camera pans past her, she is the only one *not* singing. She doesn't ever sing it, it is sung to her, which is something students might find interesting, since *The Star Spangled Banner* is sung by the president just like anyone else. *Rule Britannia* (<u>Rule Britannia Proms 2012</u>). *The Song of Marseille* (<u>La Marseillaise Roberto Alagna</u>). *Song of Germany* (<u>Deutschland Uber Alles stewardess</u>). This latter is tricky, since the first two verses were eliminated since WWII, and thus no one actually sings the original song- except by mistake (which has happened, much to the embarrassment of the athletes in the country that made the 'oops'), or on TV shows. The stewardess who in this clip sings the first verse does a good job, and in the episode it was a purposeful slight, because she sang it to a German guy who was her boyfriend and they were having an argument etc. (she was French) and he is visibly uncomfortable. After that, however, you can play the song as it is played today. <u>German Anthem World Cup 2010</u> is a good rendition because the German players on the German team are visibly singing it, while the players who are not German are kind of… not. And the largely South African fans are booing the anthem. That might be a discussion point with students if you talk about how some American athletes don't stand for *The Star Spangled Banner*. When all are downloaded and ready, look at the lyrics with students, then play the songs. They will answer the questions in turn.

The Count of Monte Cristo (1 pg., 2 hrs.): In class at the end of a quarter, semester or year. Or worked in somehow. If you do show a whole movie, this is a perfect one to go with the Napoleonic era. Buy or download the Jim Caviezel 2002 version. Great costumes, excellent good/evil dynamic, plot twists and turns, all the things that made the original Alexander Dumas book so famous. The main thing will be for students to look at each of the characters in the movie and judge their motivation. Why do they do the things they do? Why do any of us?

Casta Culture (1 pg., 15 min.): In class standalone warm-up or at home. This looks at independent Latin America, its ethnic conflict and political tribulations- which are still major issues in the region today.

Crash Course World History #31: Revolutions in Latin America (1 pg., 15 min.): In class on screen or at home online. Students look at John Green's vlog about the social and political changes that swept Latin America in the early-19th century. He looks at the *peninsulares* vs. *criollos* issue, the ethnic issue and the attempt at unity under Bolivar, and winds up with a big lesson at the end- that the Latin American movements were not very socially revolutionary at all, but they did result in political independence. An exception to the former would be Haiti, which was socially revolutionary, but it is not treated in this segment. It has a whole other episode, #30.

Chapter 17: Revolutions of Industrialization

Mill! (1 pg., 45 min.): In class on screen or at home online. Video Search: ***David Macaulay Mill***. This is the newest, latest and probably, unfortunately, the last in the David Macaulay history video series. It can be watched in a short way by only watching only the four or so animated segments, or in a long way by just letting it go, just like the others. Well worth it either way. The answer form can be answered in full by the animated segments, however, in the interests of time. In the program, British immigrants to America build a mill in Rhode Island, and the inner workings of how it operates are shown.

Industrial Manchester Game (2 pgs., 1 hr.): In class standalone. A class period must be devoted to this, it is actually an adaptation of the AP vocab curriculum to an existing game, first made by a creative but nameless teacher ~30 years ago. The narrator (teacher), speaks out the events in each round, and the students sketch out what they hear. In the game as modified, a century and a half of transformation comes alive round-by-round. In the original game, which can be found online under the search term *The Urban Game,* there are some recommendations as to what a factory should look like, etc. basically, you can make up whatever you want them to look like, put it on the board, and have the students use it as a guide. A factory is a box with a couple big windows and a smokestack on the side, with some filth puffing out. Cottages are the size of your pinky fingernail. Tenement houses should be bigger than them. Manchester grows and becomes wild looking by the end, like in real life. There was little planning… like in real life. At the end, you might vote on an artistic winner.

Inventions Flowchart (1 pg., 15 min.): In class standalone warm-up or at home. If there's one thing students can't get enough of, its technology. So, technological change being a focus in this chapter (especially the macro-change from premodern to modern, with all the social change that accompanied it), this a fun warm-up to get students thinking chronologically. It asks them to follow the threads of a single type of technology, such as the playing back of recorded sound, and group them in the right eras. There may be more than one in a single era.

Social Criticism in Art: Hogarth (1 pg., 30 min.): In class with a computer for each student or at home online. Good to introduce with the effects of industry on the working poor, or with 19th century urbanization. Students image search William Hogarth's paintings where he showed not the soaring visions of Michelangelo's heaven or the majestic scenes of Romantic era nature, but the gritty reality of urban life in London's seedy district. These are some of the most famous paintings in social history, whose message is as needed today as it was then: "Don't get caught up in bad stuff. Don't believe the lies. Practice some moderation."

Artists Take On Substance Abuse (2 pgs., 30 min.): In class with a computer for each student or at home online. A good companion to the previous Hogarth multimedia response, this will look further into how people's lives are affected by those around them who are unwilling or unable to control their addiction. The hopelessness, the despair, the devotion to loved ones despite their issues of dependency, all of it comes out in these poignant works of Industrial age social art, and students will likely appreciate it.

Traditional or Modern? (1 pg., 15 min.): In class standalone warm-up or at home. With industry came modernity, and with modernity came big social change. This chapter is a good moment to lurch into modernity in the class, by gauging what it actually means to be 'modern'. Students select one of two, and may not get all of them the first time around, despite 'being' modern. Kind of like not being able to see the Milky Way Galaxy because we are in it.

Great Clips: Industrial Britain / Industrial Working Life (1 pg., 20 min.): In class on screen or at home online. There are two segments. *Video Search*: CNN Millennium 19th century (the first is about 1 min. into the full episode). For the second, *Video Search*: CNN Millennium 19th century (it is about 34 min. in). The focus of the first looks at the inventions that changed society, such as the railroad, and how they were reflected in the Romantic era of art. Then it looks at how Brunel built mighty bridges and tunnels, etc. The second clip is about social issues related to the effects of mechanized work on people's bodies and spirits. Life by clockwork. Punch-in, punch-out, Repetition. Little social mobility. Ultimately, it links industry with getting nations prepared for competition.

The Political Compass (2 pgs., 30 min.): In class standalone warm-up or at home. Better done in school, however, because some explanation of the two values scales will likely be needed.

From left to right, we have a **social values scale**, with individualism in the center, and forces to its left and right pulling toward a collective social environment based on a certain value cluster, depending on the time and society in question. Starting on the right, Hester Prynne and her community enforced social **fundamentalism**, which is why her community forced her to wear around her neck the scarlet letter A. If the community sanctions you and is involved in your behaviors on that level, it would be something close to social fundamentalism. Usually when we hear the word 'fundamentalism,' it is in the context of religious fundamentalism. Thus, if the Pilgrims built a Christian fundamentalist community, and if Saudi Arabia is an Islamic fundamentalist community, and orthodox religious groups of all stripes have smaller-scale fundamentalist communities, they would all fall towards the far right on the social scale. Not only that, but if an indigenous society were governed by strict adherence to tribal social values (i.e.: An American, African, New Guinean, Australian tribe), then that is social fundamentalism if sanctions are imposed upon those who violate the tribe's taboos or are 'too expressive of their individualism.'

Social Conservatism means respect for tradition enshrined in law but with more freedom of thought and action than a fundamentalist order. The social desire amongst the community members is to conserve things considered good in and of themselves. **Individualism** means the attitude among the population that the rights of the individual as himself takes precedence over his membership in any community, even family, nation or civil society. If a government is structured, like in the early days of America, around that concept, then you have social individualism, abridged only by the admonition of J.S. Mill, when he declared that only when you violate the rights of other *individuals* shall your personal liberty be arrested. **Social-Liberalism** or **Left-Liberalism** is the advocating of a society based on using state power to write law and promote a social morality consciously directed to causes such as social justice, as defined by voices aimed at bringing about a more egalitarian society. This takes the form of searching for and providing aid to those deemed underprivileged, by the redistribution of social, political and economic capital from 'haves' to have-nots'. Secular values are encouraged as well, perhaps enforced by state institutions. **Radicalism** is a far-left desire and will to overthrow all that which has been conserved by society since at least the Medieval era when many of our cultures began (or began again), and put in its place a new ideology. Thus, we have the Jacobins of the French Revolution who pulled down churches and put up buildings devoted to the Cult of Wisdom. They were radical. The Paris Commune of 1871 was radical. Marx and Lenin's desire to overthrow the traditional social order was radical. The Hippie movement was called radical. The push to eliminate nation-states is called radical. Sometimes the basis for the radicalism is a desire for more intense forms of social justice than what Social-Liberals are looking for, or a willingness to use violence to meet a goal. Novelist Tom Wolfe coined the term 'radical chic' to mean middle class people promoting radical or counterculture values which, if enshrined in power and enacted in law, would destroy their culture as they know it.

The vertical scale is the **economic freedom scale**, which measures government influence on the economics of a given society. Across the top we have 'totalitarian' control, where government has a very large role in directing economic activities and people's livelihoods. On the left there is **State Communism,** which is when a socialist-communist state runs a command economy, directing everyone to their path of work, establishing quotas, and issuing punitive reprisals for those not in cooperation. Imprisoning dissenters and limiting information is a hallmark of the total control. If the Stalinist Soviet Union was a command economy in 1950, with Gulags for dissenters and quotas for workers, under a banner of radical social values, they would be in the far upper left of this chart. In the center is **National Socialism,** wherein a national community is sharply defined and made the exclusive beneficiary of the state-controlled economic system. The larger enterprises work in conjunction with the state to fulfill what the government defines as the 'national will,' and people are encouraged and conscripted to join in the effort. Hitler's Germany and Mussolini's Italy are good examples. Both state communism and national socialism define a vision of the future and an ideal society. One is internationalist (communism), the other nationalist (fascism). It is due north of individualism because it is a member's only club. You have to be an individual with the biological signature of the group, and then the idea is that the state, as it works for the national community, works for you too, because you are and want to be in the national community. On the right, **Absolute monarchs** who tax and tax the people to a large extent and punish those who do not 'live up' to their quota or expectation are, in effect, controlling the economic livelihoods of their subjects. Theocratic states where religious leaders control the work and 'donations' of the population qualify here as well, from the Egyptian pharaohs and Assyrian kings on.

On the bottom we have **Classical Marxism** on the left, the original vision of Marx's classless society, where everyone agrees each other is equal (hence on the same side of social radicalism), and gives to the society 'from each according to his ability, to each according to their need' (so there is an obligation, but it isn't state control- since there is no state). There is no government, and thus, no government control over the economy. There is no private property. There are no countries, no borders, no heaven, no identity, except as a proletarian. We are all laborers, and all there is is the *Internationale,* which is the human race. In the bottom center is **Libertarianism,** which is what used to be called liberalism before the 1960s Left appropriated the term to mean what it does today, and what this compass calls *Social Liberalism.* Textbooks sometimes call it 'classical liberalism. In libertarianism, we have government stay out of the economy altogether, low or no taxes, total free enterprise, very few controls at all. Early America had some, but very little government control over the economy, and would be called libertarian today. Adam Smith favored libertarianism. The British East India Company was free to basically do whatever it wanted, though directed by the crown sometimes. The Dutch VOC as well. Such companies had nearly complete freedom of action, such as conquer India and the Spice Islands, because, what's good for GM is good for America, right? Finally, on the lower right we have what Hobbes' called the **State of Nature**. Anarchy. No government to control the economy again, but on the far right now because, well, there's nothing more traditional in the deep history of humanity than living in wild nature! It means taking care of ourselves- we are all the descendants of survivors. Additionally, we lived in small bands and there wasn't much change generation to generation, so, it is fundamental in the sense of 'this is how we live,' and around us is an anarchy in which we participate. Marx is on the far left of the 'no government interference' spectrum because he believed the basis of natural, wild human life was cooperation. Like Rousseau, he thought cooperation is what comes to us naturally, whereas Hobbes said constant super-competition to survive was what comes naturally, a state of war of all against all, just the jungle today. Strangely enough, if you have a failed state in the present, like Somalia, where there is little government control over the economy and no regulations (or unenforced), and society is left open to cartels and gangsterism, then you drift back to this original condition in a frightening new incarnation.

The Political Compass - Values (1 pgs., 15 min.): In class standalone or at home. This warm up has students analyze the philosophical positions all the political 'isms' take, and has them match the coordinates on the compass with what people in that location generally forthrightly believe… for better or worse. A way to extend the assignment is to have students find people in history that match that philosophy and put their names on the compass. And if you really want to deepen the assignment, have students speculate on what, in the present, these philosophies say about modern issues such as: abortion rights, affirmative action, agricultural subsidies, public funding of the arts, freedom of assembly, child care, the 'corporate state', as in corporate influence on government and the political process, civil liberties, criminal justice, disease control, drug 'wars', education, energy, the environment, federalism, finance and banking, foreign aid, foreign policy, gun control, health care, housing, human trafficking, immigration, emigration, infrastructure, internationalism vs. nationalism, jobs, LGBTQ rights, media's role, military spending, minimum wage, net neutrality, non-proliferation of WMDs, big pharma, poverty, privacy rights, public land use, race relations, racism, refugee policy, religious freedom, domestic spying, social security, space exploration, special interests and lobbyists, freedom of speech and press, taxation, trade policy, transparency, veterans, voting rights, urban planning and development, terrorism, etc.

Spectre of the Gun (1 pg., 1 hr.): In class all period or at home. It is **Season 3, Episode 6**, available on *Netflix* and *Hulu Plus*, among other places. This *Star Trek* episode, written to showcase the 19th century in the American west, sees the crew beam into a re-creation of the famous Showdown at the O.K. Corral. But the underlying thing to watch for is how Dr. McCoy and Spock use 19th century empirical research and development to mess with everyday chemicals (their future gadgets don't work). This is symbolic of the Great Powers and their major firms investing in laboratories and universities at the time to increase ability and technology, the power of man over nature- sometimes it was literally expressed as the 'conquest of nature.' But it goes further in the end lesson, in which man is not only shown above nature, but over machine as well, meaning the essential factor in technological growth, is us. With great control and command, goes the implication, comes great responsibility.

Chapter 18: Colonial Encounters in Asia, Africa and Oceania, 1750-1950

ABCs of Imperialism (1 pg., 20 min.): In class on screen or at home online. This warm-up is a modern classic of the course, and University of Florida transcribed it for use online from a 19th century British book for kids learning the ABCs. Instead of 'A is for Apple,' however, it was 'A is for Army.' Every letter was preparing British youth to be the warriors, governors, explorers and administrators of the world's largest empire. Now students get to see how different childhood is, when you are expected by adults to take your places and fulfill a certain destiny in the world. *Web Search: ABCs for Baby Patriots UFL.*

Victoria's Empire (1 pg., 20 min.): In class on screen or at home online. Niall Ferguson has done many major documentaries for the BBC and other outlets, and one of them was on the British Empire's rise, rule and decline. *Video Search: Empire Ferguson 4 Heaven's Breed.* Watch at least the first 10 minutes of this hour-long episode, which touches on how the British obtained India, the technology that helped them do it, how such a small island conquered such a vast and ancient country, the "Great Game", the role of the spies who would later be the founders of MI6, and issues between the British Empire and smaller powers like Ethiopia. The second clip is from the same series but is a different episode. *Video Search: Empire Ferguson 3 The Mission.* Move to ~28 min. in and watch to ~38 min. in. This is about the Sepoy Rebellion of 1857 and its consequences.

The Darwin Controversy (1 pg., 1 hr.): In class on screen or home online. Download *A Science Odyssey Origins.* This well done documentary looks at Mendel, Darwin and later contributions throughout the 20th century. It looks at how Darwinism became less controversial over the decades.

Anna and the King of Siam (1 pg., 1 hr.): In class on screen or home online. You may have to buy the movie, but it is worth it because it is full of cross-cultural faux paus and does a good take on how British imperialism manifested itself diplomatically. Siam is Thailand, and it was a buffer between the British and French empires in Southeast Asia. This 'neutral territory', therefore, maintained its old traditions.

Eugenics: All About the Seed (1 pg., 1 hr.): In class on screen or at home online. It is **Season 1, Episode 23**, available on *Netflix* and *Hulu Plus*, among other places. In this *Star Trek episode, Space Seed,* written to reflect the Cold War controversy surrounding whether humans should practice selective breeding on themselves, the crew encounters a ship afloat in outer space and boards it. It's from 21st century Earth, and on it are people confined to a sleep state. When they are woken up, it is found they have been selectively bred in a eugenics program, and were sent away because they were 'too dangerous' because they were 'superior' (which meant aggressive and full of desire for conquest and rule). Students must weigh the costs and benefits- with the crew- of running a eugenics program. Before viewing, talk about eugenics in history, and how once Darwinian evolution appeared as a theory in 1859, the next decades saw an obsessive drawing out of possible historical outcomes, in which smarties in each nation- including America- were thinking about how to get the edge in a world that came to be seen as a jungle in which the nations ware animals battling each other in a struggle for existence. When Gregor Mendel's breakthroughs in heredity became known, and the Punnett Square that students draw in Biology class became common knowledge, it was thought by Herbert Spencer and Francis Galton that what farmers do to plants and animals- selectively breed them for desirable traits- could *and should* be done with people as well. That meant increased state control over people's reproductive habits. They spoke of tax breaks and rewards for 'desirable people' to bear children, and sanctions on 'undesirable' people for doing so, something like China's One Child Policy of recent decades, wherein only people who could afford it could have the second child, otherwise it was aborted by the state, which led to people disproportionately aborting girl 'first childs,' in the belief their one child should rather be a boy, since a boy would be more likely, they believed, to take care of them in their old age. Let them debate about eugenic government policies vs. dysgenic policies, if they get into it that far.

Chapter 19: Empires in Collision: Europe, the Middle East, and East Asia 1800-1900

Great Clips: Hideyoshi / Qing Isolationism (1 pg., 20 min.): In class on screen or at home online. There are two segments. *Video Search*: <u>CNN Millennium 16th century</u> (the first is about 20 min. into the full episode). For the second, *Video Search*: <u>CNN Millennium 17th century</u> (about 37 min. in). The focus of the first is the unification of feudal Japan and the making of it into an early modern state under Toyatomi Hideyoshi, after whom come the Tokugawas. The second looks at the overthrow of the Ming by the Manchu-Qing and their continuation of the Ming policy of developing the culture and economy by looking inward.

Asia and the Islamic Empires Matrix (1 pg., 20 min.): In class standalone warm-up or at home. Could be an introduction but more likely a review of vocab terms and keeping straight the Qing, Tokugawa, Ottoman, Safavid and Mughal dynasties, their palaces, locations, beliefs, famous rulers, and characteristics.

Great Clips: Zenith of the Qing / Opium Trade (1 pg., 20 min.): In class on screen or at home online. There are two segments. *Video Search*: <u>CNN Millennium 18th century</u> (the first is about 36 min. into the full episode). For the second, *Video Search*: <u>CNN Millennium 19th century</u> (about 36 min. in). The focus of the first is the Qing conquest over the Ming, and the prosperous 18th century in China. The second looks at the 19th century and how the Qing became decadent and corrupt, and how political ineffectiveness was exacerbated by the British demand for trade, leading to the Opium War.

To Be Industrialized, or Not To Be? (1 pg., 15 min.): In class standalone warm-up or at home. This bell-ringer is a quick one with two sections. Students match the correct crisis and reform movement with the country or empire that underwent them, by choosing which of the countries fits the clue.

Chapter 20: Collapse at the Center: World War, Depression, and Rebalancing

WWI Objectives (1 pg., 15 min.): In class standalone warm-up or at home. This bell-ringer has students figure out which country, or bloc of countries, had which objective at the beginning of WWI. After all, when war begins, people want to know from their government what they are fighting for. "Were we attacked?" "Are we defending our national honor?" "Do we see an opportunity to get our formerly independent country back?"

The Guns of August (1 pg., 45 min.): In class on screen or at home online. *Video Search: <u>The Guns of August</u>*. Barbara Tuchman wrote two important books about the run up to WWI, first was *The Proud Tower,* about European civilization in the first decade of the 20th century. While perhaps the zenith of its civilizational influence, the 'proud tower' imploded in 1914, the events of which are related in *The Guns of August.* The film adaptation by Universal Pictures collected primary source footage that really does a good job putting us there on the scene. You might ask students to contrast the History Channel-style of documentary narration vs. this 1960s way of doing it. Some will find it, well, old-fashioned. Because it is. Others may find its non-repetitiveness refreshing, which it is.

WWI Clips: Trenches / Truce / Lusitania (1 pg., 20 min.): In class on screen or at home online. There are three clips to find. For the first, *Video Search*: Tech Developments of World War I (~3 min.) OR *Khan Academy Technology in World War I* (~8 min.). Students list and note how each changed or didn't change the course of the war. The second clip is on the Christmas Truce: *Video Search*: Christmas Truce of 1914 Sainsbury. This is one of a few good (short) recreations of the famous truce on December 25, 1914, the date marked as the one by which the war would be concluded by both London and Berlin, each having won their respective victory. Clip three is found by searching Lusitania Windsor Mackay. This is the first major animated production in history, done to show the public the terrible disaster, on the scale of the Titanic only a few years earlier, with an eye to convince the average neutral American to support the Allies. Have the student look for these propaganda / POV cues.

WWI Comics (1 pg., 20 min.): In school on a computer for each student or at home. This warm-up has students do three quick researches into how the war has been portrayed in art over the course of a century. As we saw with the Windsor MacKay animation of the Lusitania sinking, propaganda and POV can be very powerful and apparent, or they can be hidden a few layers in.

American WWI Posters (1 pg., 20 min.): In school on a computer for each students or at home. Students use the website *ww1propaganda.com* to evaluate the messages the people were given by the authorities during the war years, what they meant, and why those particular messages? Categorized into a few groups, students should ask themselves to what extent *they* are propagandized by their authorities today, and to what end.

Women's Roles in WWI (1 pg., 20 min.): In school on a computer for each students or at home. Students use the website *ww1propaganda.com* to look specifically at what women were doing during the war to help the effort.

Battles of WWI (2 pgs., 1 hr.): Recommended for at home. This may be given for extra credit. It will take some time on the computer or in a book to fit the right battle with the correct description, but some students will be interested in doing it. Goes beyond the curriculum, however.

Trench War – Simulation (1 pg., 30 min.): Requires Internet. This online game done by Canada's War Museum. Students will like doing this simulation and see how trench fighters had problems with sleep, dirt, bad food, and all the rest.

WWI Dead (1 pg., 15 min.): In class standalone warm-up or at home. It's a macabre topic, the death tolls of the 20th century wars. But there is a kind of perspective in it. How do we who are studying the wars do justice to each individual soldier and civilian who paid for what we are studying with their lives? We can listen to songs like *Over There* and sing with them, or listen to songs about them, like *The Green Fields of France*, or read their diaries and memoirs. But a raw death count? Maybe it really can put things in a certain light.

The Edge of Forever (1 pg., 1 hr.): In class all period or at home. It is **Season 1, Episode 29**, available on *Netflix* and *Hulu Plus*, among other places. This *Star Trek* episode was written to reflect the idea that while an individual's destiny is his own, it might also be vital in altering the course of history. The crew goes back to 1930s New York during the Great Depression. There is much anxiety in the air, and many of the themes from this chapter are there too. Not only the depression, but the rise of totalitarianism, the public's isolationist stance, and a moral choice, which finally confronts Kirk and Spock, who have to decide whether to alter the course of history.

Germ Theory of Disease (2 pgs., 30 min.): In class on screen or at home online. First, students brainstorm all the elements they know from the Periodic Table and jot them down. Then, you can play the clip of Harry Potter singing the names of all the elements, by video searching Daniel Radcliffe Sings the Elements. After that bit of fun, we start the main event, a very good rundown of the new understanding of germ theory, and its effect on our ability to combat disease. Find the clip at: A Science Odyssey Matters of Life and Death.

The Messages of Modernism (2 pgs., 30 min.): In class on computer or at home online. First, students check out a great website for history Powerpoint presentations: http://pptpalooza.net. This site has a few by Susan Pojer of New York, which are especially good. Students will like this art ppt, which is number 48 in the website's center.

Tariffs: Tariffying or Tariffic? (1 pg., 15 min.): In class standalone warm-up or at home. Students place a dot where the tariff rate was in a given year, then connect them. Good introduction to the Great Depression, cycle of debt and payment, Smoot-Hawley, New Deal.

Rise of the Dictators (1 pg., 30 min.): In class on the screen or at home online. Four people had domination of their states in the Interwar era- Stalin, Mussolini, Hirohito and Hitler. Hirohito ruled by long tradition, the other three took power, Hitler doing it in the most democratic way, the "path of legality". First is Stalin and the Great Purges (*Video Search: Stalin's Paranoia, the Great Purge and the Cult of Personality*). Next we have Mussolini and his 'test run' of fascism. We also find out what Hitler learned from him, as he took power in Italy a decade before Hitler became chancellor of Germany (*Video Search: Mussolini March on Rome 20th century almanac*). Finally, we have another propaganda film, done by the German government to showcase the Berlin Olympics of 1936. It really was the first big television broadcast. Talk about how all Olympic opening and closing ceremonies are done to showcase the country, a tradition begun in '36. Locate it at: *1936 Olympics Opening Ceremony*.

Rise of Japan (1 pg., 20 min.): In class on the screen or at home online. Hirohito's Japan was treated by the U.S. government in a clip that was shared with new enlistees after Pearl Harbor. It has a definite POV and students will quickly see what it is. Find it at *Know Your Enemy Japan*. Only the first 20 minutes are asked about on the worksheet, but the whole thing is worth seeing. It is recommended to get a blank map of Japan and put it on the back of this handout.

The Nazi Olympics (1 pg., 1 hr.): Very good documentary where Jesse Owens himself goes back in the 1980s to Berlin as an old man. He revisits the places where he won the gold, muses about international affairs, and paints a heartwarming picture of the regular Germans of the 1930s, even saying at one point he felt freer there than in the American South.

Cartoons Go To War (1 pg., 40 min.). In class on screen or at home on Youtube. Walt Disney was a non-interventionist in WWII, like Charles Lindbergh and some others. But both Disney and Loony Tunes were employed by the government to create propaganda cartoons that justified U.S. involvement in WWII to kids and adults alike. Video search four cartoons: *Donald Duck der fuhrer's face, Loony Tunes the Ducktaters, Private SNAFU spies,* and *Disney Education for Death.*

New Alliances: Allies and Axis (1 pg., 15 min.): In class standalone warm-up or at home. Here we classify the nations not so much into which alliance they become part of, but by whether in 1939 they favored 1) the status quo (or were ready to appease Germany, the USSR and Italy in a limited way), or 2) revisionism / expansionism, or 3) Were neutral, as some countries always are.

Dear Professor... (1 pg., 20 min.): In-school on computer or at home online. If not computer access, the *Washington Post* article could be found and printed for each student. In a sense, the legacy of WWII is still with us. The old rivalries, the struggle, and some of the pain is still here, though most of that generation is in their 90s. Recently, an AP World History textbook author was visited by the Japanese government, and they wanted him to revise his textbook, *Traditions & Encounters*. This is something that may be of interest to students using his book, because it shows how seriously these topics are taken by entities around the world, and talk about a POV...

Massacre of the Innocents: WWII Dead (1 pg., 15 min.): In class standalone warm-up or at home. It's the same macabre topic, the death tolls of the 20th century wars. But in the interests of continuity, here is one for WWII, as there was for WWI.

Chapter 21: Revolution, Socialism and Global Conflict: Rise and Fall of Communism

20th Century Ideologies Simplified (1 pg., 15 min.): In class standalone warm-up or at home. This is a World History classic, been around for about 20 years, with many permutations. In this modified version, corrected for the curriculum (though some seem like they were written by the creators of South Park), we have a good opportunity to discuss political ideologies as they come to bear on Average Joe and his two cows.

Animal Farm (1 pg. two days): The movie version of the George Orwell novel Animal Farm came out in 1999. Video search it and download, or assign students to watch it at home. It is usually free on Youtube. The voice cast is great, including Patrick Stewart, Peter Ustinov, Kelsey Grammar, Julia Ormond, Julia Louis-Dreyfus, Ian Holm, Paul Scofield and more. Students will answer questions probing into the themes of totalitarianism, and how communism may not fit well with human nature.

AиIMAL FAяM (2 pgs., two days): This is for a more in-depth look at the symbolism in the movie. When students see it, they liken the events in the movie to real-life events.

Totalitarian Government (2 pgs., 30 min.): This warmup is standalone in class, however on the back is a short video clip if so desired, about censorship and whether books like Hitler's Mein Kampf should be censored. The main part of the assignment gets students thinking about the qualities of fascism, democracy and communism, and what separates the worldview of the people espousing them.

Russian Security Terms (1 pg., 20 min.): In class standalone warm-up or at home. Nothing like Russian political and security terms to get a sense of the age of ideology. Afterward look up Orwell's Newspeak Dictionary…

Lyrics of the Communist Left (1 pg., 15 min.): In class on screen warm-up or at home online. The *Internationale* can be downloaded and played for effect. The one where they sing it in the Soviet Party Congress is good. After that is a cartoon, found by searching *Propaganda Result of the XII party congress Russian cartoon*. Here we have the story of why people should want to give up their private plots of land, and why they should unite them into a collective farm. The rationale is set up with the bad capitalist choosing his way, and the good socialists figuring out why a cooperative shop is better than a private one.

Comparing Chinese & Soviet Communism (1 pg., 20 min.): Standalone assignment. Exercise to compare and contrast how things were done in the two major communist states.

Decade by Decade (1 pg., 15 min.): In class standalone warm-up or at home. As Ben Kingsley said in the CNN Millennium episode *20th Century,* the world just kept right on fighting after the end of the Second World War. The manmade disasters just kept right on roaring, from German Expulsion to the War on Terror.

Every Atomic Bomb (1 pg., 20 min.): In class on the screen or at home. There are two versions of the video, made by a Japanese animator. Students will find its bizarre, '80s-style video game format interesting. Watch the 14 min. version first and hear all the beeps. Then, watch the 3 minute one, and answer the questions.

Presidents and Premiers of the Cold War (1 pg., 15 min.): In class standalone warm-up or at home. Here is a way to compare events and personalities at the top of the bi-polar world order.

Cold War Map (2 pgs., 20 min.): In class standalone or at home. What is needed is a blank political map of the world, doesn't matter if it's Cold War era or a map from today, copied on the back of this assignment. If it's from today, however, you'll have to shine it on the screen and divide Germany in order to get the Iron Curtain in the right spot. Otherwise this can be done using an atlas or any resource like that.

Balance of Terror (1 pg., 1 hr.): In class all period or at home. Available on *Netflix* and *Hulu Plus*, among other places. This *Star Trek* episode was written to reflect the Cold War brinksmanship going on in 1966, and the mutually assured destruction concept as it was beginning to be known at that time. The Enterprise goes into the DMZ (sorry, neutral zone) separating the Federation (USA) from the Klingon Empire (USSR). Spheres of influence play a major role in this episode, and it is good to review that concept.

Who Won the Space Race? (2 pgs., 20 min.): In class standalone. Students use the clues in the name of the mission to ascertain whether the Russians or the Americans 'won' the 'first' in space. Then, they look at how many objects in the Solar System human beings have visited with spaceprobes. Finally, they are asked for what they think should be the next major focus of space exploration. Note: The first Space Race officially ended in 1975, when the Apollo-Soyuz Test Project saw both countries launch their craft, which met in orbit, and ended with a handshake between the astronauts and cosmonauts, and mutual congratulations on all the achievement.

Tear Down This Wall! (2 pgs., 1 hr.): In class on the screen or at home online. These clips all relate to the end of the Cold War. They are in an order, first looking at the Brezhnev Doctrine of not letting any Soviet bloc country leave, then the steady decline of the communist system. Then McDonalds.

Chapter 22: The End of Empire: The Global South on the Global Stage

India's Political Order (1 pg., 15 min.): In class standalone warm-up or at home. This is a good one to start Ch. 37, because it is a short warm-up recalling the various phases of India's political life. There is no "Chinese Dynasty Song" for India, unfortunately, but this can segway right into the Subcontinent's situation as of 1948.

Decolonization in India & Africa (1 pg., 30 min.): In class on the screen or at home. Four clips on decolonization's successes and woes. First, *1947 Indian Independence Color* shows us the Gandhi-Nehru-Jinnah dynamic, and the sad events which followed in the population transfer. Clip 2, *Ghana Independence Day* brings us to its rather successful transition to 'native rule,' which can be contrasted with Clip 3: *Jomo Kenyatta and the Mau Mau Oath*, wherein the British settlers in Kenya are more numerous, more established, and less happy to pull up their ties and leave. They do, however, after the violence begun the Mau Mau Uprising. Clips 4 and 5 take us to the white settler colonies in Southern Africa, where the architect of apartheid, H.F. Verwoerd, explains his reasoning, and Ian Smith, the man who led Rhodesia to independence from Britain (after Britain tried to force majority-rule on the white settlers), is shown in the 1960s and 70s, before the victory of Robert Mugabe and the ZANU-PF party, which transformed the country into Zimbabwe. Listen to Bob Marley's *Zimbabwe* if time.

Postcolonial Conflicts (2 pgs., 30 min.): In class with each student on computer, or at home online. This is a good jigsaw for students to do and present to a group or the class, each selecting one or two postcolonial conflicts and researching them. Each is worthy of further study and is good background for what is going on today, but there just isn't time. So a jigsaw can work with these, if only as a challenge to identify patterns.

Matching Political Leaders and Their Goals (1 pg., 15 min.): In class standalone warm-up or at home. This one tries to bring together all the disparate personages in this chapter and differentiate them.

Regime Change (1 pg., 30 min.): In class on screen or at home online. Students should use *Wikipedia* or other sources to locate information about when and how and why the U.S. has intervened in the Global South in the past century, and what the consequences and methods were.

Elaan of Troyius (1 pg., 1 hr.): In class all period or at home. It is **Season 3, Episode 13**, available on *Netflix* and *Hulu Plus*, among other places. This *Star Trek* episode was written to reflect the Cold War reality of nonaligned countries feeling pressure from both superpowers to join their NATO/Warsaw Pact-style alliances. Both the Federation and the Klingons want Troyius and its minerals, as members or at least exclusive associates. They both have something to offer, but the diplomats in the episode, like those in real life, don't understand each other fully. A little cultural learning will have to happen before anything can work out, and then there is still the matter of which side to pick... the choice which faced 100 and more countries during the Cold War years.

Iranian Revolution (1 pg., 15 min.): In class on the screen or at home online. This *Crash Course* episode is important because Iran is one of the countries that doesn't get as much coverage as an India or China, but there seem to always be questions about it. *Crash Course World History 226* is a good summary of Iran since the book left off with the Safavids in Ch. 27.

Chapter 23: Capitalism and Culture: The Acceleration of Globalization

Population Through Time (1 pg., 15 min.): In class on screen or at home online. This short clip can be found by searching: *Population Growth Dot Map*. It is good to use while talking about Malthus, population transition, urbanization, etc. The map places a dot for each million people, and goes through 2,000 years of history. You can clearly see how the Roman, Han and Gupta empires are the centers of world population, with sporadic dots elsewhere. As the map progresses, the dots get more numerous. Visually interesting.

Earth: Cosmic Paradise or... Other? (1 pg., 30 min.): In class with textbook or at home. Summary of the big issues in the last part of the last chapter. Almost there!

Civs and Dynasties @ a Glance (1 pg., 20 min.): In class standalone warm-up or at home. This is for classification of many civilizations and dynasties all on one handy reference sheet. How many can they get the first time? How many the second? Can the class brainstorm them together?

Extras

The Geography of Disney (4 pgs., 1 hr.*) – Standalone warm-up. Students can practice regionalization with a topic they know very well, and use geographic clues to place the films they will no doubt brag they have seen. Copy front and back for both the answer form and the clues sheet. Good icebreaker, or for an end of the year breather.

Musical Journey (5 pgs., 5 hrs.*) – A great way to cool down the year is to hit some of the humanities content that the AP World curriculum doesn't get to. While some art and famous buildings are depicted visually, there is an utter void when it comes to music, and its relationship to history. Got a week? Video search the pieces on each page, and either download or cue them up. Students who never heard any music from before The Beatles (who also classify Britney Spears is 'oldies') will hear it for the first time, and get some historical connection in the annotations on the right. The assignment is easy and should be advertised that way. All you need is a pencil and your ears. Play a 30 second to 2 min. clip for each, and watch some of their eyes light up, "I've heard that before!" Press them on where, was it on TV? Was it in a movie, or at a public event? This music is now in the public domain, so it is used often.

1) The basic things about each phase covered are as follows: Medieval chant is literally what *a cappella* is, as in, music 'from the chapel.' Singing without instruments but with each other. Renaissance music is polyphonic, so more than one instrument is heard with different music for each. Baroque, starting with Pachelbel, is lighthearted (or spiritual like Bach's *Toccata and Fugue*), known for its more detailed texture, and sometimes flightiness (like Vivaldi). Classical, starting with Haydn, is smooth, technically close to perfection, flowing, sometimes humorous.

Medieval chant starts us off Day 1. Tell them about Gregory's codification of music for churches, and recognize him as a progenitor of what would become the classical genre. The first few no one will probably know, except maybe from the Halo video game series. Some might know *Infernal*, and then more will know *Canon in D*. Get two versions of this, one actual one, and then one of the punks who plays it with electric guitar and gets 30 million views. Call this kid a punk, "how could they do this to Pachelbel!" Call Pachelbel Taco Bell too, for sure. "Err, I mean, Pachelbel, what did I say?" When you can, get videos that have something interesting going on, like for *Zadok the Priest*, someone did a montage of the coronation of Elizabeth II. For *Barber of Seville*, get the Bugs Bunny cartoon, "*Rabbit of Seville*". It's worth showing for all 7 minutes. Same with Salieri, for this one, find *Amadeus Mozart's Entrance*. Good clip. Austrian emperor tries to play Salieri's piece for Mozart, and Mozart memorizes it and plays it back, improving on it. Salieri is not happy. Everyone will know *Eine Kline Nachtmusik*, they just didn't know what it was called. *Caprice 5* is amazing because Paganini wrote it so no one but him could play it- good time to explain what a virtuoso is. For the *Sailing Fugue*, search *Boccerini Master and Commander*. It was played a lot in the movie while the ship was on the high seas. For Donizetti, search *Fifth Element Opera* so students can watch the blue lady singing *Luccia di Lamarmoor* on a tourist boat… in space.

2) Romantic era music is emotional, powerful, mirroring the majesty of nature, or harnessing the great feeling of the expression or discovery of an ideal, such as freedom. The rational Enlightenment is arrived, and now we put its ideals into practice which takes sacrifice- Romance! Feeling is king. Starting with Beethoven, who transitions in his life from Classical to Romantic, try to get a few videos where it's a training video with each note being a different color. Students like the effects, it's nice. For *Fidelio*, you could download a performance of the *Prisoner's Chorus*, or *Civilisation Kenneth Clark The Fallacies of Hope*. Find the spot in the middle where he's standing in front of a Bastille-like prison, and the *Prisoner's Chorus* plays beautifully as the political prisoners emerge out into the light. Freedom, sweet freedom. For the 9th *Symphony*, show the whole clip of the last part of *Immortal Beloved,* about Beethoven's life. It shows his abusive dad in a flashback, and Ludwig running away, running to the music, to the lake in the dead of the night, and jumping in, seeing the stars above, dreaming of this ultimate masterpiece of music, wherein we bathe in the cosmos itself. The camera then cuts back to Ludwig conducting the final symphony of his career- completely deaf. It shows the crowd behind him giving him a standing ovation. He turns around. Chopin's *Funeral March* is best heard in organ version, and it's not like Purcell's or Beethoven's funeral march, in that it's not to a person, but to his country, which was absorbed by its neighbors in 1795 and disappeared from the map of Europe until 1918. Bizet moves us into Opulence, where we have our waltzes and operas of the mid-19th century. For *Nessun Dorma,* get a Pavarotti clip and advertise the last note as the longest in an opera aria. Hold your breath! For *Carnival of the Animals* get the fish tank version, and for *Danse Macabre* find the animated skeletons doing a nighttime danse in a graveyard. Big hit. *Blue Danube Simpsons* will find a funny clip of the Blue Danube onboard a spacecraft, with Homer eating chips. Students will know this one.

3) The first theme in Day 3 is music written to mark the rites of passage one goes through in life. Say the seniors certainly have- or will- hear the *Pomp and Circumstance* march, because it's played at every graduation. A good clip is from *Fantasia*, where Donald is looking for Daisy and a flood is coming. Wedding music is well known because it's always in the movies (and in real life, of course). Sousa starts the National phase in music, where composers took folk songs and transcribed them into the classical tradition. Ives at the National Cathedral is good, search *Das Deutschlandlied organ* for the organ version. We already went through the issues surrounding the song, so no lyrics, but Haydn's music is still necessary. Have fun with the dances. *Night on Bald Mountain* has an animated clip: worst. camping. trip. ever. Get the *Sabre Dance* flashmob, when in Yerevan, Armenia some street thugs pretended to start trouble then broke out into dance for the composer's birthday.

4) Fantasian music is fantasy, and no one did it better than Tchaikovsky. Search: *Fantasia Sugar Plum Fairies* for a good clip, and *Oksana Baiul Swan Lake* to see some figure skating. For *1812 Overture*, get the version with cannons. *Sorcerer's Apprentice* is another one from *Fantasia*. Before playing Holst's *Mars*, tell the students they won't be able to distinguish it from a scifi action movie today, that's how ahead of his time Holst was. He preceded *Avatar* by 150 years, but it could literally be used in *Avatar* and it would be a great score! Get *2001 A Space Odyssey's* opening to hear *Thus Spake Zarathustra*, and if you think your class can handle it, in *Apocalypse Now* there is a crazy scene where *Ride of the Valkyries* is played by the Americans in the chopper going on the attack. *Flight of the Bumblebee Maksim* is a good clip. Maksim is a punk from Croatia (call him that and be offended by his goth / emo garb whilst at the piano). Good for students to see someone they can identify with playing piano… Moving to Impressionist with Debussy, the *Bolero* flashmob is a good clip. Before playing Schoenberg, which is now modernist, warn students about atonality, how you are not supposed to actually like it. It was avant-garde, anti-music. For *Pierrot Lunaire*, there's a clip of a woman in a skyscraper looking out… shocked because her life has no meaning. *Fantasia Rite of Spring* is Modernist-Primitivist, and good to compare with Vivaldi's *Spring*, which was lighthearted. This 'Spring' is very different- shows Darwin's vicious nature in all its brutality. WWI made all this come alive. The *Firebird* clip from Fantasia is good too, because it shows nature dying, and nature being reborn. *Rhapsody in Blue* Fantasia is good, shows Interwar New York burgeoning with stuff happening. *Battle on the Ice* should be the clip from the Eisenstein movie Alexander Nevsky, and you can contrast how the Germans are faceless brutes and the Russians are gallant defenders. And remind students this was done after the great hate of WWI. The Shostakovich piece might be the most poignant in all music, but they'll find it boring unless you tell them how in Socialist Realist music you had to have everything approved by the censors, so how could you convey the mixed feelings of the great vision of a new ideological world to build together with its realities? Listen very closely… "The people have awakened to consciousness… this revolution is very real. But ominous too…"

5) The last day sees the end of WWII bringing about Postwar Modernist music, in many varieties. Gorecki took a poem inscribed in the walls of a cell in the Auschwitz women's camp, and made a musical tribute to the innocent victims of this worst of all wars. *Palladio David Garrett* is a good version, and merges classical with some rock n' roll the students will like. Glass is minimalist, but also quite meaningful, he is meditating on the modernist condition. What does life mean? And he plays that feeling out on piano better than anyone. For Postmodern beginning with Cage, we get a free-for-all like with Modernism, but even more unstructured and purposefully bizarre. For the John Cage *4'33* piece, get the one where it's actually him at the piano. He raises his arm. Ready to play. And he doesn't play. Go with it. Pretend it's on pause, let students tell you "No, his arm moved". Whaaaat? Distract the students while this is happening. Say, "Okay, well he's got to play soon…" Start to sweat, "Uh, wow, I should have previewed this clip, sorry guys." Anything to wait it out. Use up your political capital. It's the end of the year. Let tension build. That's what Cage WANTS. At the end, he puts his hand down and people clap! Where was the music? The music, Cage says, was the music of the audience murmuring about, wondering what was going on! He flipped the script on performer and consumer. For 2cellos, search *2cellos Thunderstruck*. Say, "There is a classical music revival going on today." And look how many views it has.

If you made it this far and that's enough, ignore the last part. But the real place classical music does survive is in the production of epic movie scores.

AND NOW, 140 BELL-RINGERS, WARM-UPS, MULTIMEDIA CLIP RESPONSE FORMS, AND ONLINE ASSIGNMENTS!

Ch. 1   BIG HISTORY   Starperson _____

The long view of life and time

The chances of you existing are infinitesimally small. Yet, here you are. The World History going on around you is like a never ending TV show, every day is a new episode. We are interested in both the episode itself, what went on in it, and also how it fits into the greater context of the 'whole show'. Big History tries to establish that context. On the line, write the 1 or 2-word main subject that has meaning for us and our story:

__Big Bang_____ The Big Bang creates a new universe- we have something from nothing- the ultimate mystery
_____ The matter in the new universe obeys a series of anthropic natural physical laws- reality
_____ One natural force, gravity, pulls diffuse matter together into vast clumps- galaxies appear
_____ Gravity also pulls local matter together that once big enough, began to shine- and there was light
_____ This process will be repeated a billion trillion times in the cosmos- once for every star there is
_____ Some first generation stars die in supernovas- which launch fused metals across the arc of heaven
_____ Second and third generations of stars are born in nebulae rich in these heavy elements
_____ New objects made from the heavy metals begin to form around them- terrestrial planets
_____ One day a third generation star, yellow and medium-size, bursts to life in the Milky Way- the Sun
_____ Regular accretion pulls together celestial spheres- our Solar System of planets, moons and comets
_____ The largest gas giant, Jupiter, is so massive that it flings a lot of rogue matter out of the system
_____ The largest terrestrial planet, Earth, is metallically rich and forms in the Sun's habitable zone
_____ A wandering world called Theia half its size impacts the Earth- shattering itself and almost our Earth
_____ Matter spewed from the giant impact coalesces as a ring around Earth, and our Moon forms from it
_____ With a new 23 degree axis tilt and new metals, the emboldened Earth forms a magnetic shield for us
_____ Comets containing ice bombard the Earth for millions of years, releasing their ice into vapors
_____ An atmosphere begins to form- and one day it begins to rain- and rain- and rain- and oceans appear
_____ As our star orbits the galactic core, its course takes it to a safe haven between great spiral arms
_____ In the primitive pools and oceans, 'dead' matter miraculously comes 'alive'- and copies itself
_____ Over time, amino acids and proteins become unicellular organisms, self-contained in a 'body'
_____ Sex begins as a means of reproduction- multi-cellular organisms appear and consume
_____ Forms most wonderful inhabit the primitive Earth- and plants begin the conquest of dry land
_____ The plants photosynthesize starlight, eat CO_2 and exhale for us a 21% oxygen atmosphere
_____ Mutated fishlike creatures become land animals by pulling themselves up with their fin-arms
_____ Lungs appear and thus a kind of animal that can live both in water and on land- the amphibian
_____ Some amphibians find it easier to stay on land all the time where predators are few- the reptile
_____ The Permian-Triassic Catastrophe exterminates 98% of life: nature can give, and taketh away
_____ Survivors become huge: sea monsters and dinosaurs rule over the Earth for a long, long time
_____ The medulla drives these instinctual, territorial, reptiles- and is passed to us with mixed results
_____ The thunder lizard finds himself in front of cometary annihilation and has no space program to stop it
_____ Little furry warm-blooded creatures able to survive the impact get larger- the mammal ascends
_____ Cerebrum & cerebellum drive mammalian body & instincts like care for their young... the family
_____ As continents drift and weather changes, some are isolated on the savannas and steppes
_____ Consciousness appears when some begin to 'wake up' to their surroundings, place, and time- people
_____ They devise tools, discover fire, stand upright, and speak to each other- and then it gets cold
_____ After one of many Ice Ages, small communities of the species sapiens move out about the globe
_____ For 100k years our human Cro-Magnon ancestors survived remarkable challenges- the lucky ones
_____ In the Near East, in China, India and Egypt, new civilizations appear- material progress begins
_____ Humanity invents a way to accumulate knowledge outside of the brains of mortal men- writing
_____ For ~160 generations since civilization, our historical ancestors live, build, devise and experiment
_____ The Ancient, the Medieval, the periods of discovery and Enlightenment, and Industry, come and go.
_____ The various branches of your particular family tree arrive on American shores, at different times.
_____ A chance meeting of a certain 'egg-of-the-month' and a certain 'spermatozoa-of-the-moment' = you
_____ Thinking about the future of life and time, you realize the infinite possibilities of galactic civilization

The real miracle, therefore, is you. If one understands the order of events as presented, whereby the individual you is the result of winning an astounding sequence of biological, chemical and astronomical lottery tickets, within the superstructure of the totality of an existing ultimate reality, it is pretty clear that we are all winners. At least on one day a year, whether that be Christmas or another holiday, or simply your birthday, reflect on the fact that the chances of things being the way they are are so infinitesimally small, that each of us is indeed special. Maybe this class can help us see each other as brothers and sisters.

Ch. 1 **GENERATIONS** Present specimen _____

Measuring time through years is boring. Let's do it through generations!

A generation is the length of time between the parents' birth and when they became parents to their middle child. Today, for the average American, the number of years in a generation is 31. For Europeans it is 34, Asians 28, Middle Easterners 26 and Africans 24. Historically, the number has been 25.

What year was it exactly 100 years ago?

_____

| How many generations, *historically*, have there been in the average century?

_____

"It is a certainty that I personally had ancestors living 250 generations ago, when civilization began to take shape":

   a. True   b. False

| At the risk of doing some math, if you went back in a time machine 2,000 years, how many 'great grandparents ago' was that? (show your work):

Three primary lifestyles coexisted by 3000 B.C., namely, hunter-gatherer, nomadic pastoralist, and the emerging agriculturalist. Describe some basics about each:

_____

1) Hunter-gatherers:

What do the following tell us about what Hunter-gatherers cared most about?

Cave art (done for good luck in...):

_____

Venus figurines (good luck charms for...):

_____

2) Nomadic pastoralists:

List some domesticated animals- both farm and household- that pastoralists help adapt to living around humans:

3) Agriculturalists:

List some staple crops that early farmers domesticated to human use in different parts of the world:

Ch. 1 ~PREHISTORIC ART SHOW~ Artist _____
They called this art?

Can you draw like a caveman? Image search & sketch the masterpiece, and note its significance:

Altamira Cave　　　Location:　　　　　　　　| **Lascaux Cave**　　　Location:

Artist: _____　Rating (1-10): _____ | Artist: _____　Rating (1-10): _____

Subject: _____　Most interesting aspect: | Subject: _____　Most interesting aspect:

Cueva de las Manos　Location:　　　　　　　| **Rock State Monument**　Location:

Artist: _____　Rating (1-10): _____ | Artist: _____　Rating (1-10): _____

Subject: _____　Message / Symbolism? | Subject: _____　Message / Symbolism?

Chauvet Cave　　　Location:　　　　　　　　| **Venus of Willendorf**　Location:

Artist: _____　Rating (1-10): _____ | Artist: _____　Rating (1-10): _____

Subject: _____　Most interesting aspect: | Subject: _____　Most interesting aspect:

Stonehenge   Location:

Artist: _____   Rating (1-10): _____

Subject: _____   Most interesting aspect:

Ale's Stones   Location:

Artist: _____   Rating (1-10): _____

Subject: _____   Most interesting aspect:

Nazca Lines (Spider)   Location:

Artist: _____   Rating (1-10): _____

Subject: _____   Most interesting aspect:

Great Serpent Mound   Location:

Artist: _____   Rating (1-10): _____

Subject: _____   Most interesting aspect:

Zbruch Idol   Location:

Artist: _____   Rating (1-10): _____

Subject: _____   Most interesting aspect:

Easter Island Moai   Location:

Artist: _____   Rating (1-10): _____

Subject: _____   Most interesting aspect:

Now that you've seen some of the famous art of prehistoric cultures, what kind of themes do they have, in general?

Of all the ones we've seen, which would you be most likely to pick as a wall decoration in your room?

Ch. 2 MANSPLAININ' WORLD HISTORY?
Ourstory, anyone?

The term 'history' has been labeled a legacy of our patriarchal past (or nature), because it presents the human story with a masculine label. Some female professors, their students, and their allies in the late-20th century coined the term 'herstory' to signify history told from a female or even feminist perspective. This chapter introduces the term 'patriarchy' in the context of basically every culture in the past and even today having been patriarchal in the unequal average political or social-opportunity status of men vs. women. Is the term 'history,' then, a legacy of the patriarchal nature of society too? And if so, should it be subject to change? Traditionalists argue against changing the name 'history' to something else, because the word's tradition matters to them more than to others, who value change more so than keeping the word. If it were up to you, sitting on a council deciding what to call this World History class, what would you argue for, and why?

A similar debate took place in the 1980s in, of all things, the *Star Trek* universe. In the original 1960s show with Captain Kirk, he laid out the mission of the crew at the beginning of each episode as, "To boldly go where no man has gone before." By the 1980s, the new captain, Picard, changed it: "To boldly go where no one has gone before." Not long after, terms like 'mankind' became 'humankind.' In 1999, for example, *Time Magazine* changed its well known 'Man of the Year' award to 'Person of the Year.' Going against the grain, famed teacher Jacques Barzun argued against this de-masculinizing of collective terminology. In an essay called *The Word Man* (2000), he said:

"I adhere to the long use of 'man' as a word that means human being- people- men and women alike, whenever there is no need to distinguish them. The reasons in favor of prolonging that usage are four: etymology, convenience, the unsuspected incompleteness of 'man and woman,' and literary tradition. To begin with the last, it is unwise to give up a long-established practice, familiar to all, without reviewing the purpose it served. In Genesis we read: 'And God created Man, male and female.' Plainly, in 1611 and long before, 'man' meant human being. For centuries zoologists have spoken of the species Man: 'Man inhabits all the climatic zones.' Logicians have said 'Man is mortal,' and philosophers have boasted of 'Man's unconquerable mind.' The poet Webster writes: 'And man does flourish but his time.' In all these uses 'man' cannot possibly mean male only. The coupling of 'woman' to those statements would add nothing and sound absurd."

On the Moon, furthermore, there is a plaque that reads, "We came from Earth for all Mankind." It is dated July 20, 1969, and autographed by Neil Armstrong, Buzz Aldrin and Michael Collins. Incidentally, Neil Armstrong's first words on the Moon were, "That's one small step for man, one giant leap for mankind." Considering all this, where do you stand on Barzun's argument on preserving terms like 'man' and 'mankind' to mean both men and women?

In Western culture, the historical tradition dating to Eusebius in the 4th century and Augustine has been to divide time into **B.C.** and **A.D.**, which stand for 'Before Christ' and 'Anno Domini' (Year of the Lord). More recently, there has been a push to use B.C.E. and C.E., which stand for, 'Before Common Era' and 'Common Era.' This de-Christianizes the names of the labels, but not the division of time itself. During the French Revolution, the radical Jacobin government eliminated the entire convention, and renamed 1792 the Year 1. Which convention do you prefer, and why?

Ch. 2   HIS-STORY?   Matriarch_____

Are there more males in the history book? Okay maybe. Yeah probably. Well, definitely. But by how much?
Each person in the class take a letter. Maybe the letters should be handed out of a hat? Then, turn to the index of the textbook. Scan "your letter," and count how many names under that letter are male vs. female:

A
Male ____ *Female* ____

B
Male ____ *Female* ____

C
Male ____ *Female* ____

D
Male ____ *Female* ____

E
Male ____ *Female* ____

F
Male ____ *Female* ____

G
Male ____ *Female* ____

H
Male ____ *Female* ____

I
Male ____ *Female* ____

J
Male ____ *Female* ____

K
Male ____ *Female* ____

L
Male ____ *Female* ____

M
Male ____ *Female* ____

N
Male ____ *Female* ____

O
Male ____ *Female* ____

P
Male ____ *Female* ____

Q
Male ____ *Female* ____

R
Male ____ *Female* ____

S
Male ____ *Female* ____

T
Male ____ *Female* ____

U
Male ____ *Female* ____

V
Male ____ *Female* ____

W
Male ____ *Female* ____

X
Male ____ *Female* ____

TOTAL 'EM UP!

Y
Male ____ *Female* ____

Z
Male ____ *Female* ____

Male ____ *Female* ____

Ch. 2   ANCIENT LAW   Lawgiver _____

"Knock knock." Who's there? "The lawgiver." Crickets...

Lawgivers provide a legal basis for an orderly society. Acting as agents of the state, they fight for order in the eternal tug-of-war between order and freedom. Either extreme gets dicey: too much freedom brings anarchy, and too much order brings totalitarian control over people's lives. What's the happy medium? Societies have shaped different 'mediums' for themselves throughout the timeline. On the continuum below, place a dot where you think you'd like to live the most:

Anarchy   *Liberal freedoms*   *Tradition respected*   *Totalitarian*
_____

Is there a 'happy medium' here? If so, what defines it to you?

_____

The Babylonian Code of Hammurabi called for *An Eye for an Eye, a Tooth for a Tooth.* Why do you think this is called *Lex Talionis* (Law of Retribution)?

| Social class mattered a lot in Ancient times, and classes tended to be 'official,' as in, people in different classes had different rights. Why do you think 'An Eye for an Eye' only applied to people of the same class?

Moses became the lawgiver of the Israelites around 1100 B.C. In the Biblical Book of Exodus, he brought the law [Decalogue] down from Mt. Sinai. Match the commandment with the ethical idea behind it by drawing a line from one to the other:

#	Commandment	Ethical idea
1	*Thou shalt have no gods before Me.*	*Respect property rights*
2	*Thou shalt make no graven images.*	*Understand life and death*
3	*Thou shalt not take My name in vain.*	*Guard against jealousy*
4	*Thou shalt keep the Sabbath Day holy.*	*Monotheism*
5	*Honor thy Father and thy Mother.*	*Words have meaning*
6	*Thou shalt not kill.*	*Honor unity in marriage*
7	*Thou shalt not commit adultery.*	*Speak the truth*
8	*Thou shalt not steal.*	*Family, elders and nation*
9	*Thou shalt not bear false witness.*	*More to life than work*
10	*Thou shalt not covet what is thy neighbor's.*	*Careful who and what you idolize!*

In AP Psychology, there is reference to Lawrence Kohlberg and his theory of levels of moral reasoning. Which do you think appeals to a higher morality- Hammurabi's Code, which scares people into not doing antisocial things with threats of retribution, or the Mosaic Code, which presents ethical values to follow?

Ch. 2 PYRAMID! Vizier _____

Youtube: *Pyramid Macaulay*

This animated movie about Ancient Egypt takes place around 2500 B.C. during the Old Kingdom. It centers around the building of the Great Pyramid of the Pharaoh Khufu, the royal succession, and aspects of Egyptian culture.

Pharaoh:	*Khufu*	Describe the importance of ma'at, the balance of life,
Vizier:	*Ankath*	to the Ancient Egyptians:
Heir to throne:	*Kawab*	
Scribe:	*Hordedeth*	
Third in line:	*Balfra*	
Fourth in line:	*Jedethra*	
Fifth in line:	*Khafra*	

Geography and Environment
Religion and Worldview
Arts and Innovations
Politics and Government
Economy and Trade
Social Relationships

Use each of the above choices from the **GRAPES** chart to categorize the statements about the movie:

_____ Vizier Ankath redesigned the **architecture** of Khufu's burial chamber to foil would-be grave robbers, like the ones who robbed his father Sneferu's pyramid.

_____ Unlike the modern U.S., which obtained many of its prevailing **cultural norms** from Christianity, and has monogamous marriage written into law, in Ancient Egypt pharaohs had many wives, which is called polygamy.

_____ Kawab probably, on second thought, wishes he hadn't gone on that **trading expedition** up the Nile to Nubia.

_____ The sun-bird Amon-Re, who is seen by the Egyptians to set in the west, used a pyramidal shape upon which he created the land of Egypt- hence its **sacredness**.

_____ The Pharaoh's will, along with tradition, was the **law** of Egypt.

_____ Egypt is mostly **arid desert**, which is why these 4,500-year-old pyramids are not more worn down by rain and erosion.

The laborers who worked on the pyramid were conscripted, meaning they *had* to work on the project, but considered it a social obligation. Do you think this is a form of slavery, or a form of taxation? | Did you like the movie? Rate it and argue why it is (or is not), in your opinion, an effective way to learn about Ancient Egyptian culture:

Ch. 3   THE ORACLE   Visitor to Pythia _____

"It's not what you say, so much as how you say it"

The Oracle was visited ~700 B.C. by **Lycurgus**, lawgiver of Sparta. He sought advice on what kind of laws he should bring to his polis, and as Herodotus relates, it held him in high esteem. It said, "Love of money and nothing else will ruin Sparta." Lycurgus therefore devised a military state, in which physical arête and oligarchic hierarchy would encourage the equals to be proud, strong, and not money-grubbers. But the Oracle was right. Three centuries later, after victory over Athens in the Peloponnesian War, gold brought back from the famed city damaged Spartan values, bringing the city into slow decline.

The Oracle was visited ~594 B.C. by **Solon**, lawgiver of Athens. Like Lycurgus, he was unsure of which course to take politically because there was unrest. The Oracle told him, "Seat yourself now amidships, for you are the pilot of the city. Grasp the helm fast in your hands; you have more allies than you know." Using his connections in town, he obtained oaths from the council of magistrates, hammered out a new law code with jury trials, graduated taxes, and an equitable property resolution. After more reforms by Pisistratus and Cleisthenes, Athens not only a democracy, but the great sea power of Greece, for Solon indeed 'held fast the helm.'

The Oracle was visited ~560 B.C. by rich King **Croesus** of Lydia, minter of the first coins, whose kingdom had been subjugated by the Empire of Persia under Cyrus the Great. Croesus asked the Oracle if he should rise up against the empire, and it said, "If you make war on Persia, you will destroy a mighty kingdom!" Heartened with joy, Croesus gathered an alliance of cities and began to prepare for revolt. He sent for more advice, asking, out of curiosity, how long his monarchy would last. It said, "Whenever a mule shall become sovereign king, then, Lydian, flee, and think not to stand fast, nor shame to be chicken." Croesus began his revolt, pondering about the mule prophecy. But indeed it was *his* Lydian kingdom that was destroyed. As it turned out, the mother of Emperor Cyrus was a Mede, and his father was Persian, making him therefore a 'mule.'

At the approach of Xerxes' Persian army in 480 B.C., a group of Spartans under **Leonidas** consulted the Oracle on what to do. It said, "Either your famed, great town will be sacked by Perseus' sons (the Persians) or the whole lands of Lacedaemon (the province where Sparta is) shall mourn the death of a great king. Pray to the winds, they will prove mighty allies of Greece." In the event, Sparta was not sacked. But King Leonidas led his 300 Spartans into Thermopylae Pass, refused to retreat, died to the last man, and gained immortal fame. Later the Persian naval armada approached Cape Artemisium, and Athenian Admiral Themistocles rejoiced as a storm took out 1/5 of their ships before the battle at Salamis, where, under Xerxes watchful eye, the Athenians turned them back.

Socrates was a simple hoplite soldier until his friend **Chaerephon** (Kairo-fon) visited the Oracle ~440 B.C. and asked it, in jest, "Is there anyone alive wiser than Socrates?" to which it answered, "No." Mouths dropped. What? The Oracle can't be serious, but then it's never wrong! It's inspired by the god Apollo for Elysium's sake! Socrates got smart and made a leap of faith- he considered it might be right. But if so, how? He set off on a quest of find someone wiser, and couldn't because as he discovered, everyone's arguments crumbled under his cross-examination because he invented *logical reasoning* to counter their arguments. He discovered he had to *find the truth*, no matter where it took him, and that quest for truth began the history of philosophy- the seeking of wisdom.

While the Spartans were convinced of the Oracle's statement that they would win the Peloponnesian War in 403 B.C., **Lysander**, leader of the long Spartan siege against Athens, was warned by the Oracle, "Beware the serpent dragon, earthborn, in craftiness, creeping behind thee." A few years later after the Athenian surrender, however, he forgot about it. The war was over, after all. Then he was assassinated by a man... who had a serpent painted on his shield.

In 359 B.C. **Philip** of Macedon dreamed of fighting the Greek polis cities not because he despised them, but because he loved them, and wanted Greece to be united for once- united under him. So he visited the Oracle for advice. It said, "With silver spears you may conquer," and mentioned mysteriously that, "He who is able to tame the horse will rule." Philip readied his Macedonian warriors, but took the Oracle to heart. He used the silver of Thrace to buy himself allies and mercenaries in various polis cities. It gave him an advantage on his campaigns, which were successful. And the horse? There was a powerful colt called Bucephalus many tried to tame. But it was his young son Alexander who did it, realizing the colt was afraid of his shadow. Waiting until evening when things were calm, the horse rode like the wind. Philip gave Bucephalus to his son.

Alexander grew up. He studied with Aristotle, and knew all about the Oracle's powers. While planning his conquest of Persia in 336 B.C., he visited it for encouragement. But Pythia didn't answer. Brooding, he went back, and broke protocol. He dragged Pythia out by her hair and demanded an answer this instant! She said, "You are invincible!" That was good enough for him.

During the Hellenistic era, the Oracle retained its reputation. It was consulted by **Zeno** ~300, who asked it what direction he should take in his life. It replied, "Seek to gain the complexion of the dead." That was it. Troubled, Zeno pondered what it could mean. Literally? How could one get that pale in sunny Greece? He realized he must seclude himself in libraries, reading all the books of the ancients. After much trial, pain, hard work and scholarship, and discussion with people like Crates of Thebes, he digested the glory of the ancient classics. Having done so, he elaborated the philosophical school of Stoicism, wherein one strives to live a serious, hardworking and self-disciplined life with the goal of living in harmony with the divine reason that governs all of nature.

The Temple of Apollo, home of the Oracle of Delphi, took a beating once in a while. As Greece decayed into political disarray, it was sacked by the Celts (279 B.C.), the Romans (191 B.C.) and the Thracians (83 B.C.). Shortly thereafter, the great lawyer **Cicero**, Consul of Rome, came to seek wisdom from the battered temple. "Make your own nature, not the advice of others, your guide." While his friend Gaius Pompey fought Julius Caesar in civil war, Cicero returned to Rome, and, trusting his instincts, uncovered a conspiracy by senators led by Catiline to overthrow the government. He put this Catilinarian Conspiracy down, but when Caesar arrived, all bets were off.

Nero is reputed to be Rome's worst emperor. Caligula might be a close second, but Nero's feeding of Christians to the lions in the Circus Maximus, murder of his own mother, reputedly fiddling while watching a fire consume parts of the city below from his palace balcony, forcing Jews to kneel before a statue of him in the Temple in Jerusalem (idolatry), and other nasty stuff, if true, make him the winner. He visited the Oracle in 67 A.D., but it wasn't happy to see him. "Your presence here outrages Apollo, whose wisdom you seek. Be gone! The number 73 marks your downfall." Dissatisfied, Nero had Pythia pulled out from the temple and burned alive. A few years later, Galba led a conspiracy against Nero. His guard handed him a knife for an honorable suicide, but Nero reputedly wimped out, so the guard did him in. At the last moment, Nero was surprised because he was only 31 years old- even if the Oracle was right, how did his downfall have come so quickly? And true enough, Nero wasn't 73. But Galba was.

With the decline of Rome and the rise of Christianity, the Oracle fell into general disuse.

1. Go back and underline what the Oracle said in each passage.

2. List below the famous *people* who visited the Oracle:

3. Was the Oracle always right in these examples?

4. How might the Oracle be telling self-fulfilling prophecies?

Ch. 3　　　　　　　**GREEK TERMS USED IN ENGLISH**　　　Hoister _____

Want to activate your brain's epigens and maximize your Genetic Algorithm? Own. This. Culture.

Greek word	Words that employ the Greek meaning	Discern the Meaning from the Context:
Amphi	Amphibian, Ambidextrous	'Both'
Antiqua	Antique, Ancient	
Anti	Antidote, Antagonist	
Autos	Automobile, Autograph	
Biblos	Biblioteca, Bible	
Bios	Biology, Biography	
Chronos	Chronological, Chronometer (Clock!)	
Cosmos	Cosmopolitan, Cosmic	
Crypto	Cryptology, Crypt	
Cyclos	Bicycle, Encyclopedia	
Demos	Democratic, Demography	
Dosis	Anecdote, Dose	
Dynamis	Dynasty, Dynamite	
Ethnos	Ethnic, Ethnography	
Eu	Eudaimonia, Eutopia	

Gamos	*Monogamy, Polygamy*
Gramma	*Grammar, Monograph*
Ge	*Gaia, Geography*
Genos	*Genes, Genesis*
Heteros	Heterogeneous, Hetrodox
Homos	Homonym, Homogenous
Hydor	Hydrant, Hydraulics
Hyper	Hyperventilate, Hyperbole
Hypo	Hypodermic, Hypoglycemia
Logos	Monologue, Dialogue
Meta	Metaphysics, Metaphor
Metron	Metrics, Barometer
Morphe	Metamorphesis, Amorphous
Neos	New, Neolithic
Neuron	Neurosis, Neurology
Nomos	Astronomy, Economy
Opsis	Synopsis, Optic

Pan	Pangea, Panhellenic (Games)
Pathos	Pathology, Psychopath
Phone	Telephone, Symphony
Phos	Photograph, Photosynthesis
Polis	Metropolitan, Policy
Pro	Prophet, Proceed
Protos	Prototype, Protoceratops
Pseudes	Pseudonym, Pseudoscience
Psyche	Mind-Soul, Psychology
Pyr	Pyromania, Pyre
Sophia	Philosophy, Sophomore
Syn	Synthesis, Sympathy
Techne	Technique, Technological
Theos	Theology, Monotheism
Therme	Thermometer, Thermodynamic
Thesis	Hypothesis, Antithesis
Zoon	Zoology, Zodiac

Ch. 3 LATIN TERMS USED IN ENGLISH Hoister _____
There's a lot of them

LATIN TERMS STILL USED TODAY
(Put a little mark next to ones you've heard or used)

_____ a cappella	singing w/out instruments	_____ a priori	from what came before
_____ ad absurdum	taken to ridiculous lengths	_____ ad hoc	for this case only
_____ ad infinitum	going on forever	_____ ad lib	as one pleases
_____ ad nauseum	to the point of making us sick	_____ addendum	at the end of the book
_____ agenda	things to be done	_____ alea iacta est	the die is cast (Caesar)
_____ alias	otherwise known as	_____ alibi	I was elsewhere
_____ alma mater	school one graduated from	_____ alter ego	another me
_____ amor vincit omnia	love conquers all	_____ alumni	I went to that school
_____ anno domini	year of the lord	_____ aquila	eagle
_____ ante diluvian	very old, before the flood	_____ ante meridiem	before noon (A.M.)
_____ antebellum	before the war	_____ aurora borealis	northern lights
_____ audaces fortuna iuvat	fortune favors the bold	_____ ave atque vale	hello and goodbye
_____ audio, video, disco	I hear, I see, I learn	_____ bona fide	in good faith
_____ baccalaureus atrium	bachelor of arts (BA)	_____ carpe diem	seize the day
_____ caveat emptor	buy at your own risk	_____ casus belli	act to start a war
_____ centurion	lieutenant; soldier	_____ circa	around (ca.)
_____ cogito ergo sum	I think, therefore, I am	_____ culpa	fault, negligence
_____ curriculum vitae	in the course of life; resume	_____ cum laude	with honors
_____ de facto	in fact	_____ de jure	according to law
_____ de profundis	with deepest sorrow	_____ de rigueur	required by custom
_____ deus ex machine	god from the machine (plays)	_____ divide et impera	divide and conquer
_____ dramatis personae	cast of characters	_____ dolce vita	sweet life, relaxed
_____ e pluribus unum	from many, one	_____ emeritus	with merit
_____ ergo	therefore	_____ erratum	error
_____ Et tu, Brute?	You too, Brutus? (Caesar)	_____ et cetera	and so on (etc.)
_____ ex libris	from the library of	_____ ex cathedra	with authority
_____ ex post facto	from what is done after	_____ excelsior	ever higher
_____ exception probat regulam	the exception proves the rule	_____ exit mundi	end of the world
_____ extempore	without planning, winging it	_____ exempli gratia	for example (e.g.)
_____ facta, non verba	show me, don't tell me	_____ facsimile	make a similar one
_____ fauna	animal	_____ flora	plant
_____ gloria in excelsis Deo	glory to God in the highest	_____ finis	the end
_____ habeus corpus	you must have the body (law)	_____ honoris causa	for honor
_____ ignoratio elenchi	fallacy of irrelevant conclusion	_____ ibidem	in same place (ibid.)
_____ imperator	emperor	_____ imperium	total power
_____ imprimatur	let it be written	_____ in absentia	in the absence of
_____ in flagrant delicto	in act of committing offense	_____ in effigie	in the image of
_____ in flore	in bloom	_____ in futuro	in the future
_____ in memorium	in memory of	_____ in loco	at the place
_____ in rerum natura	in the nature of things	_____ in situ	in position
_____ in vino veritas	with wine comes truth	_____ in toto	totally, completely
_____ in vitro	in the glass	_____ incognito	in disguise
_____ inter alia	among other things	_____ inter alias	among other persons
_____ inter spem et metum	between hope and fear	_____ inter nos	between ourselves
_____ interregnum	interval between two rulers	_____ ipso facto	by the fact itself
_____ ipso iure	by operation of the law	_____ ius gentium	the law of nations
_____ justitia omnibus	and justice for all	_____ lapsus linguae	a slip of the tongue
_____ legionary	professional soldier	_____ lex loci	law of the place
_____ lex non scripta	unwritten law	_____ literati	people of letters

_____ lumen	light; enlightenment	_____ lusus naturae	freak of nature
_____ lux et veritas	light and truth	_____ magister atrium	master of arts (MA)
_____ magna cum laude	with great honors	_____ magnificat	magnificent
_____ magnum opus	greatest work	_____ mala fide	in bad faith
_____ mea culpa	mine own fault	_____ memorabilia	memorable things
_____ millennium	a thousand years	_____ modus operandi	way of operating
_____ modus vivendi	way of living	_____ moratorium	a delay
_____ morituri te salutant	you who are about to die, we salute you (said to gladiators when they fought!)		
_____ ne plus ultra	best possible example	_____ nihil	nothing
_____ nolens volens	willing or unwilling	_____ nolo contendere	no contest
_____ non campos mentis	not of sound mind	_____ non sequitur	it doesn't follow
_____ nota bene (n.b.)	an additional note	_____ o tempora!	oh the times! (Cicero)
_____ oderint dum metuant	let them hate, so long as they fear		
_____ odi et amo	I hate and I love her	_____ onus probandi	the burden of proof
_____ opera citato (op.cit)	in the cited work	_____ ophidia in herba	snake in the grass
_____ panem et circenses	bread and circuses	_____ pater noster	our father
_____ pax	peace	_____ per annum	yearly
_____ per capita	per head (per person)	_____ per cent	per hundred
_____ per diem	daily	_____ per se	in and of itself
_____ persona non grata	person not welcome	_____ post meridiem (P.M.)	after noon
_____ post mortem	after death	_____ post partum	after birth
_____ post scriptum (p.s.)	afterthought	_____ praetorian	elite guard
_____ prima facie	at first sight	_____ primum non nocere	first, do no harm
_____ primus inter pares	first among equals	_____ pro bono	for the public good
_____ pro forma	for formality	_____ pro patria	for our country
_____ pro tempore (pro tem)	temporarily	_____ probatum est	it has been proved
_____ plus ratio quam vis	reason over force	_____ quaere varum	seek the truth
_____ punctum saliens	the outstanding point	_____ quarter	four
_____ quasi	in part	_____ qui tacet consentit	silence is consent
_____ quem deus vult perdere, dementat prius - whom the gods choose to destroy, they first make mad			
_____ quis custodiet ipsos custodies? - who will guard the guardians?			
_____ qui vive?	who goes there?	_____ quid pro quo	a favor for a favor
_____ quo vadis	where are you going?	_____ quorum	of whom
_____ re	concerning (re:)	_____ redivivus	come back to life
_____ reductio ad absurdum	reduction to absurdity	_____ referendum	to be voted (referred)
_____ regina	queen	_____ requiescat in pace	rest in peace (RIP)
_____ res ipsa loquitur	it speaks for itself	_____ res iudicata	it has been judged
_____ rex	king	_____ rigor mortis	the rigidity of death
_____ salve	hello	_____ satis	enough
_____ semper fidelis	always faithful	_____ sic vita est	such is life
_____ si vis pacem, para bellum	if you wish for peace prepare for war		
_____ sic	intentionally as written	_____ signetur	let it be signed
_____ sine qua non	indispensable	_____ statim (stat!)	immediately
_____ status quo	the current state	_____ stricto sensu	in the strict sense
_____ sub poena	under penalty of law	_____ sub rosa	under the secret rose
_____ sui generis	of his/its own kind	_____ summa cum laude	with highest praise
_____ summum bonum	the highest good	_____ tabula rasa	blank slate
_____ terra firma	solid ground	_____ terra incognita	unknown land
_____ unus multorum	one of many	_____ vale	farewell
_____ vanitas vanitatum, Omnia vanitas - vanity, vanity, all is vanity (Ecc. 1:2)			
_____ veni, vidi, vici	I came, saw, conquered	_____ vera causa	true cause of
_____ verbatim	exact, letter for letter	_____ veritas vos liberabit	truth will set you free
_____ versus	against	_____ veto	I forbid
_____ via	by way of	_____ vice versa	with places exchanged
_____ vox populi	voice of the people	**Of all these, pick three you will use & note them:**	

Ch. 3   EMPERORS' MATRIX   Food Taster _____

Can I get a thumbs up?

Tracing the Roman Empire from its rise through its zenith, decline and finally collapse is fun. Match the 'caesar' with his role in history:

_____ Marched on the Republic with his legions, became dictator, assassinated ☹

_____ 1st century. Started *Pax Romana*, recognized as one of history's great admins

_____ 1st. Captain Kirk's middle namesake, he built a grand palace

_____ 1st. 'Tis said he made his 'talking' horse a senator and was hated. Assassinated.

_____ 1st. He fiddled while the city burned; a testament to the *Pax Romana* though

_____ 1st. Military man, fought and sent the Jews of Judea into diaspora

_____ 1st. Famous column honors this conquering emperor, Rome was at its height

_____ 2nd. Ominously built a wall across Britannia to bound the empire

_____ 2nd. Philosopher-emperor whose reign was the last of the greatest times

_____ 2nd. Born rich turned decadent, a "gladiator," cowardly, lustful, assassinated.

_____ 3rd. Seized power with Pannonian legion, restored order, triumphal arch

_____ 3rd. Captured at Edessa by Persians, said to have been stuffed. A low point.

_____ 4th. Split empire into two and moved to the Dalmatian coast to manage it better

_____ 4th. Having seen 'In this sign, conquer,' legalized Christianity & founded a city

_____ 4th. Fought barbarian attacks whole time until killed at the Battle of Adrianople

_____ 4th. Outlawed Olympian gods, tried to unify empire and reinvigorate the dream

_____ 5th. Watched the Visigoths come over the 7 hills to wreck the imperial capital

_____ 5th. Watched empire get dismembered, made deal with Goths against Huns

_____ 5th. Deposed by Ostrogoth chieftain to end empire- passed torch to Byzantium

Augustus Caesar	**Caligula**	**Commodus**	**Constantine**	**Diocletian**
Hadrian	**Julius Caesar**	**Honorius**	**Marcus Aurelius**	**Nero**
Romulus Augustulus	**Septimus Severus**		**Theodosius**	**Tiberius**
Trajan	**Valentinian III**	**Valens**	**Valerian**	**Vespasian**

Ch. 3 — CONRAD-DEMAREST MODEL — Social Gravity Theorist _____

Are we doomed to be doomed?

Conrad-Demarest Model of Empire – Note which example best fits **Rome**, the **Guptas** and **Han**:

1. Preconditions for the rise of empire: Agricultural potential, environmental resources, several small, antagonistic states around with none overly dominant (power vacuum), military potential:

_____ *Kept most functions of an already centralized dynastic state in place*

_____ *Evolved from a Republican form of government that became unstable*

_____ *Brought together from many conquered regional kingdoms and states*

2. Reasons for the success of building empire: In the building phase, there is a feeling of personal identification with the people, the community and the state which is being built. Values and a moral code are defined and followed with strength and even joy. The growth of the empire is considered a personal victory for the citizens. People are proud of their country's increasing power.

_____ *Emphasized proper social roles, meritocracy, mandate of heaven*

_____ *Strict social caste system enforced by linking order to religion*

_____ *Concepts of citizenship, loyalty, republican-imperial order emphasized*

3. Major rewards of empire: The rewards are economic first and foremost, wealth and trade flow to elites and in a smaller portion to all levels of citizenry, population increase, increasing complexity of society accompanies specialization by professionals, more services, and schools of thought. The expense of this cosmopolitanism is an erosion of the original core values of the founding people may lead to increasing decadence over time, but for now, prosperity. Life is good.

_____ *Urbanized life, new technology, aqueducts & water, legions offer 'a place'*

_____ *Mathematic advances, algebra, numbers, the zero*

_____ *Tribute from foreign relations, storehouses for food to lessen famine*

4. Decline and fall of empire: Empires fall because the ideology of expansion and conquest drove them to take and rule beyond their capacity (imperial overstretch), shaking the faith of the people in the power and lasting nature of their empire, decay and decadence in the culture accompanies this, and social revolution, barbarian invasion (or assault by another empire) brings it to its knees.

_____ *Yellow Turbans stir rebellion, tenant farmers, bandits and rebels attack government facilities, tax revenues fall, soldiers cannot be paid, rebel*

_____ *White Huns invade, states do not help each other, inability of rulers to control rajas, who fight each other for territory*

_____ *Population decline, barbarian settlement, latifundias offer protection, legions recruit foreign mercenaries, Gothic and Hun forces sack cities*

Ch. 3   THE CYCLE OF EMPIRE   Guiding Force _____

Are we doomed to be doomed?

Empires (and large, multicultural, civilization-sized countries) have come, and have *all* gone. Except for the ones around today, whose future may be uncertain. Is it? Let's look at the lessons of the past. Download and look at the five paintings by Thomas Cole entitled, **'Cycle of Empire.'**

	Buildings and sculptures	**Lifestyle clues**	**Conrad-Demerest Stage**
Stage I: Savage State			
Stage II: Arcadia			
Stage III: Empire			
Stage IV: Destruction			
Stage V: Desolation			

Having invented or pioneered aluminum, amphitheaters, aqueducts, arches, baths, brass work, camel harnesses, cement, city planning, concrete, crank handles, cranes, dams, domes, force pump nozzles, glass, greenhouses, hypocaust heating, mill grinding, paddle-wheel boats, reaper harvesting, sails, roller bearings, rudders, screw presses, sewers, spiral staircases, street maps, tunnels and wood veneer, among other things including legal and political systems, the Romans lost their organizational footing in the 3rd century- and fell into decadence and decline. Which phases would the 200s A.D. fit between in the above scheme?

_____

Ch. 4   THE TAO OF POOH   Uncarved block _____

FYI: 'Tao' is the traditional way of spelling 'Dao'- meaning 'The Way,' and Laozi is how our book spells the name Lao Tzu

Characters are often given traits by their authors which reflect some great concept or idea. Luke Skywalker in Star Wars is an innocent young man who, by becoming involved in an epic role not of his own making, undertakes a hero's journey. At the end of it, he comes-of-age in a rite-of-passage that can be a positive example for others to follow. The *characters* in Winnie the Pooh, written in the 1920s by A.A. Milne, were similarly made to represent various ideals. Search: *The Tao of Winnie the Pooh* and find the *Slideshare* on it.

According to Laozi (and Pooh :)
The secrets to being happy are:

4) Happiness is:

5) In everyday moments:

1)

2)

6) Let go of _____

3)

7) What does each character do based on its 'Way' (*Tao*)?

While **Eeyore** _____, and **Piglet** _____, and **Rabbit** _____

and **Owl** _____, and **Tigger** _____ ...**Pooh** _____

8) Jot down the *Tao* of each, then rate yourself 1-10 on how much **you** embody that *Tao*:

Piglet   **Tigger**   **Eeyore**   **Rabbit**

My rating: _____   _____   _____   _____

Owl   **Kanga**   **Christopher Robin**   **Pooh**

My rating: _____   _____   _____   _____

9) The two characters most like me are:
_____

10) Which characters best embody the principles of:

Yin: *Yang:*   *Wuwei:*   *Confucius:*

Ch. 4   SECRET KNOWLEDGE: METAPHORS   Virtuous _____

Own. Your. Culture.

History class is not boring. Why? Because it gives you trans-generational epigenetic inheritance, i.e.: the transfer of information from one generation to another that affects the traits of the offspring organism without alteration of the primary structure- the nucleotide sequence of that organism's DNA. Take the following three metaphors and try to match them up **without** looking:

Box 1   Box 2   Box 3   Box 4

_____ _____ _____ _____ *C'est la vie, c'est la guerre, c'est la pomme de terre.*

_____ _____ _____ _____ *Veni, vidi, vici.*

_____ _____ _____ _____ *Viel stroh, wenig Korn.*

Box 1: Translation   **2: Language**   **3: Likely Speaker**   **Box 4: Meaning**

a. Much straw, little corn.   a. French   a. Julius Caesar   a. In the extremes of condition, bad things must happen.

b. This is life, this is war, this is the whole potato.   b. German   b. Otto von Bismarck   b. It was short and sweet.

c. I came, I saw, I conquered.   c. Latin   c. Charles de Gaulle   c. Much ado about nothing.

Metaphors are really a kind of slang wisdom from the past. Trying to figure out what related ones, like these three, hold in common as implied wisdom, means you have to think about their subtlety of meaning. This meaning is sharable between cultures of like minds, so you *can* do it. What do you think all these statements have in common?

_____

In the history of Western culture, there have been people who really care about searching for the truth. We got the idea from the Greeks. Socrates valued the seeking of truth as the highest aim one could aspire to. "Full disclosure" is that which is unconcealed, unhidden, in the open, in light. Enlightenment. 20th century philosopher Martin Heidegger commented on what it means: "To raise the question of *aletheia*, of disclosure as such, is not the same as raising the question of truth. For this reason, it was inadequate and misleading to call *aletheia*, in the sense of opening, truth." So, *aletheia* is not truth? No, not quite. It is the unconcealedness that opens the way for us to find truth. One thing he said could do this well was great art. Let's think about the arts for a moment. Think about paintings, musical scores or songs, or other art, think about a work that helped you see things better, more clearly, even approaching truth:

Ch. 4   WHO MOURNS FOR ADONAIS?   Collector of thistle _____

Would you fire?

The *Star Trek* episode *Who Mourns for Adonis (S2-E2)* was written to reflect the 1960s notion that human progress through the historical timeline means we outgrow some of the myths and legends of the past, in a way that puts us almost 'on our own' in the universe. This is a tough fear to overcome, the idea that we are alone. And we certainly may not be! Our universe might be permeated with higher powers, a divine being or beings, or other biological beings spread around the vast cosmic dark. Our deepest religious beliefs have centered around the idea that we are not alone, while modern science tells us there are billions of planets out there for life to appear on, and we are probably not alone by sheer statistical probability.

Before watching, who was Adonais (Adonis) in Greco-Roman mythology?

     a. king of the gods   b. messenger of the gods   c. ever-youthful, handsome cult figure

At the beginning, when the Enterprise approached the planet, what strange thing held it in place?

_____

(this is symbolic of our culture and beliefs holding us stable, yet constrained at the same time)

Notice how Captain Kirk says, "Set us free!" This is a foreshadowing of humanity asking to be set free from the ties that bind us to our past. When they beam down to the planet, who do they encounter? _____, whose role in Greco-Roman mythology was:

     a. king of the gods   b. messenger of the gods   c. god of the sea   d. god of war

     e. god of music, wisdom, truth, prophecy, sun, light, poetry, and more. Yep, all that.

When the god informs Kirk and crew that he misses Earth and Greece, and he is happy they finally 'grew up' enough to travel in space themselves, and stumble upon him, what does he say he wants them to do?

     a. keep journeying, keep growing   b. stay there and worship him like 2,500 years ago on Earth

What specific arguments does Kirk use as to why the Humans (and Vulcan) should not be held captive?

_____

There is a bit of sadness at the end, among the crew (especially Carolyn Palamas), a bit of melancholy about having 'grown up' so much that the Olympian gods no longer had a role in their culture. What does Kirk say at the end that reveals this sadness at growing up?

| Do you think our great stories and epic tales
| of the past have a role in modern society still?
| What do you think that role might be?
|
|
|
|
|

Ch. 4   HELLENIC PHILOSOPHY: THE BEGINNING OF REASON   Observer _____
Welcome to the Great Conversation. Buckle up!

Thales of Miletus is considered the first scientist. He toured Babylon in 583 B.C. and they told him the god Marduk hurled lightning bolts, but he was confused because he was told in Greece that Zeus was the one who did that. He had never heard of Marduk before. Could they both be right? He didn't think so, so he made a leap of reasoning from "if only one could be right, one must be wrong," to, "Maybe both of them are wrong?" Maybe it was just some mysterious natural phenomenon? So he dug into the Babylonian astronomical archives, and was shocked to find that eclipses did not happen randomly, but in long, discernable patterns. He also saw that weather conditions were a good predictor of good and bad harvests. Thales was amazed, and when he went home to Greece, he predicted to his friends when the next eclipse was going to happen, but they laughed at him because "no one can possibly know when that's going to happen!" But Thales did. In the following years, he tracked the weather, and one winter bought all the olive presses in the land. Why? Because he knew there would be a great olive harvest the following spring, and wanted a monopoly on squeezing them. He was right again, having used science to get rich! Next, he hypothesized that nature arose from some self-animated substance, which moves and changes in various forms. But what was it? He knew it had to be essential to life, because life *exists*, and it must be something *arche* (very old), something omnipresent- everywhere, which underlies all things. It's... water! At least he thought it was. Because water exists as ice, liquid & vapor, and it does kind of surround the "world." Q: How was Thales' way of questioning- whether he was right or wrong- **new**?

Pythagoras of Samos studied geometry. In 520 B.C., he came up with a bizarre hypothesis: that numbers *govern* the cosmos. In other words, numbers rule! His reasoning was that since everything in the universe conforms to mathematical rules and ratios, numerical values must be embedded into the fabric of the universe. If we can understand these numerical relationships, we can come to understand the structure of the whole cosmos, and so mathematics is the supreme subject- nature's key. His own theorem is a good example ($a^2+b^2=c^2$, when c is the hypotenuse of a triangle and angle a/b is a right angle of 90 degrees). This is the underlying *principle* behind all right-angled triangles and is *always* true. From it, Pythagoras concluded laws and axioms must explain the workings of nature, so he devised dimensions, those being _, <>, and [3]. Numbers filled his mind; he saw them everywhere- and heard them too. Upon hearing a harp being played, he understood strings made certain notes in precise ratios, and when a smith hit an anvil half the size of another, the new 'note' produced followed precisely the same pattern- one octave (8 notes) apart. Further, he noted some notes are harmonious when paired, and could predict mathematically which ones they were- Music is math, and math became music to his ears! Then, Pythagoras looked up to see if there were harmonics in the heavens too, and concluded: "There is geometry in the humming of harp strings, and there is music in the movements of the celestial spheres." Later, it would be found that the elements of the Periodic Table are harmonic too, and that every 8th element has similar properties. From all this he invented a way of thinking called *deductive reasoning*, in which one starts with an axiom and trusts that, "Because X is true, these other things must also be true." Abstract thinking, he said, was more reliable than the senses: "Reason is immortal, all else is mortal." Q: If deductive reasoning is from general axiom to specific situation, what is inductive reasoning, its opposite?

Heraclitus in 480 B.C. argued that the universe is governed by a single cosmic law (divine *logos*), according to which all things come into being, move through time, and eventually die. He wanted to know what that law was, of course, which keeps the elements of the universe in orderly motion. He hypothesized it was an ongoing struggle between opposites: hot and cold, day and night- a struggle to be in balance, and for that to happen, everything must be in a state of *flux*, meaning constant change. People think the universe is a 'stable' thing- but that stability is an illusion. He thought the *essence* of the universe was water, like Thales did, but believed the *#1 Law* of the universe was change. To use an aquatic example, he said: "You can never step into the same river twice." Q: Do you agree or disagree with that?

Parmenides of Elea in 460 B.C. wanted to know what was genuinely real, and stated "all is one," like the Transformers under Optimus Prime would later on. Why? A follower of Pythagoras and the idea that numbers are the key to the universe, Parmenides used deductive reasoning too, but came up with a different answer. He said the premise that something exists means that it cannot also *not* exist at the same time, because this is a logical contradiction. This means that a state of nothing existing is impossible, a void is impossible, and something cannot come from nothing, so everything must have always existed in some form or another. Everything that *is*, must be in some way eternal, unchanging, and have some underlying unity- all is one. We sense 'change' all around us, but reason tells us change-of-essence is impossible. Thus, we cannot rely on our senses. The elements themselves move in and out of various combinations and that is what produces the illusion of change happening. 'Change' is really just a reordering of things. The elements themselves do not pass away or come into being. They recycle for all-time. Q: Would the fact that fossil fuels like coal and petroleum (gas/oil) come from decayed plant life that's been sitting in the earth for 300 million years support or argue against this conclusion?

Empedocles in 450 B.C. believed Heraclitus and Parmenides were right about change being the key thing going on in the cosmos, so he tried to identify the mysterious 'elements' that did not *ever* change, which must then be *eternal*. He identified four root elements: earth, water, air and fire. These move together and apart in different combinations by forces he called *Love* and *Strife*. That sounds weird, and was improved on by **Anaxagoras**, who a decade later proposed the universe, even these root elements, was made of super-tiny seeds, which are moved around and reordered all the time, but not by blind forces like *Love* and *Strife*, but by a transcendent *Mind* of some kind, which set the entire material universe into motion, gave it form and order, and made it go. Q: How do these arguments *differ*?

Protagoras of Abdera in 440 B.C. didn't believe something like 'truth' exists. Why? He was a lawyer, who bragged how he "could make the worse argument the better," (make a lie into truth) by simply convincing a jury *his perspective* was true. And if they believed it, that made it 'true'. So he went to Athens during the Golden Age, where there were many smart people from different cities. They came to discuss philosophy and other things, and he decided to prove to them that 'truth' was really just 'an opinion.' On a spring day, he asked a visitor from Egypt if it was hot or cold out, and he said "cold." He asked a visitor from Germania the same question, however, and this person said, "hot." Both people were telling the "truth," and so Protagoras argued the truth was *relative*, as in, relative to the perspective of the person making the statement. "Man, himself, is the measure of all things," he concluded. Truth is not *objective*- it is *subjective*. There are no absolute definitions to justice, virtue or truth. What is true for one person may be false for another. Nothing is good *in itself*, something is good or ethical only because people agree it is amongst themselves. Q: Do you think there is any *real* truth out there, or are Protagoras and the Sophists right that it's all "just an opinion?"

Democritus of Abdera waved his hand through the air in 400 B.C. and felt something. He knew that the air was not empty, because if it were, he would have felt nothing- no 'woosh'. Thus, there must be something there- too small to see, that makes up 'air.' So how small do small things get? If you take a piece of paper and cut it in half, then cut that half in half, and then that half in half, how many times can you cut it until it is gone? Technically, this is a paradox because if you cut something in half you cannot ever make it disappear, since the other half will always still be there. Eventually, however, he concluded, you'll get to something so small that you cannot only not see it, but you cannot cut it in half anymore. These things, he hypothesized, are super-tiny and of infinite number. They are the "basic building blocks" of matter, separated by voids of empty space in which they move about randomly, combining and recombining into visible matter. He called these things *atoms,* the Greek word for *uncuttables*. Parmenides was wrong, further, in saying that nothing cannot exist, since nothing isn't nothing- it's something: *a place in which atoms move* (i.e.: space). Matter is always conserved. It cannot perish. Only specific combinations of atoms change, creating and dissolving in infinite ways, on worlds throughout the void. Q: Who was more right about this, Parmenides or Democritus, and why?

Xenophanes, Anaxagoras and Aristophanes hailed the emerging victory of *reason*. Xenophanes made fun of the Olympian gods and people who believed in them because he could not reason why there would be gods engaged in precocious activities all the time, messing with people voodoo-style as they went. Anaxagoras likewise made fun of people who said the Sun *was* the god Helios, claiming instead that it is a "huge incandescent stone larger than the Peloponnese," and that "the Moon is made of the same stuff the Earth was made out of, and the sun's light is reflected off of it." Aristophanes, meanwhile, parodied the gods in his comedies. But Xenophanes emphasized that no one was really sure what was up with the supernatural world. Critical judgment is one thing, but if the world is based on purely mechanical natural forces, then there might not be an evident basis upon which to base firm moral judgments… *scary*. "And if true reality is entirely divorced from common experience, then the very foundations of human knowledge may be called into question." It seemed that the more man became freely and consciously self-determining, the less sure was his footing. "The gods did not reveal all things to us," he said, "but in the course of time, we must find out for ourselves." Q: To you, can rational clarity and mathematical elegance ever hope to coexist with the divine?

Ch. 4   HELLENIC PHILOSOPHY: SOCRATES   Contemplator _____

Toga! Toga! Toga!

Can 'mind', or else, 'minding your mind,' make you a better person? Can philosophy help you to actually live a Good life? Well, Socrates said it could. He grew up when the old gods of Olympus were being called into question by some of the Athenians. People were wondering if virtue could be taught without them. Socrates said yes, through reason, and being reasonable itself could be taught, and that good, freethinking people can be molded into being from humble beginnings. They can then question the meaning of essential concepts that we use every day, but don't think about, and in so doing, find the essence of those concepts, an essence which holds true for everyone in the world, always. No relativism here! Socrates taught about the role of reason in a person's ethical outlook on life. Q: Was Socrates' outlook optimistic or pessimistic? Why?

Born in the 5th Century B.C., Socrates died in 399 at 70, condemned to death by a jury of 501 democratic citizens. No one, except perhaps Jesus, has made more of a difference in the history of Europe. All philosophy after Socrates (and all science- which is a spin off of philosophy) was inspired by him. Half of Western culture depends on Socrates. Every single philosophical school in antiquity (except materialistic Epicureanism) claims lineage from him. What made him different was his new way of thinking- Socrates invented a skeleton key for thinking, a power tool for reasoning: he invented *the logical argument*. We use this all the time today, ironically, often without thinking! For example, when a point is proven to be true (to any reasonable person), that was done using logical reasoning. Reason is a thing, a thing that can be used, a thing that is shared, and appealed to. The American Founders appealed to the "reason of mankind" in stating why they were separating from Britain. Socrates questioned people as a lawyer questions someone in court, through cross-examination- this is the Socratic method. If A is B, and B is C, then it must be true that A is C. Sounds like one of the properties you study in math class. Because it is. Q: What achievements in the process of thinking and talking did Socrates develop?

It seems simple and innate to use logic and reason, but this art had to be discovered and practiced. It awoke from its long slumber in the mind of Socrates, who gave it expression through his words and actions. In the mind of Socrates, reason became aware of itself. He famously said: "Virtue IS knowledge, and vice IS ignorance." If you really know the Good, as in, what is Good for you, then you will do the Good thing always. Thus, what is evil? Evil is *ignorance* of the Good. This means not ignorance of facts, but ignorance of values in general. Rational self-criticism can free the human mind from the bondage of false opinion! What does Socrates mean by saying that virtue *is* knowledge and vice *is* ignorance? We all have the experience of knowing what is Good and yet choosing evil. Socrates is not ignorant of this fact of human nature, and his answer as to why we do this sometimes is found in one of the great speeches ever made: *The Apology,* given before the court of Athens. An apology is not an admission of guilt and sorrow, in this case, but a defense of beliefs and actions. "I would like to apologize" actually means, "I would like to explain myself." Q: What is virtue and what is vice, according to Socrates?

In the event, Socrates tells the democratic crowd in the Theater of Dionysus, which is now a jury, the story about how he became a seeker of wisdom (philosopher). He is on trial for atheism (not believing in the gods of Olympus), and he answers that charge by relating how pious he really is, with the following story: At Delphi, there existed the Delphic Oracle, a prophetess who gave guaranteed true answers in the form of riddles inspired by the god Apollo. Even Greeks who were skeptical of the gods (and there were many) believed in the Oracle because it always came out right. So, when he was a young man, Socrates' friend Chaerephon asked the Oracle, "Is there anyone in this world wiser than my friend Socrates?" And the oracle answered "No." Well, when Chaerephon told Socrates this, Socrates was shocked. He didn't have any true wisdom- he knew he didn't. He was just a regular person, without any great insight into the nature of things. But now comes the part that proves his belief: instead of dismissing the Oracle as a fraud, Socrates made a leap of faith. He hypothesized it was possible the Oracle did *not* lie, that it was *not* wrong, and therefore wanted to understand the meaning of the Oracle's riddle. However, to be sure it was not wrong, he decided to go out and find a person wiser than himself, to take to the Oracle, so it would explain its riddle to him more clearly. But he never got to go to the Oracle with this wise person, because he never found him. What he found, instead, was that everybody who *thought* they had wisdom lost most of it when Socrates' cross-examined them. They *believed* they were wise, but once challenged by Socrates' and his method, it turned out they were not, and so not only were they not wise, but they were doubly-flawed, because they erroneously *believed* that they were. Q: How was Socrates "wiser" than the people he talked to?

Thus, the self-fulfilling prophecy of the Oracle came to pass because the Oracle's answer made Socrates go out and *invent* the Socratic method, discover the nature of ignorance, initiate the art of cross-examination still used by lawyers and debaters today, and become the first philosopher. The Oracle's riddle was the catalyst that originated Western philosophy's whole method of understanding! An example of the Socratic method: he found a judge who sat on juries, and asked him a question:

S: Oh great and wise politician, what are you wise about? J: I am wise about justice- that's my thing. S: Ah, could you answer me the simplest question about what justice is, so I don't confuse it with injustice? J: Come on, Socrates, everybody knows what justice is. S: So then you do too? Please tell me so I might also know. J: If you insist. It means paying back what you owe and being paid back in turn what is owed to you. S: Thank you kind sir! Good day. Oh wait- before you go, I'm not sure I understand your definition. Do you mean that if I'd lent you my knife, and then, for reasons unknown, became maniacal, that it would be 'just' for you to give me back my knife while I was in that state of insanity? J: Well no! Of course not. Do I look like an idiot? S: So, by your own admission, justice is not always paying back what is owed, because in this case paying me back would be to give me back my property. Please, sir, tell me what justice is universally- by its very essence. J: Socrates, don't be a troublemaker! (man becomes angry and storms off). Q: What is the *essence* of justice?

Socrates went home, thinking that he didn't learn much about what justice is, but thinking he did learn a lot about what wisdom and ignorance are. This man thought he was wise, but he was not. The Sophists, likewise, were teachers in Athens who hired out their tutoring-skills to wealthy young dudes who wanted to be in political life. They wanted to be leaders and to be successful. To these young men, the Sophists promised to teach the skills they needed to help them get ahead in life- to be successful by hook, or by crook. To that end, they taught them all moral standards were mere conventions, that all knowledge was relative. Socrates found this educational philosophy intellectually misconceived and morally detrimental. In opposition to the Sophists' view, Socrates saw his own task as that of finding a way to knowledge that transcended opinion, to inform a morality that transcended that which is merely conventional. Q: What would justice be according to the Sophists?

a. Something absolute, which can be found through investigation   b. Something relative to the person doing the judging

Socrates found out that people come in one of two kinds: 1) fools who think they are wise, and 2) the wise who know they are ignorant. He therefore tried to help people become wiser, by teaching them, or else getting them to understand that once they realized they were ignorant, their quest for true knowledge could begin. Those who would undertake this quest were people who loved objective knowledge so much, that they would be prepared to seek it wherever it may lead them. They would become *philo-sophers* (those who love wisdom) and start asking questions. Only though self-knowledge can one find genuine happiness, and all human beings seek happiness by their very nature. Happiness is the key to living the kind of life that best serves the nature of the soul. Humble yourself, and the Socratic paradox, that you can only know by admitting you do not really know, will take form in you. Q: What is happiness, according to Socrates?

In *The Apology*, Socrates taught another paradox: he taught the jury to be sure that: "If you sentence me to death, you are actually harming yourselves- for the eternal law makes it impossible for someone good to be harmed by someone bad." A riddle? What did he mean? It's baffling, really, because he means it is literally impossible for a good person to suffer at the hands of a bad one. Socrates' answer to, "why bad things happen to good people?" is that they never do! Yes, Socrates is giving us a puzzle, and, in solving it, we can become wiser. **Solving the puzzle**: His meaning is that Apollo's command to "Know Thyself" does not mean "know what personal feelings and experiences you have had in your life" but instead, it means "know what a human being is, and therefore what you are- and what the *nature* of being human is." Put another way, it means asking, "What is the *essence* of mankind?" If you find the answer to his question, you will find the answer to why a good person cannot suffer evil. The link is that evil cannot be done to a good person because of what man's basic essence is. So what is it? Well, it is that which is left when everything else has been taken away from a person. When honor, freedom, and even life are taken away, only the *essence* is left. Socrates himself provided a great example at his execution, in which everything, even his life, really was taken away. The essence of a person is his or her virtue and wisdom, which cannot be taken away no matter what. And where are these essential things- virtue and wisdom- located? They are not located in a person's mind or body, but in their soul. The true self, therefore, is the soul- the inner self. The soul is the inner light, where 'you' exist. That is why bad people cannot harm Good people, because they cannot attack your soul. Evil from outside can attack your body, and it can harm your body, it can even kill your body. But the only evil that can ever be visited upon the essence of you, your soul, comes from YOU. It comes by your folly, your self-destructiveness, and your vice. No one *else* but you can make you foolish or vicious, or, for that matter, wise and virtuous. No one but YOU is in charge of your soul, your character, your personality. Not society, but only *you*- you are the captain of your soul, the sovereign of your life, and, ultimately, the master of your fate. Q: Do you agree or disagree with Socrates that your life is the life of your soul? Why?

Ch. 4 **WEEKS AND DAYS** Chronologist _____

Shout out to Hesiod = winner of 'most obscure pun' this year. So far.

	Greek deity	**Latin name**	*Match the months with why they're named that*
1	Hermes		J
2	Aphrodite		F
3	Gaia		M
4	Ares		A
5	Zeus		M
6	Kronos		J
7	Ouranos		J
8	POSEIDON		A
9	Hades		S

Match up the Latin-Roman equivalent names: | O

Jupiter, Mars, Terra, Pluto | N
Neptune, Mercury, Venus
Saturn, Uranus | D

Month naming choices:

Named after Julius Caesar
Februa was the feast of Roman purification
The 7th month- or a seven sided figure
Named after Augustus Caesar
The 9th month- or a nine sided figure
Juno's month has the most weddings

Maya was the goddess of blooming plants
The 10th month- or a ten sided figure
Janus was the god of doorways and new years
Aphrodite's month brought rain and new life
Mars returns to make war after a long winter
The 8th month- or an eight sided figure

Hint: Julius and Augustus wanted their months in the middle of the year when everyone is happy in summer- not at the end of the year by the Winter Solstice festival, because who likes winter anyway!

_____ Sunday   a. Thor's day named for the Nordic thunder god- Jupiter in Rome (think of Spanish)
_____ Monday   b. Day of the Moon (Mond in German), or think of 'Moon day' in Spanish
_____ Tuesday   c. Odin the Nordic god became Woden, and was Mercury in Rome (think of French)
_____ Wednesday d. Day of the Germanic 'Sonne,' became the Christian Sabbath later on
_____ Thursday e. Ares in Greece became Mars in Rome, equivalent to the Nordic Tiw (Martes in Sp.)
_____ Friday   f. Venus' Day in Rome was rendered into the Nordic Freya's Day
_____ Saturday g. No need for translation, the last one is Saturn's Day!

Ch. 5   A SOCIALIST EMPEROR?   Land reformer _____

Guess what- he was a usurper too. Bold dude.

Wang Mang had an interesting life. He overthrew the decadent and declining Han rulers, briefly, yet had many followers. So depending on who you ask, he 'usurped' the throne and deserves to be punished, or he is a 'radical reformer' who overthrew a nasty and corrupt royal dynasty- and deserves to be praised. One man's traitor, so it is said, is another man's freedom fighter.

1) Imagine the box at right is a neighborhood. In it live all the students in your class. But YOU have the authority to distribute land in it to each student, depending on--- nothing! Whatever you want, you get (it's good to be king). Using lines, divide the land into however you would if confronted with this interesting opportunity. Or take it all for yourself and have everyone pay you for the privilege of living and working on your land. Or perhaps divvy it out to your elite friends only.

So guess what Wang Mang did around 9 A.D.? As a smart Confucian scholar, he thought he could achieve social harmony through confiscating land and redistributing it so everyone had a piece.

The *wangtian* system involved abolishing all property rights as they were (government confiscation), then the redistribution of all land in China to heads-of-households.

2) However you distributed the land, now draw enough divisions so as the number of the spaces adds up to the number of students in the room, and the teacher too!

3) Did you already have an even distribution?   **Yes**   **No**
       (circle one then follow that line): | |
                                               | |

4) If you did, congratulations! Wang Mang approves!   Bad aristocrat! You just got your system overruled by Wang Mang.

How do you feel having instinctively been 'fair?'   How do you feel?

_____   a. all good   b. ripe for revolution

5) It gets better. Since everyone owns their own land, Wang Mang began handing out fees if you weren't working the land properly, or 'left the lawn messy,' or didn't plant trees for more productivity. If you couldn't pay, you had to work for the state (conscription). How do all you socialists like that policy?

| 6) Due to corruption by new administrators, Wang was overthrown himself. Would you have helped or defended Wang Mang?

Ch. 5   ROMAN CITY!   Engineer _____

Youtube: *Roman City Macaulay*

This animated movie about Classical Rome takes place around 20 B.C. during the reign of Augustus Caesar. It centers around the building of the city of:

V_____ in what is now F_____ but was then called G_____.

Engineer:	*Marcus Fabricius*	Describe the division of opinion among the Celts
Mayor:	*Gaius Valarius*	(Gauls) regarding Roman control over their land
Mayor's wife:	*Turia (yes she's blue)*	and the level of assimilation and cooperation they
Celt leader:	*Acco Beauviax*	would give:
Daughter:	*Aiden Beauviax*	
Procurator:	*Lycinus*	*Acco* *Aiden & the Druids*
Marcus' slave:	*Lorens*	
Emperor:	*Augustus Caesar*	

***G**eography and Environment*
***R**eligion and Worldview*
***A**rts and Innovations*
***P**olitics and Government*
***E**conomy and Trade*
***S**ocial Relationships*

Use each of the above choices from the **GRAPES** chart to categorize what kind of issue each of the following were (primarily):

_____ General Gaius Valerius was appointed **mayor** of the Roman city of Verbonia, while Lycinus had the greater position of procurator, which was like governor, of Gaul.

_____ The Druids had a difficult time socially **assimilating** to Roman ways of life. Some were angry, and fomented rebellion through sabotage (The bridge is burning!).

_____ In exchange for access to the Verbonia docks to send their metal products down the river and out for **trade**, the Celts promised to help the Romans build their city.

Roman cities were the most advanced of the ancient world. List six kinds of buildings they put up in Verbonia, along with what their purpose was:

	Building	*Purpose*		*Building*	*Purpose*
1)	*Forum*	*Meeting place*	4)		
2)			5)		
3)			6)		

The characters in the movie represent different opinions people have regarding progress and assimilation. If you lived back then and were a Celt, who in the movie best represents how you think you would feel about the Romans?

Ch. 5 — ARRANGED MARRIAGES – PROS AND CONS

"Hi, uh, so, I guess we're spending the rest of our lives together." Well, I hope you like anchovies on your pizza.

I. Why do people do the things they do? Psychologist Abraham Maslow studied motivation. His 'Hierarchy of Needs' was the result. Draw a triangle below, around the Maslow hierarchy, then answer the parts by placing the terms under the correct level:

Example of recent behavior

```
6                   -T-
5              --Self-Actualization--
4           ----------Self-Esteem----------
3        ------------------Belongingness------------------
2     --------------------------Safety--------------------------
1  ----------------------------Physiological----------------------------
```

Which group of terms is associated with each level? Mark 1-6:

Reputation	Employment	Metabolic	Friends	Potential	Meaning
Inferiority	Shelter	Hunger	Relationship	Accomplish	Infinity
Respect	Money	Toothache	Home	Mastery	New Dimension
Confidence	Rainstorm	Bathroom	Religion	Achievement	Spirit
____	____	____	____	____	____

II. Allan Bloom said the greatest heights a person can reach in this life are as follows: 1) Victory in a just war. 2) Consummated love. 3) Artistic creation. 4) Religious devotion. 5) Discovery of the truth. Can you envision yourself finding a goal in any of these categories? If so, can you describe it?

___

III. A big historical issue is arranged marriage vs. free-choice. In modern Western society, most people have free choice in who they become involved with and who they marry. Today, the individual is sovereign, and the community, including family and friends, exercise mainly an advisory capacity in matters of relationships and love. But there are many *kinds* of love. Match them:

A. Eros   **B. Ludus**   **C. Storge**   **D. Agape**   **E. Pragma**   **F. Mania**

___ playful love   ___ passion and desire love   ___ demanding, possessive love

___ practical love   ___ altruistic, selfless love   ___ companionship love

What kind of do you see yourself pursuing?

* **T** = Self-transcendence!

Ch. 5   MEDIA: ROMAN PLACES   Citizen _____

What do famous places tell us about the history of a culture?

Image search: **Roman Forum Reconstruction**. What is *not* present in the Forum Romanum?

a. triumphal arches   b. columned temples   c. market squares   d. stadiums

Image search: **Roman Coliseum**. Draw the first floor arch pattern on the Coliseum:

Image search: **Circus Maximus Reconstruction**. This most resembles: a. stadium   b. racetrack

Image search: **Augustus Caesar Statue**. Augustus' pose in his famous statue indicates he was an able:

     a. gladiator   b. administrator   c. artist   d. musician

Image search: **Nero Fiddles Comic**. Modern cartoonists often use the idea of Nero 'fiddling' while the city burns as an ancient analogue of politicians ignoring problems in the present day. Pick two comics and describe what they have to do with *either* ancient or modern times. What is the comedian trying to get across?

#1   #2

Image search: **Bethlehem Nativity**. Christianity began in Ancient Rome. Jesus was a Roman subject living in the Province of Judea. According to the Bible story, what kind of building was Jesus born in on the first Christmas? _____

Among the pictures, locate the Church of the Nativity. This is the building on the site of the original manger. It is made of:

a. wood   b. stone   c. metal   d. wool

Image search: **The Last Day of Pompeii Brullov**. When Vesuvius erupted, covering this medium sized city in volcanic ash, pick three people and describe their reactions to the impending doom:

1)   2)   3)

Image search: **Destruction of Pompeii Martin**. Which painting to you like better? Why?

(Regular!) Search: **Trajan's Amazing Column**. Click the NatGeo story. Trajan ruled at the height of the Roman Empire. Scan the article for clues as to what is sculpted into the victory column:

Image search: **Church of the Holy Sepulcher**. This is the church built on the site of the cave Jesus was buried in. Unlike the Church of the Nativity, this church has one of these Roman architectural innovations on the top: _____ Near what city were Calvary Hill and the cave located?

_____   _____

Image search: **Roman Christian catacombs**. Their religion banned by the Roman state for 300 years, from 30 A.D. to 325, Christians met in secret under the city. The earliest Christian art is actually located underground, in these catacombs. What kinds of things were painted by them?

_____

Wikipedia: *Christian symbolism.* What is the meaning of the following Christian symbols?

                              What it means   *How it became symbolic*

Cross (Crucifix):

Ichthys:

Alpha and Omega:

The Good Shepherd:

Dove:

Shamrock:

Search: **Quizlet AP World History Greece Flashcards**. Click the link, then the **Scatter** game. Play 3 times and mark your time for each:

Game #1 _____   Game #2 _____   Game #3 _____

Did you cut your time in half from Game 1 to Game 3?   *Yes!*   *No, and now I must carry this shame*

Ch. 6   AFRICAN TERMS IN ENGLISH   Translator_____

Zombies are real.

Zebra   **Tsetse**   **Safari**   **Kwanzaa**   **Goober**   **Banjo**   **Bwana**

Chimpanzee   **Jumbo**   **Ebony**   **Gumbo**   **Impala**   **Jenga**   **Jive**

Mamba   **Mojo**   **Zombie**   **Vuvuzela**   **Jazz**   **Voodoo**   **Mumbo-jumbo**

_____ Swahili for 'travel', you might go on one of these to see some cool animals

_____ This is a musical instrument from the Bantu culture called a mbanza

_____ A soup often associated with New Orleans creole, from Bantu (okra)

_____ Nubians in northeast Africa called this kind of wood 'h-ebeni'

_____ Mandinka Bantu for 'masked dancer,' this is also used to mean 'nonsense stuff'

_____ A primate ci-mpenzi from the Bantu language Kivili. Just don't make them mad

_____ From Tembe Bantu, '*Jas*' combines African beat with European classical instruments

_____ A Bantu word '*jev*,' meaning dance, this is like the Jitterbug (and also slang for talk)

_____ From Swahili for 'elephant,' this word also means supersized (and hello too!)

_____ Swahili for 'first fruits', adopted as an African-American holiday in December

_____ This Zulu word means 'to build', now a game you can buy at the store

_____ West African animism that contains 'vodu' (spirits) that bring luck or harm

_____ Not just a cool Chevy classic car, but a Zulu word for an antelope on the savanna

_____ Fulani Bantu for 'medicine man,' this conjures up images of stylish magic

_____ Sometimes used as a slang synonym for peanut, this comes from Bantu (nguba)

_____ Applied to a fly that carries a terrible disease that makes people blind, from Bantu

_____ Congolese for 'striped'

_____ This is a fetishized West African spirit-god that might bite you and make you one

_____ This is a venomous, fast-moving, poisonous snake. Beware!

_____ This instrument made a lot of players angry when S. Africa hosted the World Cup

_____ A 'big shot' important person- a safari leader in the Swahili language

Ch. 6 **Great Clips: Lalibela the Bee King** **Bee**_____

Video search: "CNN Millennium: 12th century" (around 17:15 min. in)

What was different about where churches were built in Africa's Christian kingdom (Ethiopia)?

_____

Which holy relics, thought lost to historians, do Ethiopian Christians say made their way into their land?

_____

_____

In the legend of Lalibela, how did people know he would be a special king?

_____

How did Lalibela get the idea for the design of the churches- in the legend?

_____

_____

What were some of Lalibela's other motivations for building and expanding his Empire of Axum?

Ch. 7 **Great Clips: Mansa Musa and Mali** **Mansa**_____

Video search: "CNN Millennium: 14th century" (around 8:15 min. in)

Describe the environment of the Mali Empire:

By which pack animal did the Arabs transport the salt to Mali on the Trans-Sahara routes across the desert?

What kind of wonderful animal did Arab traveler Ibn Battuta see in the Niger River?

During the parade celebrating Mansa Musa why did the Mansa not speak directly to anyone except his spokeswoman?

How many slaves did he brag about owning?

What other kinds of things did the Malians do with all the gold they had?

How is Mansa Musa portrayed in the Spanish Catalan Atlas, which was made with the help of reports by the Arabs and Berbers who traded with Mali?

Ch. 6   **AMERICA BEFORE COLUMBUS**   Kiva Administrator _____

School project: make a chinampa farm online and friend it. Then go to Antarcticaedu.com/20hst.htm

How did people come to America around 10,000 years ago? _____

What causes the Northern Lights? _____

Some Inuit cultures have 16 words for "ice". What animals do they make coats out of? _____

Does anyone still live on Greenland? _____

Viking Sagas say _____ discovered America around _____

Check the animated map. The European powers that claimed parts of North America at some point are:
_____

The great serpent mound is located in the state of _____

The largest tribes today, by number of modern-day enrolled members. are:

1)

2)

3)

4)

5)

The Lumbee (pop. _____) are the likely descendants of the Lost Colony of Roanoke.

The largest Florida tribe are the _____, numbering _____

The Calusa Indians of Florida painted these colors on their faces as warpaint _____

What was the largest city of Pre-Columbian times? _____ located near _____

What is a kiva? _____

The most ancient Mesoamerican culture were the _____, centered at La Venta.

The Toltec culture was centered on _____, while _____ was the Maya center.

The _____ shape was common monumental architecture from Toltec to Teotihuacan times.

The Mesoamericans were monotheistic   T   F

Connecting the Pyramids of the Sun and Moon is the Avenue of _____

Would your mom be mad if you came home with Maya piercings? _____

American archeology's founder was John L. Stephens, who discovered the pyramid of _____

Palenque was a city built by _____, who had advanced irrigation canals.

If you lived at Caracol, a Mayan city in Belize, would you have many neighbors? _____

What was the rationale for human sacrifice? _____

This sweet substance was cultivated by Mesoamericans from the cocoa plant: _____

What did Lady Xoc, Shield Jaguar II's wife, do to please the gods? _____

In Mexica (Aztec) language, an eagle chose the site for the Aztec capital of: _____

What are Chinampas? _____

Does Aztec art feature similar or different themes to Mayan and other earlier art? _____

Name and try to draw 3 Aztec gods:

1   2   3

What amazed Bernal Diaz about Tenochtitlan? _____

What is left of the earliest South American culture (the Chavin?)? _____

What did the Chimu build that is left for us today? _____

Besides drawing cool Nazca lines, what else did the Nazca spend time doing? _____

Draw 2 Nazca line shapes: 1   2

Describe the physical geography of the Inca city of Machu Picchu:

What crops did they farm? _____

What is quipu? _____

CH. 7   SILK ROAD TRIP   Germophobe _____

URL: Antarcticaedu.com/12HstSilk.htm   At each ---- area, note which ethnic group the
                                         silk changed hands to in the relay, following
                 * Chang'an   the pattern below:

                   * Xi'an
                 * Lanzhou   Han Chinese
         * Mati Si   --

              * Dunhuang
                                             Chinese Buddhists
     * Crescent Lake

* Turfan   --

* Bezeklik

* Urumqi

       * Kazil

           * Kashgar

               * Lake Karakul
                                         ----
               * Almaty
                                         ----
                 * Bishkek
                                         ----
                   * Dushanbe
                                         ----
                   * Tashkent

                   * Samarkand
                                                                    * Taxila
                     * Bukhara   * Khotan   to India→

                   / * Ashkabat \   * Bactra
                  /   \   ------------------
                 /   \   * Qom
                 ----
                                                * Ecbatana

                                                * Ctesiphon
                 ----
                                                * Bahgdad

         --------------------------------   * Palmyra
                      * Edessa

    Antioch *

CH. 7　　　DISEASES IN HISTORY　　　Patient Zero _____
We all fall down.

429 B.C.	*Plague of Athens*	100,000 including Pericles die of Typhus during Peloponnesian War
165 A.D.	*Antonine Plague*	5,000,000 die of Smallpox in Roman Empire; diffused on Silk Road
250	*Plague of Cyprian*	3,500,000 die of Smallpox in Roman Empire; diffused on Silk Road
541	*Plague of Justinian*	40,000,000 die of Bubonic Plague in Byzantium; weakening it
1346	*The Black Death*	100,000,000 die of Bubonic Plague- worst pandemic of all time
1489	*Granada Typhus*	20,000 Moorish and Spanish soldiers die of Typhus at Granada
1507	*Great Dying: Carib.*	3,000,000 Taino and Caribs die over two decades of Flu & other
1520	*Great Dying: Aztecs*	8,000,000 die in Mexico and Caribbean of Smallpox and Flu
1527	*Great Dying: Incas*	200,000 die in South America of Smallpox and Flu
1545	*Cocoliztli Epidemic 1*	12,000,000 indigenous Americans die of hemorrhagic Ebola
1555	*Brazilian Smallpox*	2,000,000 indigenous Brazilians die over 20 years
1566	*Typhoid Epidemic*	2,000,000 die across Mesoamerica of Typhoid Fever
1576	*Cocoliztli Epidemic 2*	2,000,000 die in New Spain (Mexico) of hemorrhagic Ebola
1577	*Black Assizes*	10,000 die of 'Goal Fever' (Typhus) in English prisons and courts
1596	*Plague of Seville*	1,200,000 die in Spain of three rounds of Bubonic Plague
1617	*Great Dying: North*	1,500,000 North American Indians die over 200 years of Bubonic Plague, Smallpox, Measles, Chickenpox, Hepatitis, and Typhus
1629	*Italian Plague*	1,000,000 die in Milan and other cities of Bubonic Plague
1633	*Colonial Epidemics*	American Colonies are hit with smallpox and measles 10 times
1641	*Ming Plague*	1,000,000 die in China of Bubonic Plague, Ming collapse
1665	*Plague of London*	100,000 die in a year, mass exodus from city
1679	*Plague of Vienna*	76,000 die in a year, mass exodus from city
1708	*Northern Plague*	200,000 die during Great Northern War of Bubonic Plague
1720	*Plague of Marseilles*	100,000 die in Southern France of Bubonic Plague
1738	*Balkan Plague*	60,000 die in the Balkans of Bubonic Plague
1771	*Russian Plague*	100,000 die in Moscow and a "Plague Riot" furthers the trouble
1789	*Australian Smallpox*	Thousands of Aboriginal Australians and New Zealanders die

1812	*Napoleonic Epidemic*	50,000 French soldiers die of Typhus returning from Russia
1817	*Cholera Pandemic 1*	150,000 people die from China to India to Europe
1829	*Cholera Pandemic 2*	200,000 people die of Asiatic Cholera, half in Russia
1847	*Coffin Ships*	30,000 Irish and others die on the way to America of Typhus
1852	*Cholera Pandemic 3*	1,100,000 die mostly in Russia; in Britain John Snow finds well
1855	*Plague Pandemic*	20,000,000 die, 12m in India alone, of Bubonic Plague
1863	*Cholera Pandemic 4*	700,000 die in MENA and Europe, 50k in USA
1864	*Civil War Fever*	55,000 die of Typhoid inc. Lincoln's son; 13k at Andersonville
1875	*Fiji Epidemic*	75,000 die of measles on Fiji
1881	*Cholera Pandemic 5*	10,000 die in India and Europe, Robert Koch est. germ theory
1889	*Flu Pandemic*	1,000,000 die worldwide of "Asiatic Flu," vectors mapped
1899	*Cholera Pandemic 6*	1,000,000 die in India, MENA and Europe over 10 years
<u>**1900**</u>	<u>*Frisco Plague*</u>	<u>113 die, city freaks out - would you?</u> Yes No
1916	*European Typhus*	3,000,000 die of Typhus on the Eastern Front during WWI
1918	*Spanish Flu*	75,000,000 die worldwide in nastiest flu outbreak (H1N1)
1919	*Russian Typhus*	3,000,000 die of Typhus during Russian Civil War
1945	*European Typhus*	Millions die of Typhus in Europe during WWII
1957	*Asian Flu*	2,000,000 die worldwide
1961	*Cholera Pandemic 7*	300,000 people die but spur preventative measures
1968	*Hong Kong Flu*	1,000,000 die worldwide
1960	*AIDS Pandemic*	30,000,000 dead mostly in Africa but now worldwide
2008	*Zimbabwe Cholera*	5,000 die of cholera outbreak in Southern Africa
2009	*Swine Flu*	9,000 die worldwide of Swine Flu (H1N1), like Spanish Flu
2010	*Haitian Cholera*	10,000 die in Haiti of Cholera in aftermath of earthquake
2013	*West African Ebola*	12,000 or more die of hemorrhagic Ebola outbreak

List the 3 worst ever:	Go back and **square** all the times *Typhus* has affected prisons and soldiers in war, then **circle** Plagues!	Some infectious diseases are of recent (last 200 years) origin. **Name** two:	This list only has major outbreaks- some diseases are **endemic** to certain regions, meaning they:

Ch. 7 — REVENGE OF PHASE 1? Germ Freak _____

They're all around us. (if you ain't one now, you will be soon)

From Ancient Athens to Andersonville Prison Camp in the Civil War, to WWI (3 million deaths) and WWII, typhus epidemics have broken out many times during war when conditions get unsanitary. And it's only one of a number of infectious diseases people have had to contend with. Most have been lessened as society has transitioned through Stage 2 and into Stage 3 and 4 of the epidemiological transition. Some, however, fear the return of Stage 1 diseases due to new strains (mutation) and increasing resistance to antibiotics. Here are the average yearly totals for 5 years:

Disease	Type	Vector	Deaths/year
African Sleeping Sickness	Parasite	tsetse fly	34,000
AIDS (HIV)	Virus	bodily fluids	1,200,000
Anthrax	Bacteria	airborne	a few
Bubonic Plague	Bacteria	flea bite	200
Chickenpox	Virus	airborne	7,000
Cholera	Bacteria	unsanitary	130,000
Common Cold (200 types)	Virus	airborne	a few
Dengue Fever	Virus	mosquito	20,000
Diphtheria	Bacteria	airborne	5,000
Dysentery	Bacteria	unsanitary	80,000
Ebola	Virus	bodily fluids	11,000
Enterovirus (Polio+64)	Virus	mucus	a few
Gonorrhea	Bacteria	bodily fluids	4,000
Hepatitis A, B, C	Virus	blood	380,000
Herpes	Virus	bodily fluids	a few
HPV	Virus	bodily fluids	266,000
Influenza (Flu)	Virus	airborne	500,000
Legionnaires	Bacteria	airborne	a few
Leprosy	Bacteria	airborne	a few
Lyme	Bacteria	tick bite	4,000
Malaria	Parasite	mosquito	1,200,000
Measles	Virus	airborne	110,000
Meningitis	Bacteria	bodily fluids	303,000
Norovirus (Stomach Flu)	Virus	foodborne	210,000
Pertussis	Bacteria	airborne	61,000
Pneumonia	Virus	airborne	4,000,000
Rabies	Virus	dog bite	60,000
Salmonella	Bacteria	foodborne	a few
Schistosomiasis	Parasite	unsanitary	200,000
Scabies	Parasite	crowdedness	a few
Sepsis	Bacteria	reaction	3,000,000
Smallpox	Virus	airborne	none since '78
Streptococcal pharyngitis	Bacteria	airborne	a few
Syphilis	Bacteria	bodily fluids	120,000
Tetanus	Bacteria	blood	60,000
Tuberculosis	Bacteria	airborne	1,500,000
Typhoid Fever	Bacteria	foodborne	181,000
Typhus	Bacteria	lice bite	none since '47
West Nile Fever	Bacteria	mosquito	280
Yellow Fever	Virus	mosquito	30,000
Zika	Virus	mosquito	none

Directions: For each of the types below, identify the top five most fatal infectious diseases today.

Bacteriological infection
1)
2)
3)
4)
5)

Viral infection
1)
2)
3)
4)
5)

Parasitic growth
1)
2)
3)
4)

While a gruesome topic, there are some good movies related to outbreaks of infectious diseases. The following might be consulted for 'entertainment:'

Panic in the Streets (1950)   *12 Monkeys (1995)*
The Andromeda Strain (1971)   *Outbreak (1995)*   *The Omega Man (1971)*
Black Death (2010)   *The Stand (1994)*   *Contagion (2011)*

If these infectious diseases are making a comeback, why do you think that is?

Ch. 8   DYNASTIES OF CHINA   Mandate holder _____
From the mists of time to today

>1600 B.C. _____ :

    1046 B.C. _____ :

        256 B.C. _____ :

Warring States (1.5m)
-------------------------- 221 B.C. _____ :
      |
      | Yellow Turban Uprising (4.5m) --------
      | 581 A.D. _____ :

3 New Philosophies
     /|\
    / | \   618 _____ :
   / | \
  / | \   An Lushan (21) --------
 / | \   960 _____ :
/ | \
1   2   3
/ | \   1227 _____ :
/ | \
/ | \   1368 _____ :

                      1644 _____ :

                      1912 _____ :

                      1949 _____ :

                      Today?

Below, translate the names of the dynasties onto the timeline, to see how long in history it lasted, relatively:

-1500   -1000   -500   1   500   1000   1500   2000

Ch. 8   CHINESE PROVINCES   Name _____
Translate the following to understand Chinese state names, then a label map in English:

Dong = eastern   *Xi* = western   *Bei* = northern   *Nan* = southern   *Zhong* = central
Hai = sea   *Hu* = lake   *He* = *great river*   *Jiang* = river   *Shan* = mountain   *Tian* = heavenly
An = calm   *Ning* = peace   *Yun* = clouds   *Ming* = bright   *Qing* = pure   *Jing* = capital

1. Anhui =   _____ Emblem
2. Beijing =   _____ _____
3. Chongqing =   Ultimate _____
4. Fujian =   Happy
5. Guangdong =   Big _____ (Land)
6. Gansu =   Pleasant
7. Guangxi =   Big _____ (Land)
8. Guizhou =   Noble
9. Hainan =   _____ _____
10. Hebei =   _____ _____
11. Heilongjiang = Black Dragon _____
12. Henan =   _____ _____
13. Hong Kong = Spice Harbor
14. Hubei =   _____ _____
15. Hunan =   _____ _____
16. Jiangsu =   _____ Awakening
17. Jiangxi =   _____ _____
18. Jilin =   Lucky Forest
19. Liaoning =   Distant _____
20. Neimongol = Inner Mongolia
21. Ningxia =   _____ Summer
22. Qinghai =   _____ blue _____
23. Shanxi =   _____ _____
24. Shaanxi =   Same as Shanxi but in a different dialect
25. Shandong   Waters _____
26. Shanghai = Upon the _____
27. Sichuan =   Four corners
28. Taiwan =   Gulf Island
29. Tibet =   Tibet
30. Tianjin =   _____ Gateway
31. Xinjiang =   New Frontier
32. Yunnan =   _____ _____
33. Zhejiang = Winding _____

Ch. 9   **ARABIC TERMS IN ENGLISH**   Translator_____

Get your checkbook out, this warm up ain't free

Admiral		*Caravan*		*Algorithm*		*Assassin*
	Candy		*Cheque*		*Alcohol*	
Algebra		*Apricot*		*Elixir*		*Crimson*
	Adobe		*Hazard*		*Ghoul*	
Average		*Azimuth*		*Arsenal*		*Gerbil*
	Alchemy		*Giraffe*		*Jar*	

_____ The word 'emir' meant high-ranking official, and this is a high-ranking naval officer

_____ From Arabic folklore (1001 Arabian Nights), this is a mischievous creature

_____ Predecessor to scientific *chemistry* all about trying to mix-up metals to make gold

_____ Greek term for healthy potion adopted by alchemists and related back to Europe

_____ Arabic for 'distilled,' this was later a generic name applied to beer, wine and spirits

_____ 'Al-barquq' is the Arabic term for a type of peach, adapted into English for this fruit

_____ Term for 'military storage facility' adapted when Italians fought Arabs at sea

_____ The 'Hashishin' were a sect in North Africa that struck when you least expected it

_____ The compass direction a celestial object is from the viewpoint of the observer

_____ Literally 'restoring broken parts,' this favorite style of math balances equations

_____ Cane sugar came from India and was brought to Europe in this tasty form

_____ A convoy of travelers journeying together, these are still common in the Middle East

_____ In money transactions, this replaces currency. Traders used them for long distance.

_____ Red color for dyeing silk from China and wool from sheep

_____ This desert rodent is found in North Africa, you might have one as a pet someday

_____ From the Persian name al-Khwarizmi (9th c.), who sought patterns

_____ This safari animal was brought by Arabs to Italy (1200s), and their name for it stuck

_____ Meaning 'brick,' this is the Arabic term for the traditional Middle Eastern mud-brick

_____ Container for holding oils, sugar and candies, brought from Arabs to Spain

_____ Meaning 'damage' b/c insurance claim writers wanted to know what to expect

_____ Originally az-zahr, meaning 'dice,' throwing them meant 'taking a risk' or 'peril'

Harem   **Zenith**   **Lemon**   **Magazine**
Lime   **Mattress**   **Zero**
Macabre   **Sugar**   **Tariff**   **Orange**
Sofa   **Mummy**   **Hookah**
Hummus   **Jasmine**   **Lute**   **Serendipity**
Sheik   **Ream**   **Sultan**
Nadir   **Syrup**

_____ Both a climbing plant and a girl's name, like that of the princess from Aladdin

_____ Term for 'tax on imported goods' comes from 'ta'riff,' to notify as a tabular receipt

_____ Must've been a sweet day when Arabs brought 'Sukkar' to the West from India

_____ Food made of chickpeas, comes as a spread for bread or crackers

_____ From India to Persia, Arabia to Al-Andalus this sour yellow fruit diffused

_____ Sailors realized they wouldn't get scurvy if they had lots of these green sour fruits

_____ Musical instrument that diffused from Middle East to Al-Andalus in the Middle Ages

_____ From the term 'khazn' = 'to store,' whether ammo or stories between glossy covers

_____ This is a 'matra,' a cushion for lying on, related to the Ottoman, an Islamic dynasty

_____ 'Mumiya' a substance used to embalm dead bodies to preserve them

_____ As in the freaked-out or terrible dance of death, adopted during the Bubonic Plague

_____ The worst point in someone's good fortunes or career, low point

_____ This fruit associated with Florida came from the east- and the Sanskrit term 'naranj'

_____ Measure for 'bundles of paper,' that diffused from China to Spain via the Caliphate

_____ From Arab name for Sri Lanka, this means 'by fortunate accident'

_____ Another name for couch, this term came from Arabic via Turkey to the West

_____ Term for 'women's quarters' in a large, possibly multifamily household

_____ Terms for Arabic rulers, one a 'king' (left), the other a 'chief' (right) _____

_____ From the term 'sharab'– to drink- if you actually drank this it'd be sticky-sweet

_____ 'Samt' – The direction in the celestial sphere vertically upwards from the observer

_____ Water pipe for smoking, popular in a culture where alcohol is banned

_____ 'Sifr' originally, this placeholder in math originated in India and via the Arabs

Ch. 9   LARGEST EMPIRES IN HISTORY   Administrator _____
Will the empire strike back?

Is the 'age of empires' over? The European empires all seemed to fall after WWII, except for perhaps the Soviet Empire, which collapsed 45 years later. Empires grew over time, from the ancient Persian to the modern British. Use the directions below to fill in the time-growth graph:

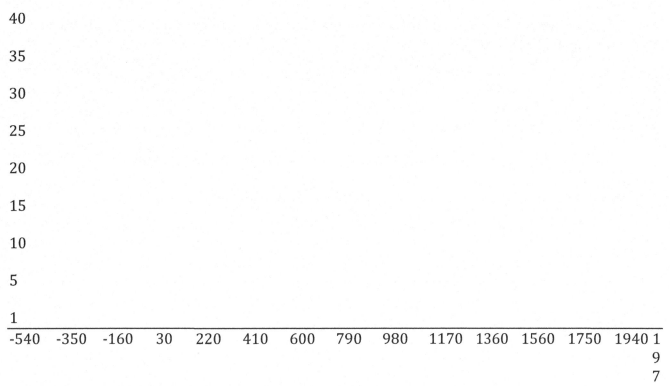

Use the information below to plot the rise and fall of the great empires of history:

Having overthrown the Babylonian Empire in 1540 and expanded to Lydia and Egypt, the Persian Empire grew to 6 million square megameters in -350, then was overthrown by Alexander in -332

The Hellenistic Seleucid Empire comprised much of the former Persia, and bounced back to a height of 5 million in -160, and slumping to 0 by 30.

The Romans rose starting in -509 to a height of 5 million in 150, continued at 5 to 476, when it fell to 3 (when only Byzantium survived), and Byzantium steadily lost land until 1453 when it hit 0.

The Islamic Caliphate grew from 622 to a height of 11 million in 790, then dropped to 2 in 980 when it split apart, and continued at 2 until being conquered by the Mongols about 1250.

The Mongol attack on China started in 1220, rising from that year to a height of 24 million in 1350, after Russia, Persia and parts of the Islamic Caliphate had been taken. It dropped to 0 by 1552.

The Spanish Empire rose from 0 in 1491 to a height of 14 million in 1810, then the Mexican and other Latin American revolutions dropped it to 0 again in 1900.

The British Empire began to rise in 1560 to 15 million in 1850, stagnated to 1800 then rose again to 36 million by 1920, then dropped to 0 in 1975.

Make an observation about the duration of the empire and its size over time:

Ch. 9 THE HAJJ — Pilgrim _____

What do pilgrims do in Mecca?

In 1853, Captain Sir Richard Francis Burton of the British Army did something "no non-Muslim had ever done" – he visited Mecca. The penalty for this is harsh. In 1855, he wrote of the journey.

So why would ABC correspondent Michael Wolfe, a news reporter from America, be allowed to make the Hajj pilgrimage to Mecca?

_____

What country is Mecca in? _____

As we accompany the correspondent on the Hajj, summarize the meaning of the various rituals:

OBLIGATION	RITUAL / MEANING
Plain towel dress	
Road checkpoints	
Prayer in Public	
Seven Circuits around the Ka'ba	
Zamzam Well	
Tent city of Mina	
Camping on the Plains of Arafat	
Gathering 49 Pebbles	

Ch. 9 # STAR NAMES **Stellar student** _____

Use the clues, like –os is Greek, al- is Arabic, or how it 'sounds,' to determine if the bright star's name came from Greek, Roman or Arabic language

1. **Sol**   Latin for 'Sun'   _____
2. **Sirius**   *Seirios*= Searing (glowing)   _____
3. **Canopus**   King Menelaus' navigator   _____
4. **Alpha Centauri**   The *'Alpha'* star of Centaurus   _____
5. **Arcturus**   *Arktouros*= Guardian of the Bear   _____
6. **Vega**   *Waqi*: Swooping eagle   _____
7. **Capella**   *Capra*- Latin for goat 'Capricorn'   _____
8. **Rigel**   *Rijl*: foot of Jauzah (Orion)   _____
9. **Procyon**   *Prokyon*= 'Pro' = precedes the dog   _____
10. **Achernar**   *Akhir an-nahr*: End of the river   _____
11. **Betelgeuse**   *Ibt al-Jauza*: Hand of Jauzah   _____
12. **Hadar**   *Hadar*: Present, settled out east   _____
13. **Altair**   *Al-tair*: Flying eagle (not *Aquila!*)   _____
14. **A-Crux**   First star of the Southern Cross   _____
15. **Aldebaran**   *Al-dabaran*: Follower (of Pleiades)   _____
16. **Antares**   *Aut Ares*= red like Ares   _____
17. **Spica**   Latin for Libra's ear of wheat   _____
18. **Pollux**   Castor's twin, son of Zeus   _____
19. **Fomalhaut**   *Fom al-Haut*: Mouth of the fish   _____
20. **Deneb**   *Dhanab ad-Dajaja*: Tail of the hen   _____
21. **Mimosa**   *Mimosa*- 'Dramatic actor' in Latin   _____
22. **Regulus**   *Regal*- king, *'regal-us'* – prince   _____
23. **Adara**   *Aoara*: Young Middle Eastern lady   _____
24. **Shaula**   *Al-Sawla*: Tail of the Scorpion   _____
25. **Castor**   Pollux' constellation Gemini twin   _____

Of the Top 25 brightest stars, how many names derive from the following:

Greek: _____   Did you figure out the secret for using the symbols to verify if you picked right? What was it?

Roman: _____

Arabic: _____   Which star name would you name your pet?

Ch. 9 **ISLAM-RELATED TERMS** **Guesser** _____

You better not just be guessing.

_____ We were the first dynasty of Muslim caliphs, ruling from Damascus after Ali's death.

_____ We believe Ali was the true successor to Muhammad, and make up 20% of Muslims.

_____ We were a tribe of wealthy merchants in Arabia, and count Muhammad as one of us.

_____ We are those who have submitted to Allah and practice Islam.

_____ I am the holy city of Muslims, on the western coast of Arabia.

_____ This religion, meaning 'submission,' is the fastest growing in the world today.

_____ This is the pilgrimage Muslims take to Mecca, which is also the Fifth Pillar.

_____ The black cube at the center of the Great Mosque, reputed to be Abraham's temple.

_____ We are Arabic tribes then and now, who practice pastoral nomadism.

_____ After murdering the Umayyads, we founded a new dynasty based at Baghdad.

_____ This is the Arabic term for 'king,' the chief Muslim civil and religious leader.

_____ This book contains the sayings of Muhammad during his life.

_____ This is the 622 AD 'flight' from Mecca of Muhammad, to escape the Quraysh.

_____ Term for 'struggle,' often indicative of war for the faith, compared with 'crusade'.

_____ Muslim teacher of sacred law (sharia) and Islamic theology.

_____ Book containing the recitation Muhammad spoke of the words of Allah.

_____ The official, sacred law of Islam, applicable in each sufficiently Islamic society.

_____ The majority of Muslims, 80%, who believed Abu Bakr was rightful successor.

_____ Term for the entire part of the world under Muslim rule.

Abbasids	*Bedouins*	*Caliph*	*Ka'ba*
Hadith	*Hajj*	*Hijra*	*Islam*
Jihad	*Mecca*	*Medina*	*Mullah*
Muslim	*Quran*	*Quraysh*	*Sharia*
Shi'a	*Sunni*	*Umayyad*	*Umma*

Ch. 10   CYRILLIC ALPHABET   _____

How do you learn the Cyrillic alphabet? I don't know, but there must be some methodius

Byzantium had a major impact on early Russia. Even though the first political rulers of Kievan Rus were Varangian Norsemen (Vikings) like Rurik, much more cultural influence came from the Byzantines. Below, note Byzantine cultural diffusion to the early Rus in the following domains:

Religion & Architecture: **Concept of Government & "The Third Rome"**

Alphabet (Locate and write the characters of the Cyrillic alphabet and put their English sounds underneath them):

___

1. Write your name using Cyrillic characters:
_____

2. Write 'Good Day' in Cyrillic: | In Russian, 'Good Day' is 'Dobry Den'. Write that below:

3. Transliterate the following Russian cities & names into the English Latin Alphabet:

_____ Москва   _____ Рюрик

_____ Санкт-Петербург   _____ Игор

_____ Новосибирск   _____ Олга

_____ Екатеринбург   _____ Владимир

Ch. 10　　　　　　　　**MEDIEVAL PHILOSOPHY**　　　　　　　Worrywart _____
Don't worry, soon you'll be in the afterlife.

Augustine of Hippo saw the Roman world crumbling around him. In 415, barbarians were everywhere; they even burned down his town and its church. He wrote a book, *Civitas Dei,* in which he comforted people by reminding them reality consists of two 'worlds,' not one- the heavenly 'City of God,' and the earthly 'City of Man.' While the earthly 'City' may be in ruins, the heavenly 'City' is eternal. Still, a convert to Christianity, he wondered, if God was all-powerful and good, then why is there evil in the world? Evil, he reasoned, was not created by God because evil is not a thing, per se, so much as a deficiency or absence of good. The evil of a thief is that he lacks honesty, just as the evil of being blind is that a person lacks sight. Still, why would God create a universe in which horrible things happen to people and by people? The answer was because God wanted us to be free and self-determined, so he gave us freedom of will (freewill). Having freewill means being able to choose, and sometimes that means choosing between good and evil. God left open the possibility that people might choose evil, and so there is a struggle between our rationality and morality on the one side, and temptation and vice on the other. Rationality is the ability to evaluate choices through the process of reasoning, but often we don't grow up enough mentally to be rational. So we do evil instead. Having the possibility of not being good, furthermore, gives us a greater appreciation of goodness, as we act in the image of God, and in homage to God, who we see is not the maker of the evils in the world- *we are.* Q: Would you choose to have freewill, or for your actions to be predetermined? You'd bear less responsibility if they were pre-determined...

Boethius was a Roman philosopher who lived in 525, at a time when the Ostrogoths ruled Italy. He studied Aristotle and became chief advisor to Theodoric, the Ostrogoth king. He wrote *The Consolation of Philosophy* while in prison awaiting execution for treason. He wondered- if God lives in an eternal present, meaning he knows the future as well as the present and the past, that means he knows what we are going to do before we do it. If this is true, and he is ever-present and knows everything, how can it be said we have freewill like Augustine said? Boethius got to thinking: "If I have freewill, it means I am free to go to the theater, or stay home and do homework." That's my freewill. But at the very same time, if I say "I am going to the theater tonight," that statement is not true or false, at least not in the same way as "I went to the theater yesterday," which is either true *or* false. We live in the flow of time, but God, by contrast, knows what to us as past, present and future in the same way we know the present, and we are so much more regulated by time that we cannot overcome it. We don't transcend time, but God does. Q: If you believe humans have souls that continue after the body dies, do you think a human soul will transcend time in heaven too?

Avicenna, speaking of souls and what they might be, was Persian but wrote in Arabic and lived in Bukhara, one of the Silk Road towns in Central Asia. In 1030, after a lifetime studying Greek philosophy, a funny thought struck him: "If I were blindfolded and suspended in air, touching nothing and having no sense of touch at all, I would not know I had a body. I would, however, know I had a 'self,' that 'myself' exists, and that means there is part of me that is not of the body. That is my soul- a human soul distinct from the body." Avicenna called this the Flying Man Experiment. He knew Aristotle argued otherwise, saying body and soul are one unit (monism), but he disagreed and said, like Plato, that they were two (dualism). Q: If your soul (assuming you have one or believe you do) could be trans-morphed into an animal, what kind of animal would it be and why?

Anslem in 1077, who would later become Archbishop of Canterbury, always knew Christians had faith in the existence of God. But he wanted to prove it using rational argument, too. He wanted to prove it with logic. He imagines himself discussing the following: *Anselm*: "Do you agree that if God existed he would be the greatest thing that there could be, that than which nothing greater can be thought?" *Fool*: Yes. *Anselm*: And do you agree that 'that than which nothing greater can be thought' exists in your mind?" *Fool*: Yes, in my mind- but not in reality. *Anselm*: But would you agree that something that exists in reality as well as in the mind is greater than something that exists in your mind alone?" *Fool*: Yes, I suppose so- candy in my hand is better than candy that's just in my imagination. *Anselm*: "So if 'that than which nothing greater can be thought' exists only in the mind, it is less great than if it existed also in reality?" *Fool*: Yes. The being that really exists would be greater. *Anselm*: "So now you are saying that there is something greater than 'that than which nothing greater exists'?" *Fool*: That doesn't even make sense. *Anselm*: "Exactly. And the only way around this contradiction is to admit that God (that than which nothing greater exists), does exist- both in thought and reality." Q: How would you answer Anselm's ontological argument?

Averroes in 1186 lived in Al-Andalus as a *qadi* (judge). He read Aristotle and applied his philosophy to Islam. If Muslims accept that the Quran is true, but parts of it are demonstrably false, the text must be a poetic truth and must be interpreted using philosophical reasoning. This he argued meant philosophy and Islam are not incompatible. He argued humans do not have immortal souls, but humanity is immortal through a shared intellect, which may last forever, but you and I will perish when our bodies die. Q: Do you think most Muslims viewed Averroes with admiration or with suspicion? Why?

Jewish philosopher Moses Maimonides in 1190 thought we anthropomorphize God too much- give him human traits when he is actually far beyond us. Do not take the Torah as literal truth and think God is even a corporeal thing. Maimonides used negative theology to argue what God is by arguing what he is not. First of all, he has no attributes. He is not good or powerful. This is because an attribute is either accidental or essential. If you are sitting, have long brown hair and a long nose, those are accidental attributes. You would still be "you," essentially, if you were standing, had red hair and a small nose. Being human, a rational moral animal, is what you are *essentially*. God has no such accidental attributes. What about essence? Essential attributes define, but Maimonides argued God is undefinable. Ergo, God has no attributes at all. We can say "God is a creator," because this states what God does, rather than a thing that God is. We cannot say what he is. Q: Do you agree?

Thomas Aquinas in 1291 wondered if the universe had always existed, or if it had been created at a certain point in time. He combined classical philosophy and Christianity into *scholasticism*, the idea that Christians have a duty to study nature, using science and observation, because God is happy when they do, since they are studying his great Creation. Aquinas read Aristotle, who argued the universe always existed, is eternal, and has always been changing and moving. Movement and change do not come from nowhere, and there was never a time without motion. Thus, there was no First Cause, as Plato thought, and as Christians also believe, understanding that God created the universe from nothing in *Genesis 1:1*. Aristotle was simply wrong, to Aquinas, based on belief in the Bible. But Aquinas wanted to prove this by applying reason. How did he do it? He knew Aristotle defined the infinite as that which has no limit, like an infinity of numbers has no limit because there is always the possibility of adding "1" to each new highest number. Thus, actual infinity is impossible. However, Aquinas, a Christian, believed human souls are immortal, and live on when the body dies. So, there may be an actual infinity of souls. In the battle of Aristotle vs. the Bible, both win. The world did have a beginning, but God created it in such a way that it existed eternally. God could have made the universe without human beings, but then he made them. Q: Of all of the above, from Augustine to Aquinas, which argument do you find most compelling?

Ch. 10   SLAVIC TERMS IN ENGLISH   Speaker _____

Russian, Polish, Czech, Serbo-Croatian, Ukrainian and more!

Robot   **Troika**   **Sable**   **Polka**   **Boyar**   **Parka**   **Slave**

Tundra   **Kremlin**   **Vampire**   **Mammoth**   **Paprika**   **Trepak**

Cossack   **Taiga**   **Tchotchke**   **Zemstvo**   **Spruce**   **Matryoshka**   **Pierogi**

Dacha   **Pavlovian**   **Czar**

_____ The Russian word for 'King,' which comes from the name of Julius Caesar.

_____ Furry animal you might use to make a Russian-style winter hat called a *ushanka*.

_____ A very cold biome in which the ground is always frozen, even in summer.

_____ A large prehistoric animal, like a furry elephant, that lived in northern climates.

_____ A kind of food, like a turnover, filled with things like beef, kraut or potato & cheese.

_____ A kind of tree that in the original Polish meant 'from Prussia' (z Prus).

_____ A Russian psychologist gave his last name to mean 'a conditioned response.'

_____ The Czech word for worker, which became the term for a non-human worker.

_____ A type of jacket or coat that bundles people up in cold climates.

_____ A Russian nobleman pre-1917, whose title was taken away by the communists.

_____ Large home, often in the woods or in a location like on a seaside.

_____ A cold forest wherein trees are cone-bearing.

_____ A Russian-style doll that has many smaller dolls inside of it.

_____ Many Slavic villagers were kidnapped and sold in the Middle East into servitude.

_____ In an old Russian city, this was the central fortress, the most famous in Moscow.

_____ Term for chili peppers brought to Hungary in the past, now used as a kitchen spice.

_____ Dracula was from the region, and this is a term for a sly, night-living blood-sucker.

_____ A three-individual triumvirate, from the Russian.

_____ A Russian dance, very fast, famous from Tchaikovsky's *Nutcracker* ballet.

_____ A Polish dance; comes from the term for 'Polish woman;' also a pattern of dots.

Ch. 10 **CENTRAL EUROPEAN SIGHTS** Tourist _____
Youtube: Expedia Prague; Rick Steves Budapest; Rick Steves Krakow

Which cities are the following sites in? Your choices are these medieval capitals in Eastern Europe:

Prague, Czech Republic *Budapest, Hungary* *Krakow, Poland*

Each row of sites is in one of the above cities. As you watch the video for the first city, note which one in each row is in that city. Then, rate how interesting or nice the 'sight' is:
(3 = I would definitely explore this site   2 = Looks okay, I'd check it out   1 = Boring, blah)

Neo-Gothic Parliament
Who needs such a fancy capitol?

_____ ____

Astronomical Clock
Think it has an alarm?

_____ ____

Barbikan Gate
To defend against Mongols

_____ ____

Planty Park
When you don't need a city wall

_____ ____

Szechenyi Baths
The Roman tradition lives!

_____ ____

Tyn Church (Gothic)
Whoa... seriously Gothic

_____ ____

Charles Bridge
Statues of saints over the Vltava

_____ ____

St. Mary's Church (Gothic)
Mongols shot the trumpeter here

_____ ____

Castle Hill
Royal residence on the Danube

_____ ____

Cloth Hall Market
Did Walmart have to replace it?

_____ ____

Fisherman's Bastian
Elaborate, skeletal, Neo-Gothic

_____ ____

St. Vitus Cathedral
Mausoleum of Bohemian kings

_____ ____

St. Wenceslas Statue
Good King Wenceslas was real...

_____ ____

Chain Bridge w/ Lions
First over the mightiest river of Europe

_____ ____

Wawel Hill
Kings, Queens and culture icons

_____ ____

Matching: Draw a line noting how the various phases of architecture in these cities evolved:

Romanesque (800-1100)   a. Arcaded archways built on a human scale

Gothic (1100-1400)   b. Fortress-like buildings to protect from marauders

Renaissance (1400-1600)   c. Revival of the medieval style in a later era

Neo-Gothic (1800s)   d. Lots of pointy spikes and spires, gargoyles, huge

Which city would you like to visit most, out of the three, and why? And you better not put 'none!'

Ch. 10   **CATHEDRAL!**   **Chronicler** _____

Video Search: Cathedral Macaulay (~57 min.)

This animated movie about the building of a Gothic cathedral in medieval France takes place in the 12th century. during the reign of Augustus Caesar. It centers around the building of the city of:

     a. Memphis   *b. Verbonia*   *c. Aberwavyrn*   *d. Beaulieu*

1st Chronicler: *Pierre*	1. In 1214, a great fire swept through the city, burning the early-Medieval church, which was built in this style
Good Bishop: *Philippe*	
Bad Bishop: *Gervais*	a. Romanesque b. Gothic c. Baroque
Architect: *Master Guillaume*	
Daughter: *Aiden Beauviax*	2. The holy relic that Pierre believed saved him from the flames was:
Merchant: *Thibaut*	
Friar: *Roland*	a. Veil of Mary b. Finger of John the Baptist
2nd Chronicler: *Ansel*	

Ongoing: Note the kinds of tools and simple machines used to build the cathedral:

3. The length of time the Gothic churches took to build was:

    a. Months   b. Years   c. Decades

4. Master Guillaume, based on the real-life Abbot Suger, faced a real problem when he ran out of marble. What was the major 'other' problem the cathedral faced when Bishop Gervais took over?

---

5. What role did the building of the church have on the community the church was to become the centerpiece of?

6. Below, Note some of the unique *Gothic* aspects of the cathedral, that help define this architectural style:

7. In the end, the merchant is inspired by the example of St. Francis of Assisi, who founded a famous Christian order. What was he inspired to do?

←got OCD?

Ch. 10 THE VIKINGS — Northman

Erika, sweetie, I'm gonna be late and can't find my helmet. Have you seen it? Oh, Thor's gonna love this.

The Vikings erupted onto the stage of history in the late-700s and raided and traded, explored and settled, for 300 years. On a blank map of Europe, sketch their travels and trials. They are called Vikings in English because some raided England, and they were from the area of Scandinavia called Vik. It would be like if you visited Japan with some friends and later they called all Americans "_____" (insert the name of your city!). They are really *Norse,* the Northmen, who today live in, among other places, Norway, and hold high the Nordic gods Thor and Odin.

1) The Vikings as Explorers. Locate modern Oslo, Norway and put it on the map. South of that on the Southern coast, put the district of Vik. The Sagas tell of the exploration of Iceland, Greenland and Vinland. Draw a dotted line from Vik to Iceland and label Iceland. Continue the line from Iceland west across the North Atlantic (and off the map), label it → to Greenland and Vinland.

Three places, three stories. Iceland they settled permanently, Greenland they settled in 982, but left when the Medieval Warm Period (temps 2 degrees above average) ended in the 1300s. they left stone ruins. In Vinland they are believed to have arrived in the year 1000 but left nothing behind. Historians are pretty sure they got there by what they said about it, how long it took there, etc., and while some said it was impossible to cross so vast a distance in a Viking longship, in 1893 a replica was built and the trip was duplicated- just to show it could be done!

2) The Vikings as Raiders. In 795 they raided Dublin, Ireland, also the abbeys of Lindisfarne and Iona in Scotland, and in 820 they raided York, England, bringing the Danelaw with them. Draw a dotted line to these places from Scandinavia and label them. In 845 they rowed up the River Seine all the way to Paris and raided it under Ragnar. Evidence of products made in other places are found in Scandinavia to this day. Draw a line from the North coast of France to Paris and label Paris.

3) The Vikings as Settlers. By 911, the Vikings (known to the French in the more proper way as the Nortmanni- Northmen), had arrived and settled the northern coast of France, henceforth called Normandy. Their chieftain, Rollo, entered into a feudal contract with King Charles the Simple of France, and became Duke of Normandy, ancestor of the famous Duke William, who conquered England and became King William I.

4) The Vikings as Mercenaries. When Viking long ships crossed the Straits of Gibraltar and into the Mediterranean, they found a Muslim Caliphate in Spain, and conflict between Muslim Saracens and Christians on Sicily. The Christians asked the Vikings for help, and the Vikings agreed- but not for free! After striking a deal, they became mercenaries and defeated the Muslims at the Battle of Cerami and the Battle of Palermo, winning Sicily in 1071. Roger, the Viking chieftain became Count of Sicily. His brother, Robert Guiscard, became the most famous Norman in the Mediterranean. Two decades later, the Normans ended Muslim rule over Malta.

5) The Vikings Travel East. Trace a dotted line through the Baltic Sea from Scandinavia to Northwest Russia, near where modern St. Petersburg is. Then, trace it down from there to the Black Sea. Just north of the Crimean Peninsula, the Varangian (Viking) chieftain Rurik was invited by the Rus tribes to be their first king, as the tribes squabbled over which of their chiefs should be king of the budding nation. Rurik made his headquarters in Novgorod, and many of the first Russian kings had Viking names, like Oleg and Olga. Only later did Vladimir and Yaroslav- Slavic named kings- appear.

6) The Vikings adopt Christianity. Over time, the Vikings adopted Christianity, some of the last Europeans to do so. Kenneth Clark said that a humorous situation arose in cemeteries of the time, in the transition period, when the gravestones had Norse runes on one side, with homages to Odin and Thor, and Christian symbol on the other side. He said they were "hedging their bets." What did he mean in this context?

Ch. 10 COMPARISONS: BYZANTINE AND LATIN CHRISTENDOM   Judge _____

Let's get medieval

Match the vocab term from the chapter with its appropriate place on the comparison chart:

Monasticism	*Bezant*	*Caesaropapism*	*Charlemagne*
Canon Law & feudal decree	*Corpus Iuris Civilis*	*Empire*	*Feudal*
Grand imperial capital	*Iconoclasm*	*Justinian & Theodora*	*Kingdoms*
Missi Dominici	*Sassanians/Muslims*	*Papal supremacy*	*Small cities*
Theme system	*Vikings/Magyars/Moors*		

COMPARISON

	Western Christendom	Byzantium
Type of state(s)		
Urban scenario		
Primary leaders		
Law		
Religious hierarchy		
Social-religious movements		
Military strategy		
Economic order		
"Threats"		

Ch. 10   SURNAMES   Chosen one _____

You've been named, sir. So what's my surname, sir?

Website: *http://forebears.io/surnames*

Which countries do people with your last name live in? Put the name in the search box and then click on the name result to get a world map and a list.

What are the 'top-3' countries with your last name- and how many people are said to have it?

1)   2)   3)

Website: *Ancestry.com/learn/facts*   Put your name in the search box ☺

What does it mean? _____

Which states is it most prevalent in? _____

You have a LOT of last names. No really, you do! The one you actually use is likely your dad's pappy's grandpappy's last name. But that's just tradition. You have equal claim on many others! How many of the following do you know? You have equal access, after all, to all of them:

Mom's maiden name   *Mom's mom's maiden name*   *Dad's mom's maiden name*

_____   _____   _____

Website: *Internationalheraldry.com.*

Some names even have a coat-of-arms due to a heraldic past in the Middle Ages or beyond. Below left, sketch the coat-of-arms and add the labels: crest, wreath, mantle, helmet, supporters, shield of the arms, compartment, and motto.

   (it's the bluish image partway down the page)

| Now for the best part- design you own! You can make it any way you want, but make it symbolic of you and your personality and code of honor!

Ch. 10 CASTLE! Mason _____
Youtube: *Castle Macaulay*

This animated movie about Medieval England takes place around 1283, during the reign of Edward I. It centers around the building of the castle of an Edwardian castle.

Aberwyvern was in *W*_____ which was a *rebellious   cooperative* region.

Lord Aberwyvern: *Kevin La Strange* | To some, the castle was a defensive fortress. To others
Lady Aberwyvern: *Catherine* | it was an offensive weapon. Who might have these
Engineer: *James of St. George* | perspectives on the castle and why?
Welsh chieftain: *Daveth of Gwyneth* |
Blacksmith: *Andrew* | *Defensive*   *Offensive*

***G**eography and Environment*
***R**eligion and Worldview*
***A**rts and Innovations*
***P**olitics and Government*
***E**conomy and Trade*
***S**ocial Relationships*

Use each of the above choices from the **GRAPES** chart to categorize what kind of issue each of the following were (primarily):

_____ Kevin La Strange was appointed **lord** of the English territory of Northwest Wales by King Edward I.

_____ The Welsh had a difficult time socially **assimilating** to English ways of life. Some were angry, and fomented rebellion by attacking the castle.

_____ Lots of jobs were available in the building of the castle and the town, namely, tanner, miller, cooper, blacksmith, armorer, mason, carpenter, architect and more. Products were made by the townspeople and **traded**.

Edwardian castles were the most advanced of the Medieval world. List six kinds of parts they had that helped them in their task of securing an area:

	Part	*Function*		*Part*	*Function*
1)	*Drawbridge*	*Protective barrier*	4)		
2)			5)		
3)			6)		

What kind of weapons were used in the siege?   Did the castle withstand the siege?

_____   _____

Why did castles like Aberwyvern decline?   What happened to the importance of the town?

Ch. 10   **CASTLES GRAND!**   Vassal _____

http://www.antarcticaedu.com/19hstcastles.htm

In the first picture, which one is the castles and which is the palace? | Which is more *luxurious*?
_____ | _____

Why did the English build so many castles in Scotland and Wales?

_____

All castles were large and had moats: *a. True*   *b. False*

The English never built castles in Ireland as they did in Scotland and Wales: *a. True*   *b. False*

What's changed in the last 100 years at Harlech castle in England?

_____

Chepstow is unique for being _____

All the royal coronations are held at _____

During the Romantic era in the 19th century, medieval castles   The largest castle in Britain is

        a. were scorned   *b. were revived*   _____

Would YOU want to have your wedding reception in a castle's grand hall?

_____

What is special about Windsor Castle in London? | The infamous prison in Central London that
                                                | dates from the middle ages is this:
                                                |
                                                |
                                                |

Bodium castle is noted for its: When King John signed the Magna Carta, why was he angry?

_____   _____

If you were a Harry Potter fan, which castle in England would you most like to visit? _____

If France and England had a contest as to which was the more imposing castle, would you pick St. Michael's Mount or Mont St. Michel?
                                        _____

How are French and English *gardens* different? | Scroll through the rest of the castles. Which
                                                | is your favorite?

Ch. 11   CENTRAL ASIAN TERMS IN ENGLISH   Pasha _____
Turkish, Altaic and Mongol

Shish-Kebab   **Altai**   **Kiosk**   **Pastrami**   **Ottoman**   **Yogurt**   **Pilaf**

Coffee   **Ataman**   **Baklava**   **Pasha**   **Balkan**   **Khan**   **Batman**

Janissary   **Cossack**   **Yurt**   **Urdu**   **Caffeine**   **Shaman**   **Kumis**

_____ Originating in Yemen, this bean, *'kahve,'* keeps Starbucks and Dunkin in business

_____ A city in Turkey and a unit of measurement... that became a superhero

_____ This aged milk-based substance is often modified with fruit

_____ Originally *'cafeneh,'* this is the psychoactive stimulant in coffee

_____ Turkish dessert popular in Greek and Middle Eastern restaurants

_____ Turkish name for Russian and Ukrainian soldier-adventurers and vagabonds

_____ From *'Yeniceri,'* meaning a new soldier, these were slave fighters for the Sultan

_____ 'Ruler' in Turkish, pronounced with a soft 'k' so 'han'

_____ From *'kosk,'* a pavilion that sells things like tickets and soda on street corners.

_____ A footstool that you might put your feet up on while you chill out pasha-style

_____ You can eat *'Pastirma'* a deli meat with *'Pilav,'* boiled rice w/ spices: _____

_____ A *'saman'* is a magician who can manipulate natural forces

_____ Meat and vegetables on a stick

_____ Leader of an armed band- adopted as *hetman* by Poles and Ukrainians from Turkish

_____ From *'pasa,'* this is a polite like 'sir'

_____ 'Mountain chain,' this refers to the peoples of Greece, Romania, Bulgaria and Serbia

_____ Dog breed and mountain range

_____ A 'dwelling place,' this is used as a portable home on the steppes or in armed forces

_____ From *'kumyz,'* a fermented drink made of horse blood and yogurt

_____ From Turkish *'orda,'* meaning the Khan's entourage

Ch. 11   Great Clips: Genghis Khan and the Mongol Conquests   Khan _____

Video search: "CNN Millennium: 13th century" (around 1 min. in)

Before Watching

Genghis Khan (ok, Chinggis) united a nation and mobilized it as a fighting force. That doesn't happen too often in history. Aside from the world wars of the 20th century, the Mongol conquests resulted in terrific loss of life, on the order of 16,000,000.

1. What are the characteristics of the steppe biome?

2. What kinds of things did the Mongols eat and what was missing?

    Eaten   *Missing*

3. Describe Mongol psy-ops and battle tactics:

---

4. If you survived the initial conquest, life under Mongol rule was not the worst imaginable. What did the Mongols do that helped the economies of the places they conquered?

Ch. 11   Great Clips: The Pax Mongolica   _____

Video search: "CNN Millennium: 13th century" (around 13 min. in)

Pax Mongolica means "Mongol Peace." The unity of Asia and Russia under Mongol rule opened the way for a vast trade network to develop.

1. Note some advice to merchants traveling along the Silk Road warning them about silver and paper money:

2. Why did the Mongols built notary-post stations at a day's ride on the Silk Road?

3. What did William of Rubruck say about the capital?

4. The Mongols were religiously:

    a. tolerant   *b. strict*

---

4. Charlemagne invited scholars to Aachen last chapter, how were the Mongol khans similar?

Ch. 11 **Great Clips: Yuan Dynasty China** _____
Video search: "CNN Millennium: 13th century" (around 20 min. in)

Before Watching, think again about why great dynasties and empires fall. Foreign invasion? Decadence (getting "soft")? Some kind of catastrophe like a volcano? Yes, yes and yes! So which was it for the Yuan?

Why might tough nomadic warriors "get soft" after settling in China as a ruling class?

_____

Kublai Khan's luxurious palace was called _____.

This Italian (Venetian) traveler visited it:

_____

Why did the Chinese hate the government of the Great Khan?

_____

How did the Chinese express their culture under Mongol rule?

_____

Decadence is the term that is used when ruling elites and/or regular people (but in this case the Mongol elites) start setting up lavish and luxuriant lifestyles for themselves. What was Kublai Khan's family life like?

_____

What happened when Kublai and his wife Chabi sent a fleet of ships to conquer Japan?

_____

All empires fall, it seems. The Yuan fell in 1368. What does it mean that "Kublai conquered China, but then China conquered him?"

_____

Ch. 11 **Great Clips: Tamerlane's Central Asian Empire** _____
Video search: "CNN Millennium: 14th century" (around 18 min. in)

Four times in history, powerful Turkish clans or conquerors emerged from Central Asia. The Saljuqs against the Byzantines, the Ghaznavids into India, the Ottomans against the Byzantines, and the forces of Tamerlane.

After Watching

Samarkand in Central Asia is decorated by mosques and mausoleums with   red   blue   purple   domed roofs.

Central Asia's rule over East and West, North and South, had one last, second wind in the early-15th century. Fifty years after the Mongol collapse in China, this conqueror came out of nowhere:

a. Genghis Khan   b. Kublai Khan   c. Timur

| The empire built by the Turks of Central Asia
| was ruled by this Turkic ethnic group:
|
| a. Turkmen   b. Uzbek   c. Kazakhs

He slaughtered _____ at Delhi in _____, and at Isfahan in _____, Timur built a skull pyramid of 70,000 heads. But that's okay, he encouraged trade...

What was Timur's religion (hint: different than the Mongols):   Unlike the Mongol Empire that lasted 200 years, what happened to Timur's empire when he died?

Ch. 12   **RENAISSANCE LITERATURE**   Fashionista _____
Your new favorite books

http://hudsonfla.com/litrenaissance.htm

Write the name of the famous work, then match the letter from the correct description of the work:

_____ ____
Francesco Petrarch

A. Taught Renaissance people how to dress fashionably

_____ ____
Giovanni Boccaccio

B. Contained images of the human body and machines that fly

_____ ____
Baldisseri Castiglione

C. Pioneered the use of the essay format of writing

_____ ____
Martin Luther

D. His daughter died young, and his sadness went into this work

_____ ____
Niccolo Machiavelli

E. First to reveal that the earth moved around the sun

_____ ____
John Calvin

F. Posted reasons why Catholic leaders were corrupt on church door

_____ ____
Desiderius Erasmus

G. Wanted people to focus on making themselves better- not perfect

_____ ____
Nicholas Copernicus

H. Grief over his beloved Laura is the subject of his internal struggle

_____ ____
Thomas More

I. Rambunctious comedy and satire about how school is a huge farce

_____ ____
Ignatius Loyola

J. Ten stories, ten days. All different topics, hard to classify

_____ ____
Leonardo da Vinci

K. A 'reaction against reformers,' this is handbook of the Jesuit Order

_____ ____
Francois Rabelais

L. Ripped on the institutions and made fun of just about everyone

_____ ____
Montaigne

M. Advised Lorenzo d'Medici how to gain and keep power

_____ ____
Jan Kochanowski

N. Taught hard work and perseverance were the keys to a good life

Of all these books, which would you pick to read if you had to read one and why?

All done? Go to Bentley 5e → student view → scroll bar to 21 → "Who Am I" game, Interactive Map, Outline.

Ch. 12 **Great Clips: Zheng He's Treasure Ships** **Eunuch Admiral** _____
Video search: "CNN Millennium: 15th century" (around 2 min. in)

Review: who was trading on the Indian Ocean during the Postclassical Era? | Why was the Ming dynasty considered a 'restoration' of native Chinese rule?

What was the *Quilin* 'dragon' that Zheng He brought back? _____

What were the purposes of the Ming rulers sending Zheng He all around the world?

_____

How did the Treasure Fleet's ships compare with Columbus ships (which sailed 70 years later)?

_____

Ch. 12 **Great Clips: Italian Renaissance Fashions** **Courtier** _____
Video search: "CNN Millennium: 15th century" (around 10:30 min. in)

Before Watching

What is 'fashion' anyway? Why do you think some people care so much about being in fashion?

| What was the role of wealthy noble patrons in the Renaissance movement?

What kinds of things was Leonardo da Vinci interested in? | Summarize what the Renaissance was all about:

Great Clips: Building a Russian Empire **Officer** _____
Video search: "CNN Millennium: 16th century" (around 15:00 min. in)

Before Watching

What was St. Basil's Cathedral, the most iconic Russian building (get it? iconic?) constructed to commemorate?

| What themes did early Russian cinema have that
| supports the idea of strong, centralized state?

Ivan IV instituted the *Oprichnina*, which started a grim tradition in Russia. What was the role of the *Oprichnina*?

Ch. 12   **Great Clips: Mehmed II and the Rise of the Ottomans**   Sultan _____

Video search: "CNN Millennium: 15th century" (around 25 min. in)

Before Watching

Having invaded the Byzantine Empire in the mid-11th century, the Seljuk Turks won territory in Anatolia and stayed. Two centuries later, the Ottomans unified another group of Turks, who migrated to Anatolia as well and renewed the battle with the Byzantines. They took land in the Balkans and finally assaulted Constantinople in the 15th century.

1. How many centuries had Turks lived in Anatolia before ending the Byzantine Empire in 1453? _____

After Watching

2. How did the Ottoman Turks 'get through' the walls of Constantinople?
_____

3. How are elementary school children taught about Turkish heroes?
_____

4. How did the 'Whirling Dervishes' worship Allah?
_____

3. The Turks' treatment of the Byzantine Greek population of the city can be characterized as:

    a. tolerant   b. brutal

5. What new drink appeared in this era in the Turkish Empire and why did Muslims especially like it?
_____

Ch. 12   **Great Clips: Akbar and the Mughal Dynasty**   Syncretist _____

"CNN Millennium: 16th century" (around 28 min. in)

Before Watching

The history here is complex. The medieval Islamic Caliphate (which ISIS is claiming to be recreating today) declined with the Abbasids after Mongol attack and the rise of the Gunpowder Empires (Ottoman, Safavid and Mughal). When Babur I led a war of conquest into Northern India in 1526, his forces came from the family palace in modern-day Kabul, Afghanistan. The immediate issue was how to rule a majority of Hindus with a victorious Muslim minority.

6. The attack of Babur can be seen aiding in the diffusion of this religion to Northern India: _____

After Watching

7. For the harem women in Afghanistan, why were the Indian dancing girls 'culture shock?'
_____

8. What did Babur I 'see' India as a place for?
_____

9. Why did Babur declare a jihad against a group of Indian princes?
_____

10. Akbar the Great was   *more*   *less* tolerant of Hinduism than his grandfather Babur.

11. How many wives did Akbar have? _____

12. How successful were Akbar's religious roundtable meetings?

13. Why did Gulbadan Begum 'flee' to Mecca?
_____

Ch. 12 NEW HORIZONS VOCAB REVIEW   Cosmologist _____

Honey, why do you still act like you're the center of the universe? Copernicus disproved that 500 years ago! #HowAstronomersFight

---

1. ____ Struck mid-14th century Europe and led to a labor shortage

2. ____ Muslim traveler and legal scholar (*qadi*) who visited the Swahili Coast and India

3. ____ Best way to transport heavy goods

4. ____ Straits through the Spice Islands by which ships reached China

5. ____ Was called Khanbaliq during the Yuan era

6. ____ Mongol rule allowed for increased travel of this type

7. ____ Venetian merchant whose accounts of China spurred a spirit of exploration

8. ____ Eunuch who sailed for the Ming emperors until they grounded his fleet

9. ____ Nestorian Christian priest who served as envoy for the Ilkhans of Persia

10. ____ Wealthy family such as Medici or Sforza who commissioned works of art

11. ____ Fibers of this make textiles that are easier to clean and more sanitary

12. ____ Europeans made use of this during the Hundred Years' War

13. ____ Term for the colder period that followed the Medieval Warm Period

14. ____ Grand Prince of Moscow who ended dominance of the Mongol Horde

15. ____ Sculpted the *David* statue and painted the Sistine Chapel ceiling

16. ____ Not a Renaissance artist, this person wrote *The Prince*

17. ____ River in Russia that facilitated the spread of Russian culture eastwards

18. ____ Year in which the Spanish *Reconquista* was completed

A. Beijing   **B. Bubonic Plague**   **C. Cotton**

D. 1492   E. Gunpowder   F. Ibn Battuta

G. Ivan III   H. Land (i.e.: Silk Road)   I. Little Ice Age

J. Machiavelli   K. Marco Polo   L. Melaka

M. Michelangelo   N. Rabban Sauma   O. Sea (i.e.: Indian Ocean)

P. Patron   Q. Volga   R. Zheng He

Ch. 13   **EXPLORERS' MATRIX**   Poop deck janitor _____

Completing the map of the world one conquest at a time...

Explorer	Time	Sailed from...	Significance / Accomplishment
Bartholomeu Dias			
Vasco da Gama			
Christopher Columbus			
Amerigo Vespucci			
Vasco de Balboa			
Ponce de Leon			
Hernando de Soto			
Francisco Coronado			
Ferdinand Magellan			
Pedro Cabral			
Alfonso Albuquerque			
John Cabot			
Jacques Cartier			
Hernando Cortes			
Francisco Pizarro			
Francis Drake			

Henry Hudson			
Walter Raleigh			
John Smith			
William Bradford			
Samuel de Champlain			
Father Marquette			
Robert de La Salle			
James Cook			
Abel Tasman			
William Bligh			
Vitus Bering			
William Barents			
J.-F. de La Perouse			
Lewis & Clark			
Francis Parkman			
F. von Bellingshausen			
Robert Peary			
Roald Amundsen			

Ch. 13 FIRST AROUND THE WORLD?   Navigator _____
You thought it was Magellan? Think again!

Video Search: **Magellan Voyages of Discovery: Circumnavigation.** In 1519, with 251 sailors traveling an average of 100 miles/day, the *Victoria, San Antonio, Santiago, Trinidad,* and *Concepcion* set out on a mission to find a western route to the riches of the Spice Islands. Note the roles played by the following along the way:

Ferdinand Magellan　　　*Chevalier Antonio Pigafetta*　　　*Lapu-Lapu*　　　*Juan Sebastian Elcano*

_____

Note the issues, problems or victories Magellan and the crew went through at each of the following key points on their way to- eventually for some- circumnavigate the globe:

Atlantic Ocean
_____

South America
_____

Pacific Ocean
_____

Philippines Islands
_____

The Spice Islands
_____

Indian Ocean
_____

Return in Spain

Knowing what you do about the voyage, would you have signed up for it? Weigh the possibility for 1) glory, 2) hardship, 3) adventure, 4) the knowledge that you are the first to do something amazing:	*Who should get the credit for the first voyage around the world? Magellan or the guys who survived?*

Ch. 13   **CRASH COURSE #23: COLUMBIAN EXCHANGE**   Diffuser _____

Benefits of the Columbian Exchange | Harmful effects of the Columbian Exchange

1.

2.

3.

4.

5.

6.

7.

8.

9.

10.

Below: Is the world better off as a result of the Columbian Exchange? Why?

Use the book or online to find out what crops, people, animals and diseases traveled in which direction:
Search term: Columbian Exchange. Click on the encyclopedia article and list the items below. Be careful to list them on the right side!

Domestic Animals from New to Old →
(brought back to Europe by Columbus)

← Domestic Animals from Old to New
(brought to America from Europe)

Cultivated Plants from New to Old →

← Cultivated Plants from Old to New

Diseases from New to Old →

← Diseases from Old to New

Ch. 14   **Great Clips: Jamestown**   Settler _____
Video search: "CNN Millennium: 17th century" (around 8 min. in)

How did Jamestown get its name? _____

Describe the dress that the workers at Jamestown today wear- which is what the settlers wore:

_____

Describe some of the troubles the Jamestown colonists had:	What was the relationship between John Smith and Chief Powhatan?

What was the first American law, summarized into one line, regarding work in the colony?

_____

What was the 'salvation' of the Jamestown colony?

_____

Great Clips: Brazilian Slavery and Sugarcane
Video search: "CNN Millennium: 17th century" (around 18 min. in)

Like the United States, Brazil has a large African population largely due to the slave trade of the colonial era:

        a. True   *b. False*

What was the economic reason to transport slaves from Africa to Brazil?	Why didn't the Portuguese enslave Native Americans to harvest sugar?

Describe the difficult and laborious conditions harvesting sugar entailed:	What kinds of African cultural expressions did maroon communities retain in the rural areas of Brazil?

Ch. 14   LABOR SYSTEMS   Laborer _____

"This is going to be a lot of work." –student   *"Uh, no it's not." –actual laborer*

Match the following labor system references in AP World History to the appropriate term:

1. _____ One commonly become a servant or slave here, the ancient name for modern Iraq, by being captured in battle (POW), being indebted to someone, or by inheriting the status.

2. _____ Conscript labor was used here on large public projects such as the Great Pyramid, wherein the workers had no choice in the matter but the work was considered a duty to the state.

3. _____ Following a famine, this monotheistic group sought refuge in Egypt until being assigned slave status and migrating out under the guidance of the lawgiver Moses.

4. _____ These dwellers around the Greek city of Sparta were forced into doing agricultural work to support the Spartan military class, the full-citizen equals.

5. _____ Following the Punic Wars, captured fighters from Carthage, Greece, etc. were brought to Italy to work on these large, commercial farms- which became a cause of social unrest.

6. _____ After the Vedic Age the concept of a Dalit outcast group and a Sudra working caste evolved here, which mandated the kinds of work people were allowed to do.

7. _____ Conscript labor was used here on large projects such as the Great Wall and the Grand Canal, famously by Emperor Qin, which helped lessen his popularity and led to his overthrow.

8. _____ Arab merchants transported African slaves to the Middle East from this coast during the 7th-15th centuries, the Zanj Rebellion being an example of a failed revolt.

9. _____ Feudal aristocrats were often supported by the labor of these Medieval Europeans, who could be required to be bound to the land itself, or to a cottage owned by a lord.

10. _____ Having conquered Central Mexico, this empire ritually sacrificed captured people and employed forced labor, which drove many tribes to help Cortes against them.

11. _____ This conscript system, employed first by the Inca and then by the Spanish, led many laborers to contract mercury poisoning in the silver mines of Potosi.

12. _____ Hacienda plantations dotted the landscape of Spanish America, which became the centers of this labor system of conscripted agricultural work.

13. _____ Chiefdoms here commonly used slaves and cattle as currency and measures of wealth, from the Igbo and Yoruba in the west to the Zulus and Xhosa in the south.

14. _____ The Middle Passage of Triangular Trade across the Atlantic saw the most African slaves brought to this Portuguese colony to harvest and process sugar in engenhos.

15. _____ A plantation economy developed here based primarily on cash crops like tobacco early on in the 17th century and cotton by the 19th.

American South	*Africa*	*Aztec*	*Brazil*	*China*	*Egypt*	*Encomienda*
Hebrews	*Helots*	*India*	*Latifundia*	*Mesopotamia*	*Mita*	*Serfs* *Swahili*

16. _____ Under this labor system, a European's sea ticket would be paid by a sponsor in America, who would then work for that sponsor upon arrival for an average of 7 years.

17. _____ While most were privately held, corporations could own slave plantations too, as this company did in the Spice Islands, traffic from which necessitated establishment of the Cape Colony.

18. _____ Islamic empires used slave armies such as the Egyptian Mamelukes and this force of European men kidnapped as children from the Balkans while under Turkish rule.

19. _____ Russian and Ukrainian villages were raided for workers and women to be sold in Middle Eastern slave markets, such as Roxelana, which is why this word comes from 'Slav'.

20. _____ The Spanish and Italian coasts were raided- usually at night- for slaves destined for North Africa by *these*- until the U.S. Navy defeated them in the early-1800s.

21. _____ War debts in France inspired the state to force the peasantry who couldn't pay taxes to work for part of the year on public works projects such as road maintenance.

22. _____ In the industrializing world, this concept reflected the idea that the business of laborers and employers, freely associating, should not be regulated- but considered slavery "peculiar."

23. _____ Following the abolition of slavery in the U.S., workers came from this region in a new phase of indentured work to labor on railroads, until, following race riots, Congress stopped the flow.

24. _____ Serfdom as a labor system continued here longer than elsewhere in Europe, factoring into a heightened consciousness of class, which continued into 20th century socialism.

25. _____ Rapidly industrializing Japan encouraged an attitude of teamwork and loyalty within the framework of these large corporate conglomerates, channeling competitive spirit into business.

26. _____ Employed as the *Levee en masse* during the French Revolution, and known as 'calling people up' in WWI, WWII and Vietnam, for example, if this happens to you, it's forced soldiery.

27. _____ During the Second World War, the Germans and Japanese used slave labor in these institutions of state, where people were forced to produce war materiel.

28. _____ From the 1930s to the 1970s, millions of Soviet citizens were sent against their will to these work camps in Siberia, where they harvested resources for the state.

29. _____ Slang for a command economy in which the labor of the people is placed at the will of the government, and to not cooperate makes a person an enemy of the state.

30. _____ Attracted by ads for better work, this occurs when women are kidnapped, smuggled across international borders, and enslaved as prostitutes.

31. _____ In a modern incarnation of a non-regulated, laissez-faire capitalism, these are large factories employing low-wage workers in substandard conditions for long hours in East Asia.

32. _____ Conception of a modern corporatist state as a place in which the masses are held in debt bondage as 'human livestock' to labor for the wealth of transnational elites.

Asia   Axis camp   Barbary pirates   Corvee   Drafted   Dutch East India   Gulag   Indenture   Janissaries

Laissez-faire   Russia   Sex trafficking   Slave   Sweatshop   Tax farm   Workers' paradise   Ziabatsu

Ch. 14   **PIRACY ON THE SPANISH MAIN**   First Mate _____
Video Search: *History Channel True Caribbean Pirates*

1. Transatlantic piracy began after this explorer linked Spain to the Bahamas in 1492:

   a. Magellan   b. Cortés   c. Columbus   d. Da Gama   e. Diaś

2. When adventurers from France, England and Holland came to the Caribbean and cooked meat, they became known as this, the mascot of the Tampa Bay NFL team: _____

3. Modern Haiti and the Dominican Republic used to be this island, on which animals were released:
   a. Cuba   b. Puerto Rico   c. Hispaniola   d. San Salvador   e. Aruba

4. Why did the original 'Pirates of the Caribbean' get so angry at the Spanish?

_____

5. In England's 1654 invasion fleet, this future pirate captain happened to sign up to fight on the Spanish Main:
   a. Erik the Red   b. Leif Erickson   c. Captain Hook   d. Henry Morgan

6. After things go wrong for the English fleet, they turn their sights to this island, which England would rule for 300 years, until the 1960s:
   a. Puerto Rico   b. Cuba   c. Jamaica   d. Hispaniola

7. In order to fight the Spanish *legally*, Captain Morgan required this kind of license: _____

8. In the 1668 fight against the English, the Spanish at Portobelo, Panama did *not* have this kind of weapon:
   a. Musket   b. Grenade   c. Cutlass   d. Canon   e. Sword

9. How did the buccaneers spend their wealth back in Jamaica?

_____

10. If someone gave you $50,000, what would *you* do with it?

_____

| 11. Why were the Buccaneers upset after the successful 1671 Sack of Panamá Viejo? | 12. How did the meeting go between Captain Morgan and King Charles II? | 13. What did the Treaty of Utrecht do? |

Ch. 14 **HOW TO PIRATE SOURCES** Swashbuckler _____
Time to cite your site

Today we are going to do some research online and cite our sources in a bibliography. Online, search: **21 Famous Pirates That Put Jack Sparrow To Shame**. In the article, summarize the most famous pirates in a 'Who, What, When" format:

1) François L'Olonnais When:

What:

How do you pronounce this name phonetically?

2) Bartholomew Roberts When:

What:

How do you pronounce this name phonetically?

3) Henry Morgan When:

What:

How do you pronounce this name phonetically?

4) Edward England When:

What:

How do you pronounce this name phonetically?

5) Anne Bonney When:

What:

How do you pronounce this name phonetically?

6) Edward Teach When:

What:

How do you pronounce this name phonetically?

7) Calico Jack   When:

What:

How do you pronounce this name phonetically?

8) Hayreddin Barbarossa   When:

What:

How do you pronounce this name phonetically?

9) Mary Read   When:

What:

How do you pronounce this name phonetically?

10) Francis Drake   When:

What:

How do you pronounce this name phonetically?

Now, pick one of the pirates, the one most interesting to you, and go to the **Wikipedia article** on that pirate. Most teachers and professors prefer you do NOT use Wikipedia in your bibliography, but especially with current research on a topic, Wikipedia can lead you to a strong source that you can use in your bibliography. Search the death or demise of your pirate. Specifically, what happened to them in the end? Write a summary of what happened to them below:

Now, cite your source by putting a little superscripted '1' at the end of your statement. Since you don't want to use Wikipedia, find out where Wikipedia got the information by finding the superscripted number indicating a bibliographical notation, which is located in the particular section on the demise of your pirate. **Click on that notation**, and when your page scrolls down to the bottom of the article, write THAT source below, next to the superscripted 1:

Ch. 24 **INCA GOLD (OR SILVER)** Miner _____

Video Search: *Ascent of Money Ferguson Episode 1 Bullion to Bubbles (first 13 min.)*

1. "The power of finance is everywhere we look?" What is *finance* in this context?

_____

2. In Inca society 500 years ago,   *gold   silver   labor   money*   was the unit of value.

3. We recall Ponce de Leon searched Florida for the legendary Fountain of Youth, which he never found, although with the number of retirees who come to Florida each year, the joke is people are still searching for it there. Similarly, Francisco Pizarro and the Spanish conquistadores came to the Andes in 1532 for a specific reason. What was it?

_____

4. What did the Spanish find in Potosí?	5. Why were the Incas mystified by the Spanish obsession with mining silver?

6. The mita system of peonage that the Spanish ran in Potosí, meant that each able-bodied Inca male had to do this:	7. Why *didn't* the amazing mine the Spanish found not save the empire from decline?

8. This iron law of economics is true in every society in the history of the world:

   a. Money has as much value as the metal content in it

   b. Money is only worth what other people will give in exchange for it

9. What are Americans 'trusting' the U.S. Treasury *not* to do?

_____

10. If the U.S. Treasury 'betrayed the public trust,' what would you likely see happen?

a. Prices would drop for products in stores, because no one would have any money to buy things

b. Prices would rise for products in stores, because so much money was circulating in society

11. Will you try to pay for college as you go, or take loans out from the government or a bank?

Ch. 15   **CHRISTIAN DENOMINATIONS**   Adherent _____
One religion, many ways of expression

```
                                                              Evangelical 1950------------
                                                             /
1. Think of churches in your         |-Lutheran 1517 --------------------------------------
   city- which denominations         |
   have you noticed?          P      |
                                     |                Mennonite 1537-----------------------
                                     |               /
                              r      |-Anabaptist 1525-------------------------------------
                                     |               \
                                     |                Amish 1693------------------------
                              o      |
                                     |
                                     |                          Calvary Chapel 1965--------
                                     |                         /
_____        t      |                         |-Church of God 1914--------
                                     |                         /
2. What year did the Catholic-       |                Pentecostal 1901---------------------
   Orthodox split happen?     e      |               /
                                     |-Anglican (Episcopal) 1534----------------------------
_____               |               \
                              s      |                Methodist 1738------------------------
3. What year did Luther post         |                 \
   the 95 Theses triggering the      |                 |-Salvation Army 1880---------------
   Reformation?               t      |                  \
                                     |                   Nazarene 1907--------------------
                              a      |
4. What year did Calvin 'clean       |
   up Geneva by preaching            |                          Adventist 1844--------------
   predestination and purity?  n     |                         /
                                     |                 Church of Christ 1801---------------
_____               |                /
                              t      |        Baptist 1607--------------------------------
5. What year did Henry VIII          |       /
   Break from the Pope and           |-Calvinist (Reformed, Presbyterian) 1536-----------------
   Begin the Anglican Church?        |       \
                                     |        Congregationalist 1607---------------------
                                     |
_____               |

**Early Church** ---------Catholic ----------------------------------------------------------
         |      |      |                      \
         |      |      |                       Uniate 1596--------------------------------
         |      |      |                      /
         |      |      Orthodox 1054 -----------------------------------------------------
         |      |
         |      Oriental 451------------------------------------------------------------
         |
         Church of the East (Nestorian) 431-------------------------------------------
```

Ch. 15 **HENRY VIII: THE TYRANT KING?** Courtier _____

Video: Henry VIII The Most Iconic King of English History

1) What kind of feeling was there in England when Henry VIII became king in 1509?

2) In America, we like to say if you work hard enough, you can achieve almost anything. How is that different than England was in the 1500s?

3) What were some of the sources of Henry's paranoia, which led him to lash out at plotters like the Duke of Buckingham (off with his head!)?

4) What's the role of Thomas Wolsey in Henry's administration?

5) (13:00) Henry is often portrayed as 'bad' in the books because he was upset about not having a son to succeed him on the throne. After hearing about his situation, what do you think about that?

   a. I still think Henry is 'bad'   b. It's complicated   c. Everything was Anne's fault

6) Anne Boleyn and Henry seem: a. to be faking their love   b. to actually be in love

7) Whose counsel swayed Henry more?   a. Wolsey his friend   b. Anne his mistress

8) What did Anne convince Henry about the Catholic Pope?

9) Why did Thomas Cromwell (Henry's key advisor after Wolsey's demise) seek the legal, legislative approval of Parliament to 'authorize' the 1534 *Act of Supremacy* giving Henry rule over the English Church?

10) How did Henry get injured? _____

11) What was Jane Seymour's role in Henry's life?

12) The 1540s were dominated by _____

14) All in all, how do you think Henry VIII should be written about in history books?

13) How does it all pan out for the royal line of the Tudor dynasty? Does it survive?

Ch. 15   A NEW WORLDVIEW   Cosmologist _____

Honey, why do you still act like you're the center of the universe? Copernicus disproved that 500 years ago! #HowAstronomersFight

Video Search: ***The Universe: Beyond the Big Bang (S01E14).***

The History Channel series *The Universe* brings astronomical topics to life for viewers with CGI and commentary. In this particular episode, the 'season finale,' the program interviews Neil DeGrasse Tyson, Michio Kaku, Brian Greene and other big names in astronomy to review the essential moments which changed our view of our position in the cosmos. As they appear in the program, figure out which of the major figures below made the breakthrough discovery. They are in chronological order:

_____ Earth is in the middle of the observable universe

_____ The planets travel in loop-de-loops called epicycles as they orbit around the earth

_____ The Sun is in the center, the Earth is a planet, and moves around the sun w the rest

_____ The orbits of the planets, including the Earth, are elliptical (ovals) instead of circles

_____ Used telescope to observe Venus' phases, Jupiter's moons, sunspots & other proofs

_____ Postulated gravity was the invisible force that pulls apples & objects around the Sun

_____ Theorized relativity and space-time, that they're connected, and gravity bends light

_____ Argued the universe had been small at its beginning, as if hatched as a 'cosmic egg'

_____ Andromeda is actually a galaxy outside ours, and most galaxies are red-shifted...

_____ Backed Steady-State theory; discovered stellar nucleosynthesis- we are made of star!

_____ Wrote the Big Bang Theory of the expanding universe and denied the Steady-State

_____ Predicted a 'glow' from the Big Bang permeates the entire universe in every direction

_____ Discovered the universal 'glow' by accident while trying to eliminate all 'noise'

Albert Einstein
Aristotle
Arno Penzias & Robert Wilson
Edwin Hubble
Fred Hoyle
Galileo
George Gamow
George Lemaitre
Isaac Newton
Johannes Kepler
Nicholas Copernicus
Ptolemy
Robert E. Dicke & Team

All done? At right, draw the heliocentric universe *with as many spherical moons* as you know around each planet.

Ch. 15   CLIP: NEWTON'S DISCOVERY   Light being _____

Video: Cosmos Ep. 3: When Knowledge Conquered Fear (~17:00 min. in, at the London coffeehouse)

Recall that coffee diffused through Europe after King Jan Sobieski of Poland led a European alliance against the Turks, who were besieging Vienna, in 1683. The Turks left all their tents and supplies in their retreat, including coffee. It diffused fast, so the story goes. A year later, coffee was all the rage in London, and a particular coffeehouse saw a historic meeting between three luminaries of the Scientific Revolution: Sir Christopher Wren (architect of St. Paul's Cathedral), Robert Hooke (pioneered microscopes) and Sir Edmond Halley (Halley's Comet).

What problem were they trying to solve? | Are the buildings of Cambridge built in the Classical
   | or Gothic architectural style?
   |
_____ | _____

Isaac Newton was born in 1642 on: a. New Year's Day   b. the Fourth of July   c. Christmas

Newton experimented with light and investigated other questions about nature, often as an escape from this person, who he argued with:

     a. his mom   b. dad   c. stepmom   d. stepdad

The following was *not* one of the things young Newton was working with that didn't pan out:

     a. astrology   b. alchemy   c. Biblical codes

What was the elegant mathematical solution to the problem of why planets orbit the way they do that Newton gave Halley when he came to visit Cambridge?

_____

In America, we have the National Geographic Society. In England, they have the _____

The Society was bankrupt in the 1680s because it couldn't sell enough of a book on the history of:

     a. dinosaurs   b. amphibians   c. mammals   d. reptiles   e. fish

What do you think Newton's Latin-titled book, *Philosophiae Naturalis Principia Mathematica*, means in English?

_____

Of the three from the coffeehouse, which took destiny into his hands and paid out his own money so that Isaac Newton's book on the laws of gravity could be published?

     a. Sir Christopher Wren   b. Sir Edmond Halley   c. Robert Hooke

How old will you be when Halley's Comet returns (2061)? | Where do you think you'll live?
   |
_____ | _____

Ch. 15 THE AGE OF REASON   Big idea person _____
What's the big idea?

During the Renaissance, Niccolo Machiavelli shocked everyone who read his book *The Prince* (1511), by advising his local lord, Lorenzo di Medici, to 'throw morality away if it doesn't suit you, and do what you need to do to keep and increase your power.' Today many people are Machiavellian- they lie, cheat and steal if they can get away with it. The Medieval formulation of being a good person for God's sake and yours was basically thrown out the window by Machiavelli.

In your society, what do you think would happen if the electricity shut off and all institutions of state- police, firefighters, schools, EMS, etc.- all disappeared for a year?

_____

Around 150 years later, Thomas Hobbes in England, after much thought, concluded absolute monarchy was a legitimate form of government because you need a strong leader to stop anarchy in society. He wrote a book called _____ advocating strong leadership.

Kings favored Hobbes' philosophy because it justified their rule. Leviathan is a 'monster composed of men,' and each country is a monster. That 'monster' is made of the collective abilities of all the people that live in it, and its head is the sovereign, which coordinates the actions of 'the monster.' Hobbes justified his argument for strong leadership by saying in prehistoric times, which he called the *State of Nature*, some people were probably well-behaved but many were not. So, anarchy reigned until local rulers called chiefs appeared- the first 'sovereigns.' The primary reason government exists is to control anarchy.

Why do you think "even good people might have to become bad in a state of anarchy"?	Aside from providing order, what else do you think government should be responsible for?

Around 50 years later, however, John Locke argued something different than Hobbes. To him, there was something more important than kings: *natural rights.* What are the three natural rights?

1.   2.   3.

Locke argued people were "blank slates" when they were born, and the way they grew up "made them who they were". Draw a box at right: 1) For the following four things, start at the top of the box and work clockwise, writing them in the order they become important in shaping a person's values and character: *1. Family, 2. Friends, 3. Job/co-workers, 4. media (TV, Internet, music, movies, news stations)*. Now draw yourself inside the box. Draw arrows coming from each influence to you. Now draw arrows going back out to the influences, 'counteracting them.' Now write 'Human Agency' next to you. That power is the dignity each person has, that Locke said must be protected, despite believing in the Blank Slate theory.

Ch. 15   **GOVERNING STRATEGIES**   _____

How do they get us to accept them- and who do they think they are anyway?

Match characteristics of the four common ways of maintaining legitimacy and inspiring loyalty:

Tradition	***Force***	***The Social Contract***	***Nationalism***
"the way"	"the stick"	"the handshake"	"the kiss"
____|____	____|____	____|____	____|____

A. This is the Enlightenment method of making an implied deal, a tacit agreement between citizen and state, in which the state promises to defend and protect the life, liberty and property of the citizen in exchange for the citizen promising to not do illegal things and perform their civic duties when called upon.

B. This method entails the state using its power to compel its subjects to behave a certain way, else they be punished by its might.

C. When the relationship between a state and its people are enshrined in unwritten customs no one quite remembers the origin of, or in written customs that trace back to a specific and perhaps religious source, this creedal kind of community exists.

D. This method of loyalty is not a product of government so much as of biological identity in a community of like-cultured people who share a similar vision for their community's future, and act to organize the apparatus of state in a way that benefits that community future by safeguarding it by harnessing the collective power and ability of its members.

Of the following, on a 1-10 scale with 1 being "not at all important to me" and 10 being "very important to me," how loyal, proud or respectful are you to the following political entities:

_____ Your city   Which is called _____

_____ Your county   Which is called _____

_____ Your metro area   Which is called _____

_____ Your state   Which is called _____

_____ Your region   Which is called _____

_____ Your country   Which is called _____

_____ NATO   Which stands for _____

_____ The UN   Which stands for _____

_____ Your school   Which is called _____

_____ This class   Which is called _____

_____ Your planet   Which is called _____

Below, sketch the shape of the one that you rated the highest:

Which one was most important to you as it informs your identity most, and why that one?

Ch. 15   WORD PROJECT BUILDER
Word up

Today we are going to make a project on the Renaissance, Reformation and Scientific Revolution on Microsoft Word.

1. Open Microsoft Word and create a new document.
2. At the top of the page, title your document 'Renaissance Era,' then find and click Insert → Table (3 columns, 6 rows).
3. Across your top row, type 'Humanism' in column 1, 'Vernacular' in column 2, and '95 Theses' in column 3. Center them.
4. Now go online and find a short definition of each of these, and type them into the corresponding boxes in the 2nd row.
5. Next, do an image search for each of the three, locate an *interesting* image, such as a person, art or building that represents humanism as a concept, or a book written in vernacular, and drag it from the Internet into your document's 3rd row.
6. You can resize the images by double clicking on them and making each no more that 2.25 inches wide (the bottom value).
7. Across the 4th row, type 'Council of Trent' in column 1, 'Heliocentric Theory' in column 2, and 'Boyle's Law' in column 3.
8. Now go online and find a short definition of each of these, and type them into the corresponding boxes on the 5th row.
9. Next, repeat Step 5-6 for these new ones, and put their images in the 6th row. All done!
10. Type name / date / hour in the upper right, make sure the document is 1 page only, and print it to media (File → Print).

Ch. 16 — ABSOLUTELY AWESOME! (IF YOU'RE THE KING).

Honey let's build a new palace." Oh yes, that would be divine! "You're right!" And mine! Ah haha!

The building up of empires overseas brought wealth to the royal families of the home countries. The end of the 30 Years War brought peace and the Westphalian Order, which helped create a 'balance of power' and stability in Europe. Monarchies gained strength from all this. While England and the Dutch Republic were not technically absolute monarchies but constitutional ones, there were times people in England felt like their kings were going a little overboard (and even executed one, Charles I). Famously, the American colonists would later also argue their government was acting like absolutists, but even they had it pretty good in comparison with others. They at least had the right to claim they had rights! But Russia, France and Austria were three rising powers that *actually were* absolute monarchies. **Part I: An Absolutist Story.** Using the word bank below, note the names of some famous monarchs, the names of the royal dynasties and the palaces they built for themselves with their country's wealth:

Dyn:	Bourbon	Habsburg	Romanov	Stuart
Peeps:	Catherine II	Charles I	Charles V	James II
	Louis XIV	Louis XVI	Philip II	Peter I
Caps:	London	Paris	St. Petersburg	Vienna
Pals:	Buckingham	Schonbrunn	Versailles	Zimni (Winter)

England *France*

Royal dynasty:

Significant monarchs:

Imperial capital:

Name of palace:

Austrian Empire (inc. Spain) *Russian Empire*

Royal dynasty:

Significant monarchs:

Imperial capital:

Name of palace:

Part II: Using the word bank below, fill in the blanks <u>on the back</u>. Good luck!

Assemble	Associate	Balances	Capitalism
Consent	Currency	Equality	Executive
Gravity	Judicial	Newton	Legislative
Liberty	Life	Natural	Popular sovereignty
Order	Press	Property	Religion
Speech	Stability	Wealthier	Yes

Part 2: An Enlightening Story

Can you apply science to society? If there are physical laws in nature, like _____, discovered by Isaac _____, does it mean there *could* also be "natural laws" of society?   Yes   No

HOBBES (1650): "Purpose of government is to establish _____ and protect _____."

LOCKE (1690): "Yep, and the _____ to be who you want; and have _____.

These 3 social "rights" are considered _____, like the force of gravity!

Plus, government should have the _____ of the governed to be legit.

That means _____ _____ is a reasonable Enlightenment value.

MONTESQUIEU (1750): A stable state (in politics) can be had best if government is

Divided into a _____ branch that makes legislation, an _____ branch which enforces the legislation, and a _____ branch that judges whether the legislation is good or bad by evaluating the laws when they are applied in court cases. In this way, government has checks and _____.

and this system is called _____ _____ _____.

VOLTAIRE (1760): People should have freedom of conscience, and so I believe that within a country, citizens should have Freedom of _____, which, broadened, stands for freedom of belief and thought.

People should be able to express their opinion too, verbally as _____ or written as '_____.'

Meanwhile, people should be able to _____ peaceably, and express their group opinion too.

This means by extension that people should be free to _____ with who they want.

SMITH (1776): Prosperity can be generated within a country if a sound system of economics is instituted, creating a game in which everyone plays by the same rules. Harnessing peoples' drive to make themselves _____, by earning _____ to satisfy their desire to have things, the invisible hand of the market will generate national wealth through free actors doing what they want.

"My system," Mr. Smith says, is called _____, and in it, it is best if government takes a back seat role and even just stays out of the way!"

ROUSSEAU (1780): No one should have social privileges that are denied to others. In this way, we can ensure a 'level playing field' for everyone, and in so doing, achieve social:

Ch. 16   **AMERICAN HISTORY DIAGNOSTIC TEST**   **You** _____

*If any of the questions contain errors, write N/A and note why the question is invalid.
After answering the questions below,* Youtube: <u>Mark Dice Fourth of July</u> *to see if you were right.*

1. What country did the 'Mericans declare independence from? _____

2. What is the purpose of the Fourth of July celebration? _____

3. When Jesse Ventura, John Wilkes Booth and the other Founding Fathers signed the Declaration of Independence, what year was that?
_____

4. What's the purpose of Fourth of July weekend? _____

5. Name two of the Founding Fathers of the United States: _____ / _____

6. What year did the Declaration of Independence get signed? _____

7. Fourth of July weekend we celebrate the Civil War victory of the North over the South, the freeing of the slaves, right?
_____

8. Fourth of July weekend we celebrate John Wilkes Booth, Jesse Ventura and the other Founding Fathers- who's your favorite Founding Father?
_____

9. Fourth of July weekend we're celebrating our independence from China. What are you doing to celebrate that victory over the Chinese?
_____

10. When we won WWII celebrating the victory over the Axis of Evil on the Fourth of July, what do people usually do to celebrate the victory over the Nazis that special weekend?
_____

11. What is Independence Day? _____

12. What year was independence declared? _____

13. Name any American Founders you know:
_____

14. Do you know any of the Preamble of the Constitution- and what the phrases mean? Write as much as you can:

Ch. 16   IN CONGRESS, July 4, 1776.   Delegate:

The unanimous Declaration of the thirteen united States of America,

1. Is there a capitalization error in *United* here? Why or why not? _____

When in the Course of human events, it becomes necessary for one people to dissolve the political bands which have connected them with another, and to assume among the powers of the earth, the separate and equal station to which the Laws of Nature and of Nature's God entitle them, a decent respect to the opinions of mankind requires that they should declare the causes which impel them to the separation.

2. To whom are the founders directing the Declaration? Who is the intended audience? Circle your answer above.

We hold these truths to be self-evident, that all men are created equal, that they are endowed by their Creator with certain unalienable Rights, that among these are Life, Liberty and the pursuit of Happiness; That to secure these rights, Governments are instituted among Men, deriving their just powers from the consent of the governed, --That whenever any Form of Government becomes destructive of these ends, it is the Right of the People to alter or to abolish it, and to institute new Government, laying its foundation on such principles and organizing its powers in such form, as to them shall seem most likely to effect their Safety and Happiness.

3. What three "Natural Rights" does Jefferson refers to? _____

4. When does a person / people have a right and the duty to overthrow the government? Circle that part in the doc:

Prudence, indeed, will dictate that Governments long established should not be changed for light and transient causes; and accordingly all experience hath shown, that mankind are more disposed to suffer, while evils are sufferable, than to right themselves by abolishing the forms to which they are accustomed. But when a long train of abuses and usurpations, pursuing invariably the same Object evinces a design to reduce them under absolute Despotism, it is their right, it is their duty, to throw off such Government, and to provide new Guards for their future security; Such has been the patient sufferance of these Colonies; and such is now the necessity which constrains them to alter their former Systems of Government. The history of the present King of Great Britain is a history of repeated injuries and usurpations, all having in direct object the establishment of an absolute Tyranny over these States. To prove this, let Facts be submitted to a candid world.

5. Now like a good lawyer making their case, Jefferson outlines the specific reasons George III and the British government are guilty of despotism and eligible to be overthrown by the enlightened American colonists. Circle all the times Jefferson directly uses the word, "He" in this section:

He has refused his Assent to Laws, the most wholesome and necessary for the public good.
He has forbidden his Governors to pass Laws of immediate and pressing importance, unless suspended in their operation till his Assent should be obtained; and when so suspended, he has utterly neglected to attend to them.
He has refused to pass other Laws for the accommodation of large districts of people, unless those people would relinquish the right of Representation in the Legislature, a right inestimable to them and formidable to tyrants only.
He has called together legislative bodies at places unusual, uncomfortable, and distant from the depository of their public Records, for the sole purpose of fatiguing them into compliance with his measures.
He has dissolved Representative Houses repeatedly, for opposing with manly firmness his invasions on the rights of the people.
He has refused for a long time, after such dissolutions, to cause others to be elected; whereby the Legislative powers, incapable of Annihilation, have returned to the People at large for their exercise; the State remaining in the mean time exposed to all the dangers of invasion from without, and convulsions within.
He has endeavoured to prevent the population of these States; for that purpose obstructing the Laws for Naturalization of Foreigners; refusing to pass others to encourage their migrations hither, and raising the conditions of new Appropriations of Lands.
He has obstructed the Administration of Justice, by refusing his Assent to Laws for establishing Judiciary powers.
He has made Judges dependent on his Will alone, for the tenure of their offices, and the amount and payment of their salaries.
He has erected a multitude of New Offices, and sent hither swarms of Officers to harrass our people, and eat out their substance.
He has kept among us, in times of peace, Standing Armies without the Consent of our legislatures.
He has affected to render the Military independent of and superior to the Civil power.
He has combined with others to subject us to a jurisdiction foreign to our constitution, and unacknowledged by our laws; giving his Assent to their Acts of pretended Legislation:
For Quartering large bodies of armed troops among us:
For protecting them, by a mock Trial, from punishment for any Murders which they should commit on the Inhabitants of these States:
For cutting off our Trade with all parts of the world:
For imposing Taxes on us without our Consent:
For depriving us in many cases, of the benefits of Trial by Jury:

For transporting us beyond Seas to be tried for pretended offences
For abolishing the free System of English Laws in a neighbouring Province, establishing therein an Arbitrary government, and enlarging its Boundaries so as to render it at once an example and fit instrument for introducing the same absolute rule into these Colonies:
For taking away our Charters, abolishing our most valuable Laws, and altering fundamentally the Forms of our Governments:
For suspending our own Legislatures, and declaring themselves invested with power to legislate for us in all cases whatsoever.
He has abdicated Government here, by declaring us out of his Protection and waging War against us.
He has plundered our seas, ravaged our Coasts, burnt our towns, and destroyed the lives of our people.
He is at this time transporting large Armies of foreign Mercenaries to compleat the works of death, desolation and tyranny, already begun with circumstances of Cruelty & perfidy unparalleled in the most barbarous ages, and totally unworthy the Head of a civilized nation.
He has constrained our fellow Citizens taken Captive on the high Seas to bear Arms against their Country, to become the executioners of their friends and Brethren, or to fall themselves by their Hands.
He has excited domestic insurrections amongst us, and has endeavoured to bring on the inhabitants of our frontiers, the merciless Indian Savages, whose known rule of warfare, is an undistinguished destruction of all ages, sexes and conditions.

6. According to the Declaration, has King George III given up his legitimacy in ruling the American Colonies?

_____

7. List 5 specific verbs used above to describe the alleged oppressions suffered by the Colonists:

_____

In every stage of these Oppressions We have Petitioned for Redress in the most humble terms: Our repeated Petitions have been answered only by repeated injury. A Prince whose character is thus marked by every act which may define a Tyrant, is unfit to be the ruler of a free people.

8. What did the colonists try doing before declaring independence? _____

Nor have We been wanting in attentions to our British brethren. We have warned them from time to time of attempts by their legislature to extend an unwarrantable jurisdiction over us. We have reminded them of the circumstances of our emigration and settlement here. We have appealed to their native justice and magnanimity, and we have conjured them by the ties of our common kindred to disavow these usurpations, which, would inevitably interrupt our connections and correspondence. They too have been deaf to the voice of justice and of consanguinity. We must, therefore, acquiesce in the necessity, which denounces our Separation, and hold them, as we hold the rest of mankind, Enemies in War, in Peace Friends.

9. How did the American colonists feel toward the British *people*? _____

10. Now comes the exact moment of the birth of the American Republic. Circle the statement when it is born:

We, therefore, the Representatives of the united States of America, in General Congress, Assembled, appealing to the Supreme Judge of the world for the rectitude of our intentions, do, in the Name, and by Authority of the good People of these Colonies, solemnly publish and declare, That these United Colonies are, and of Right ought to be Free and Independent States; that they are Absolved from all Allegiance to the British Crown, and that all political connection between them and the State of Great Britain, is and ought to be totally dissolved; and that as Free and Independent States, they have full Power to levy War, conclude Peace, contract Alliances, establish Commerce, and to do all other Acts and Things which Independent States may of right do. And for the support of this Declaration, with a firm reliance on the protection of divine Providence, we mutually pledge to each other our Lives, our Fortunes and our sacred Honor.

11. What do independent states have the right to do, according to the document, that mere colonies do not?

_____

12. At this moment, the American Revolution truly began. Skirmishes had already occurred, even battles, like Bunker Hill, but this was the *revolution*. Signing the document (think of John Hancock) was like signing your own death warrant. Knowing confiscation of property and war would be the likely response on the part of the British Crown, what did the Americans pledge to each other?

_____

Ch. 16   **GOT RIGHTS? PROVE IT!**   Defendant _____

Which Amendments do the Following Violate?

_____ 1. You graduated from high school and started a pizza restaurant with some friends. You calculated you would break even for three years, build a customer base, then start making money. On the day you opened for business, a new law passed raising the minimum wage from $8 to $15, and you couldn't afford to pay your employees. You went out of business after six months, wrote a letter of protest to the newspaper, and they published it. Both you and the editor were fined $500 dollars by the Secretary of Commerce for criticizing the new minimum wage law in print.

_____ 2. You always liked and respected military service. Then some soldiers appeared at your door claiming they had orders to move into your house for two weeks. You didn't know them. They were nice about it, but you knew something was wrong. You suspected they would raid your refrigerator and watch TV all day and night, and possibly throw their laundry all over the floor.

_____ 3. You are pulled over for speeding while going on vacation to the Great Smoky Mountains in Tennessee. The state trooper tells you to open your trunk and inspects it. He finds a briefcase with $300 inside and takes it, but lets you go without a ticket.

_____ 4. A police officer comes to your door and says the government just outlawed firearms.

_____ 5. Your neighbor got arrested for possessing a small bag of marijuana. The police come to your door and demand you give them your cell phone so they can check who called you, or who you called, and when. They did not have a warrant from a judge, but claimed they had the right to confiscate your property because they were investigating a criminal case.

_____ 6. It doesn't specifically say in the Constitution that we, "have a right *not* to be harassed by telemarketers who threaten us over the phone if we don't buy their products," but its absence in print doesn't mean that right doesn't exist, and that we would necessarily lose in a court case.

_____ _____ 7. You were looking at merchandise on the shelves at Walmart and bumped into another customer with your cart. They sue you for medical injuries in the amount of $10,000, which you think is way too much. They said you caused "soft tissue damage" and "mental trauma". You get a summons to come to the courthouse. You go to a room where they offer you this plea bargain: "If you pay $1,000, we will drop the lawsuit here and now." You refuse and demand to go to court to be heard by the judge or jury. They say, "C'mon, we don't have time for all that!"

_____ 8. You get arrested for breaking and entering into your school to perform a senior prank at midnight. They schedule your hearing for two years in the future.

_____ _____ 9. You get arrested because a CVS was vandalized. The police put you in a room with bright lights shining in your eyes. They leave you for 24 hours, and there is someone always watching you. They feed you gruel, and make jokes about your ethnic background. Finally, sleep deprived, they interrogate you but you say nothing in response to their questions. They say, "Answer the question! You HAVE to answer! Oh, we gonna be here for as long as it takes."

_____ 10. There is nothing in the Constitution about education or marriage and family issues. Each state decides how to regulate those kinds of things for themselves, which is why some laws in the USA are different depending on what state you are in.

The Bill of Rights

Amendment 1 – The Freedoms

Congress shall make no law respecting an establishment of religion, or prohibiting the free exercise thereof; or abridging the freedom of speech, or of the press; or the right of the people peaceably to assemble, and to petition the Government for a redress of grievances.

Amendment 2 - Bearing Arms

A well-regulated Militia, being necessary to the security of a free State, the right of the people to keep and bear Arms, shall not be infringed.

Amendment 3 - Quartering Soldiers

No Soldier shall, in time of peace be quartered in any house, without the consent of the Owner, nor in time of war, but in a manner to be prescribed by law.

Amendment 4 - Searches and Seizures

The right of the people to be secure in their persons, houses, papers, and effects, against unreasonable searches and seizures, shall not be violated, and no Warrants shall issue, but upon probable cause, supported by Oath or affirmation, and particularly describing the place to be searched, and the persons or things to be seized.

Amendment 5 - Rights of Persons

No person shall be held to answer for a capital, or otherwise infamous crime, unless on a presentment or indictment of a Grand Jury, except in cases arising in the land or naval forces, or in the Militia, when in actual service in time of War or public danger; nor shall any person be subject for the same offence to be twice put in jeopardy of life or limb; nor shall be compelled in any criminal case to be a witness against himself, nor be deprived of life, liberty, or property, without due process of law; nor shall private property be taken for public use, without just compensation.

Amendment 6 - Rights of Accused in Criminal Prosecutions

In all criminal prosecutions, the accused shall enjoy the right to a speedy and public trial, by an impartial jury of the State and district wherein the crime shall have been committed, which district shall have been previously ascertained by law, and to be informed of the nature and cause of the accusation; to be confronted with the witnesses against him; to have compulsory process for obtaining witnesses in his favor, and to have the Assistance of Counsel for his defence.

Amendment 7 - Civil Trials

In Suits at common law, where the value in controversy shall exceed twenty dollars, the right of trial by jury shall be preserved, and no fact tried by a jury, shall be otherwise re-examined in any Court of the United States, than according to the rules of the common law.

Amendment 8 - Further Guarantees in Criminal Cases

Excessive bail shall not be required, nor excessive fines imposed, nor cruel and unusual punishments inflicted.

Amendment 9 – Rights not Specifically Enumerated

The enumeration in the Constitution, of certain rights, shall not be construed to deny or disparage others retained by the people.

Amendment 10 - Reserved Powers

The powers not delegated to the United States by the Constitution, nor prohibited by it to the States, are reserved to the States respectively, or to the people.

Ch. 16 — PHASES OF THE FRENCH REVOLUTION — Gerondist _____

Dis bonjour à mon petit ami... Monsieur Guillotine!

_____ The 'old order' government of absolutist rule by King Louis XVI and Marie Antoinette, which went into severe debt after helping the Americans defeat George III.

_____ Because modern state-funded militaries are expensive, and the Seven Years' (French & Indian) War required heavy expenditures, Louis XVI's government incurred this.

_____ Without this, the widespread recognition and belief in the natural rights of life, liberty and property, the French Revolution would probably never have happened.

_____ The French Parliament, called together after centuries of non-use, in order to decide which of the three estates would shoulder the burden of paying the new taxes.

_____ The Third Estate delegates met here after storming out believing the nobles and royals defrauded them into covering the taxes, and swore to fight for a constitution.

_____ Believing a legislative body could lead the push for a constitution, the delegates of the Third Estate established this, which superseded the Estates General.

_____ After the king fortified his position with foreign troops, on July 14, 1789, this prison in Paris, symbolic of political oppression and containing weaponry, was stormed.

_____ In the countryside, this overtook the nobles when their privileges were abolished and their chateaus were broken into and looted by mobs of zealous peasants.

_____ Document drafted by Lafayette, Jefferson and Mirabeau, and passed by the National Assembly, affirming natural rights, a separation of powers, and individual freedoms.

_____ Victory for the enlightened revolution! This new supreme law of the land, transformed France from an absolute to a constitutional monarchy.

_____ Founder of the women's movement, this reformer asked why the *Declaration of the Rights of Man and Citizen* did not grant equal rights to half the population.

_____ Sneaking out of the capital to a Royalist base in the east of France, in disguise, the king and queen were recognized, arrested, and lost a lot of popular support.

_____ Of the two republican clubs active in the Assembly, this was the more moderate, favoring abolition of the monarchy but a stable society based on popular sovereignty.

_____ Of the two clubs active in the Assembly, this was the more radical, favoring abolition of Christianity, permanent overthrow of the monarchy, and a new calendar.

_____ In Autumn, 1792, this wave of killings was perpetrated against people suspected of being Royalist supporters, which struck fear in the hearts of moderate people too.

_____ This organization with an Orwellian name (because they hunted down 40k 'enemies of the revolution' and guillotined them) took power and began the *Reign of Terror*.

_____ Leader of the Jacobins, he assumed control of France and directed the guillotining of targeted 'enemies', as well as replaced Christianity with a 'Cult of Reason'.

_____ This 'Massive Draft,' saw all unmarried, able-bodied men between 18 and 25 were brought into the French military to fight an Austrian invasion to stop the revolution.

_____ In this marching song, which would become the French National Anthem, people marching to fight planned to use invaders' impure blood to irrigate their fields.

_____ King Louis XVI and his wife, this queen, were both executed by guillotine along with the rest of the royal Bourbon family, by the radical National Convention.

_____ In the 'hot month' of 1794, French moderates became disgusted with the radical turn of the revolution, arrested the leaders like Robespierre, and guillotined them!

_____ This rather weak council governed after the radicals were thrown out. During their time, Napoleon was gaining momentum as a military leader by fighting the Coalition.

_____ This 'seizure of power' occurred when Napoleon declared himself emperor, summoned the pope to Paris, and ceremoniously crowned himself and Josephine.

_____ Toulon, Marengo, The Pyramids, Ulm, Jena, Austerlitz, Friedland and Borodino all crowned Napoleon with glory, making these a series of _____ for France.

_____ Acre, Smolensk, Moscow, the Battle of the Nations, and Waterloo all sealed the fate of Napoleon and his *Grand Armee*, making these a series of _____ for France.

_____ The first time Napoleon was existed it was to this island off the coast of Italy. From it he escaped and raised the banner of French conquest once again for 100 Days.

_____ The French Revolution was over after Napoleon was exiled here for the 2nd and final time. But he left the *Civil Code,* which became the basis for French law to this day.

Ancien Regime	**Bastille**	**Committee of Public Safety**	**Constitution of 1791**
Coup of 18 Braumaire	**Declaration of the Rights of Man and Citizen**		**Defeats**
Elba	**Enlightenment Consciousness**		**Estates General**
Flight to Varennes	**Girondists**	**Great Fear**	**Jacobins**
Le Directoire	**Levee en Masse**	**Marie Antoinette**	**Marseillaise**
Maximilian Robespierre	**National Assembly**	**Olympe de Gouges**	**September Massacres**
St. Helena	**Tennis Court Oath**	**Thermidorian Reaction**	**Victories**

War debt (funny 'cause war debt caused *both* the British and French monarchies to issue new taxes…
which both times led to…)

Ch. 16   TEXT ANALYSIS: AMERICAN REVOLUTIONARY SONGS   Macaroni _____

Hold up- music can be made for something other than commercial gain? © = chorus

The Liberty Song (1770). 1. Circle a line you see in this Enlightenment-era song that reminds you of things the American founders complained about in the Declaration of Independence:

Come, join hand in hand, brave Americans all, | 2. What line in the text best supports the idea that the singers
And rouse your bold hearts at fair liberty's call; | of this song believe they have unalienable natural rights?
No tyrannous acts shall suppress your just claim, |
Or stain with dishonor America's name. |
In freedom we're born and in freedom we'll live. |
Our purses are ready, steady, boys, steady; |
Not as slaves but as free men- our money we'll give. | _____

Yankee Doodle (1774). Sung by the British to make fun of the Americans by saying American lowlifes thought sticking a feather in their hat made them dressed well, the Americans turned the song around and embraced it as a rallying cry ('Macaroni' back then was slang for being fashionable and lookin' sharp- are you a macaroni?).

Yankee Doodle went to town, a-riding on a pony, stuck a feather in his cap, and called it macaroni!
Pa and I went down to camp, along with Capt. Gooding, and there we saw the men and boys, as thick as hasty pudding.
© Yankee Doodle keep it up / Yankee Doodle dandy, mind the music and the step / And with the girls be handy.
There they'd fife away like fun, and play on cornstalk fiddles; some had ribbons red as blood, bound around their middles.
And there was Cap'n Washington / Upon a slappin' stallion, giving orders to his men / I guess there was a million! ©

3. The song does *not* describe the American military recruitment camp as: *a. crowded*   *b. cheerful*   *c. somber*

The Revolutionary Alphabet (1775). 4. Circle what the letters A, B and C stood for in the Revolutionary Alphabet:

A is for: Alphabet   American   **B** is for: British   Boston   **C** is for: Congress   Cell phone

5. When the song says, "Stand firmly A to Z," what do you think that means | 6. Here are the rest: Defense, Evils, Fate,
in the context of the song and the times? | George, Hypocrites, Justice, King,
| London, Mansfield, North, Oaths, (The)
| People, Question, Rebels, Stuarts, Tories,
| Villains, Wilkes, York, Zero. Each proper
| name is a British government official the
| colonials were angry at. Go through the
| list and try to judge how many names
| like this there are:
|

My Country 'Tis of Thee (1831)

My country, 'tis of thee, sweet land of liberty, of thee I sing;
Land where my fathers died, land of the pilgrims' pride, from every mountainside, Let freedom ring!
My native country, thee, land of the noble free, thy name I love;
I love thy rocks and rills, thy woods and templed hills; my heart with rapture thrills, like that above.
Our fathers' God to Thee, author of liberty, to Thee we sing.
Long may our land be bright, with freedom's holy light, protect us by Thy might, great God our King.

7. If anyone in your class is from Great Britain, they will surely recognize the melody of this song. Why? because it is the exact same melody as that of the British National Anthem, *God Save the Queen*. Why do you think the Americans kept that melody after the Revolutionary War, but changed the words? Nostalgia. In history, nostalgia plays an interesting role. We tend to remember the past with 'rose-colored glasses' sometimes, and many Americans were attached to the melody of their old British anthem. They certainly were no longer attached to the words, however! List the adjectives they ascribed to their new country in the song, and the nouns about it they sang about:

The Star Spangled Banner (1814)

O' say can you see by the dawn's early light,
What so proudly we hailed at the twilight's last gleaming,
Whose broad stripes and bright stars through the perilous fight,
O'er the ramparts we watched, were so gallantly streaming?
And the rockets' red glare, the bombs bursting in air,
Gave proof through the night that our flag was still there;
O' say does that star-spangled banner yet wave,
Over the land of the free and the home of the brave?

O' thus be it ever, when freemen shall stand
Between their loved home and the war's desolation.
Blest with victory and peace, may the Heaven-rescued land
Praise the Power that hath made and preserved us a nation!
Then conquer we must, when our cause it is just,
And this be our motto: "In God is our trust."
And the star-spangled banner in triumph shall wave,
Over the land of the free and the home of the brave!

America the Beautiful (1893)

O' beautiful for spacious skies,
For amber waves of grain,
For purple mountain majesties
Above the fruited plain!
America! America!
God shed his grace on thee
And crown thy good with brotherhood
From sea to shining sea!

O' beautiful for pilgrim feet
Whose stern impassioned stress
A thoroughfare of freedom beat
Across the wilderness!
America! America!
God mend thine every flaw,
Confirm thy soul in self-control,
Thy liberty in law!

O' beautiful for patriot dream
That sees beyond the years
Thine alabaster cities gleam
Undimmed by human tears
America! America!
God shed his grace on thee,
And crown they good with brotherhood
From sea to shining sea.

8. When Francis Scott Key wrote the words to the American national anthem, he was in a British prison overlooking Baltimore, Maryland, where a battle was taking place. If the British flag was flying in the morning, he and a doctor, Benes, who was his cellmate, would know the Americans had lost the battle. But what did they see as the dawn's early light lifted over Baltimore and Fort McHenry?

_____

9. Usually, only the first verse is sung. There are more, and the first verse ends in a question mark, though it is rarely sung that way. Some have said, even in our time, it is a question that never really ends, that it is as applicable in our time as it was back then. What question is the anthem asking?

_____

10. What is the last stanza's 'answer' to the question asked in the first?

_____

11. Originally a poem called *A Poem for July 4*, this song was written by Katherine Lee Bates, an English professor at Wellesley College, after she took a train trip across the country and was stunned at the amazing landscapes that awaited her. When a church choirmaster in New Jersey read the poem, he thought, "Wow, I just wrote a musical piece called *O Dear Mother Jerusalem*, and if I put the poem to that song, it will be a perfect fit!" It was, and we've been singing it ever since. If you had to summarize it in one line, what is Professor Katherine Bates asking *America(ns)* to do in the poem?

_____

12. There is a debate about the national anthem. Some athletes don't want to stand while it is being played, and many argue it is too violent a song, what with the bombs bursting in air and so forth. Some argue it should be replaced, perhaps by *America the Beautiful*, perhaps by another song. Still others, usually from a globalist or Marxist perspective, say we don't even need national anthems anymore. What do you think?

Ch. 16   **TEXT ANALYSIS: EUROPEAN NATIONAL SONGS**   **Citoyen** _____

Hold up- music can be made for something other than commercial gain?

Examine the lyrics of the national songs and comment on geographical attributes/cultural expressions. Then 'like' the song by putting a number by the name (1-3, with 3 being "Like it!" 2 being "ok" and 1 being "can I *unhear* that please?"). Video search the song title and artist, and begin:

British Anthem. Okay, *God Save the Queen* is NOT revolutionary, in fact, it's symbolic of the pre-revolutionary worldview. It was adopted in the 1750s during the French and Indian War, to encourage a sense of British identity after the Act of Union merged England, Wales and Scotland.

God Save the Queen

God save our gracious Queen,
Long live our noble Queen,
God save the Queen!
Send her victorious,
Happy and glorious,
Long to reign over us,
God save the Queen.

Thy choicest gifts in store
On her be pleased to pour,
Long may she reign;
May she defend our laws,
And ever give us cause
To sing with heart and voice,
God save the Queen!

1. In *The Star Spangled Banner,* the American anthem, tribute is paid to the flag of the United States. What national symbol is the focus of the British anthem?

2. Looking at the lyrics, how do we know England was a *constitutional* monarchy and not an absolutist one like Bourbon France or Habsburg Austria at the time?

3. Hey isn't this a rip-off of the American song *My Country Tis of Thee?*
    a. Yes   b. No because they had it first! and it was the Americans who changed the lyrics!

Rule Britannia

When Britain first, at Heaven's command
Arose from out the azure main;
This was the charter of the land,
And guardian angels sang this strain:
Rule, Britannia! rule the waves:
Britons never will be slaves.

Still more majestic shalt thou rise,
More dreadful, from each foreign stroke;
As the loud blast that tears the skies,
Serves but to root thy native oak.
Rule, Britannia! rule the waves:
Britons never will be slaves.

The Muses, still with freedom found,
Shall to thy happy coast repair;
Blest Isle! With matchless beauty crown'd,
And manly hearts to guard the fair.
Rule, Britannia! rule the waves:
Britons never will be slaves.

4. This British national song is the finale every year at the *Last Night at the Proms,* which is the annual celebration of British nationhood. Since they don't have a 4th of July-style Independence Day (because they were never ruled), they gather for this festival. While the French and Napoleon especially focused on building a powerful army, which branch of the service did the British find most important?

_____

5. Why do you think that is?

_____

6. What do you think the words 'azure main' mean in this song?
    a. the assured place   b. the blue sea

French Anthem: La Marseillaise, (Song of Merseilles, 1792)

Allons enfants de la Patrie,	Let's go, children of the nation,
le jour de gloire est arrive.	the day of glory has arrived.
*Contre nous de la **tyrannie**,*	against us stands **tyranny**-
l'étendard sanglant est levé! (2x)	its bloody flag is raised! (2x)
Entendez-vous dans les campagnes?	Do you hear it in the fields?
Mugir ces féroces soldats?	the soldiers baying in the distance?
Ils viennent jusque dans vos bras,	they come to us, into our arms,
Egorger vos fils et vos compagnes!	and slit the throats of women and son!
© Aux armes, citoyens!	© To arms, citizens!
Formez vos bataillons.	Form your batallions.
Marchons, marchons!	March on, march on!
Qu'un sang impur,	Invaders' impure blood,
abreuve nos sillons! (x2)	waters the furrows of our fields! (x2)
Amour sacré de la Patrie,	Sacred love of the Fatherland,
Conduis, soutiens nos bras vengeurs	Lead, support our avenging arms
Liberté, Liberté chérie,	Liberty, cherished Liberty,
Combats avec tes défenseurs! (2x)	Fight with thy defenders! (2x)
Sous nos drapeaux que la victoire	Under our flags, may victory
Accoure à tes mâles accents,	Hurry to thy male accents,
Que tes ennemis expirants	May thy expiring enemies,
Voient ton triomphe et notre gloire! ©	See thy triumph and our glory! ©

7. Queen Marie Antoinette's brother, the Austrian emperor, invaded France to stop the revolution.

On a long march from the city of Merseilles to Paris, the people were singing this song. What do you think they meant by 'Tyranny'?

a. The Americans
b. Absolute monarchs of Europe
c. The French revolutionaries

8. The British anthem was reverential. What is the tone of the French anthem?

German Anthem: Das Deutschlandlied (Song of Germany, 1841)

Deutschland, Deutschland über alles,	Germany, Germany above all,
Über alles in der Welt,	Above all in the world,
Wenn es stets zu Schutz und Trutze	When, for protection and defense,
Brüderlich zusammenhält.	Brothers stand together.
Von der Maas bis an die Memel,	From the Meuse to the Nemen,
Von der Etsch bis an den Belt,	From the Adige to the Belt,
Deutschland, Deutschland über alles,	Germany, Germany above all,
Über alles in der Welt!	Above all in the world!
Deutsche Frauen, deutsche Treue,	German women, German loyalty,
Deutscher Wein und deutscher Sang	German wine and German song
Sollen in der Welt behalten	Shall retain in the world
Ihren alten schönen Klang,	Their old beautiful chime
Uns zu edler Tat begeistern	And inspire us to noble deeds
Unser ganzes Leben lang.	During all of our life.
Deutsche Frauen, deutsche Treue,	German women, German loyalty,
Deutscher Wein und deutscher Sang!	German wine and German song!
Einigkeit und Recht und Freiheit	Unity and justice and freedom
Für das deutsche Vaterland!	For the German fatherland!
Danach lasst uns alle streben	Towards these let us all strive
Brüderlich mit Herz und Hand!	Brotherly with heart and hand!
Einigkeit und Recht und Freiheit	Unity and justice and freedom
Sind des Glückes Unterpfand;	Are the foundation of happiness;
Blüh' im Glanze dieses Glückes,	Flourish in the radiance of this happiness,
Blühe, deutsches Vaterland!	Flourish, German fatherland!

9. While the British anthem was about reverence for Queen and country, and the French anthem was a soldier's marching song, Germany was only uniting for the first time in the 19th century, so their anthem's theme is "what makes our nation great?" What are some things identified in the song?

10. After WWII, the new Allied-sponsored governments of East and West Germany wanted to *discourage* nationalism in the country, which makes an interesting case study in "what do we do with unifying features of national life, like the anthem?" The government decided to get rid of two of the stanzas. Which two do you think they got rid of, ← and why?

Ch. 16 **THE COUNT OF MONTE CRISTO** Code name_____

Would you forgive- or take revenge- on your best friend?

1. Who was on the island of Elba, and why was he under British dragoon guard?

_____

2. What city in France acted as the *Farallon's* port-of-call:

_____

3. Why was Danglars angry at Edmond when they got back?

_____

4. Identify two sources of the animosity between the two BFFs:

_____

Dramatis Personae	**CHARACTER TRAITS**	**MOTIVATION**
5. Edmond Dantes (Don-tess):		
6. Fernand Mondego:		
7. Mercedes (Mer-seh-dess):		
8. Danglars (Don-glaa):		
9. Morrel (More-ell):		
10. Villefort (Vill-for):		
11. The Priest:		
12. Jacopo (Yakapo):		
13. Luigi Vampa:		

14. If you were done wrong by your best friend, and had the opportunity to take revenge like Edmond did, would you? Would you? Why or why not?

| 15. Dantes found the treasure & made a new identity for himself and a new symbol. If YOU found the treasure, what would YOUR new identity be? Make it up ☺

16. On the back of this paper, sketch out a ***symbol*** you would make up for yourself ---------------→

Ch. 16 CASTA CULTURE Seeker _____

Status in Latin America and the reasons for revolution

'Casta' is like 'class' in America during the days of segregation, or the 'caste' system of India. Each society has had some kind of class system, and while modern constitutions tend to lessen their potency or at least their official sanction, they prevailed in the 1800s and in some ways still today. Draw a triangle in each of the boxes, and note the *casta* hierarchy as it was in each country:

Haiti - 1804
(blacks, gens de coloeur, grand blancs, petit blancs)

Mexico – 1810
(criollos, indigenous, mestizos, peninsulares)

1. Which classes of people would most likely be opposed to any major change in society (conservatism)?

a. blacks and indigenous peoples   b. peninsulares and grand blancs   c. criollos and mulattoes

2. In the Haitian Revolution, there was a time when the mulattoes (*gens de coloeur*)- who were not slaves but were of part African descent- sided with the whites (*blancs*). Why do you think that might be?

_____

3. When the French radical revolutionary government under the National Convention (the Jacobins) abolished slavery in the French colonies, the *grand blancs* and many *petit blancs* spoke of declaring independence (much like the creoles of Mexico would, and like Rhodesia would much later do too) to keep the existing system going. When Napoleon assumed power in France, he reinstituted slavery anyway though, much to the happiness of the *grand blancs* and *petit blancs*, but much to the anger of the *gens de coloeur* and especially the black would-be slaves. An army under Napoleon's brother Leclerc arrived to enforce it, but when the army arrived, so many died of Yellow Fever they had to abandon the island. The black leaders declared independence, and began to rule the island. This twist of fate is most similar to:

a. when germs helped Cortes defeat the Aztecs   b. when Cornwallis surrendered to Washington

4. Despite turning on Padre Hidalgo and supporting the Spanish authorities after Hidalgo's men started looting their property, and despite not supporting Padre Morelos' 1813 *mestizo* uprising either, the *criollos* as a class tended to support independence from Spain more so than than other *castas*. Why?

_____

5. Circle the ruler below who was not a *caudillo,* but who was installed by the French after Cinco de Mayo:

Augustin Iturbide   *Vicente Guerrero*   *Antonio Lopez de Santa Anna*   *Manuel de la Pena*

Benito Juarez   *Maximilian I*   *Benito Juarez*   *Porfirio Diaz*

Ch. 16   **REVOLUTIONS IN LATIN AMERICA**   Bolivarian_____

Crash Course World History #31

1. The three social or political institutions in Latin America in 1800 were:

   _____   _____   _____

2. Transculturation in Latin American society is most like:

   a. religious syncretism in Akbar's India   b. Tokugawa Ieyasu expelling Christians from Japan

3. Social categories like *peninsulares* and *creoles* describe:

   a. Europeans and people of European descent   b. mestizos   c. Indigenous Americans

4. Pedro I was the first king of _____, which revolted from _____.

5. Which social group did Napoleon anger in Mexico by instituting Enlightenment principles there?

_____

6. What role did Father Hidalgo have in Mexican independence?

_____

7. In 1820, why did the *peninsulares* join forces with the *creoles* against Spain?

_____

8. What do the terms *junta* and *llaneros* mean in the revolt of South America against Spain?

_____

9. With the revolts of <u>these areas</u> in south South America under San Martin, all of Latin America was independent of Spanish control (except Caribbean islands…)

_____

10. How did the item Mr. Green found in the secret compartment illustrate Latin American revolutions?

11. Who was the open letter directed to and what did that person do in history?

12. After independence, most Latin American countries became representative democracies   T   F

13. Why weren't the Latin American revolutions all that 'revolutionary'- at least socially?

_____

Ch. 17   MILL!   Laborer _____

*Video Search: **Mill David Macaulay***

This animated movie is about the early Industrial Revolution in America, where much of the know-how was brought over in the minds and dreams of British entrepreneurs.

Idea man: *Priam Huntington*	1. How did Priam and Shadrack obtain the money to build their mill?
Investor: *Josiah Gresham*	
Priam's wife: *Elizabeth Gresham*	_____
Partner: *Shadrack Moore*	
Manager: *Mary Methuen*	2. List three parts of a spinning machine:
Best weaver: *Sarah Methuen*	
Competitor: *Zach Moore*	_____
G2 owner: *Daniel Huntington*	
***G**eography and Environment*	3. Why were 'water rights' such a big issue at the Huntington Mill vs. Northgate trial?
***R**eligion and Worldview*	
***A**rts and Innovation*	
***P**olitics and Government*	
***E**conomy and Trade*	
***S**ocial Relationships*	_____

Use each of the above choices from the **GRAPES** chart to categorize the statements about the movie:

_____ 4. Huntington Mill's creation was certainly an economic boon to the community, but this category is most representative of the **technological accomplishment**.

_____ 5. The American government instituted an **embargo** on English products, which was good for Huntington Mill.

_____ 6. The **judge decided** in favor of Northgate Mill in the court case. This is an example of a _____ decision.

_____ 7. When Sarah and her friends went to Northgate, they became a new group like the Lowell Girls, who, in real life, were very like them, living in a **new way of life.**

_____ 8. The mills had to be **located** on rivers.

_____ 9. When the girls went on strike, the company had to consider their viewpoint. The investors were far away, and didn't much care, but took **financial consideration**.

10. At the end, when (spoiler alert) Zach asks Sarah to go with him out west and she refuses, she stays back to take care of her ailing aunt. Describe what Zach does, where he goes, and if the movie becomes kind of like an American fairy tale:

11. Did you like the movie? Rate it and argue why it is (or is not), in your opinion, an effective way to learn about early industrialization:

Ch. 17   INDUSTRIAL MANCHESTER GAME   Tenement dweller _____

"Aye lads, as ye can see, nearby industry provides a wee lovely coating of soot on this tenement." –19th C. real estate agent

Sketch appropriate symbols for the items to draw as a model to follow.

Round 0: In prehistoric times, there was a Celtic tribe called the *Brigantes* living in the area where Manchester is now. When the Romans expanded to Britain following in the footsteps of Julius Caesar, they built a fort called *Mamucium* to project power in the area, much as English castles would in the Middle Ages. On your papers, **sketch** the old fort somewhere near a corner. And from it, to both ends of the paper, **draw** a narrow river, ~1-inch-wide, labeled *Medlock*. Then, **draw** 10 peasant homes scattered around near the old fort. Each cottage should be about the size of your pinkie finger nail. This is the pre-industrial town.

Round 1: The first invention that changed things in Manchester was Jethro Tull's seed drill (1701). It improved the speed of planting crops, by using a circular motion to drill a hole in the ground while sowing a seed to a predetermined depth. Repeating this process until all the rows were planted was much faster than doing it by hand. This increased productivity meant fewer farmhands were needed, and those workers left to find new jobs in cottage industries in Manchester. **Add** 10 houses clustered around a church.

Round 2: The next invention to alter the landscape of Manchester was Richard Arkwright's water frame (1769), which was an improved way to power machines like Kay's flying shuttle to weave strands of wool or cotton into thread. The threads could then be sown into clothes and other textiles. Along the river winding through Manchester, **add** a mill by drawing a building larger than a house, connected by an axle to a water-wheel in the river. The water power turned a turbine inside the building, to which the machines were connected by a series of gears and belts like those on a car engine. **Place** 10 houses around the mill.

Round 3: Manchester didn't become the first great industrial city by accident. It was blessed with coalfields very nearby. Since medieval times, smiths used coal to get fires going hot enough for smelting metal so they could shape it into something. It was also used as a heat source. Lord Bridgewater owned coal mines near Manchester. **Make** a symbol for his coal mines in three places near the edges of the map. Then, because a lot of miners- men, women and children- got sick or died, **provide** a graveyard of little crosses near the church, which is where cemeteries were generally located so people could visit their deceased relatives.

Round 4: Lord Bridgewater wants his coal easily transportable to other river systems in England. He funds a canal leading from the river straight off the map. **Draw** this canal with parallel edges, and put waves marks in it. You helped Bridgewater invest, and get a 200 percent ROI over the next decade. **Build** 3 fancy houses with a little driveway, horse & buggy and trees, and mark yours with a special symbol.

Round 5: The problem with water mills is they had to be located along, well, water. By digging a little channel arm off the river, the water flow could be controlled. But the next invention changed all that. James Watt's steam engine (1781) had coal evaporate water into steam, and channel the increased pressure to turn the turbines that ran the textile machines. This caught on fast- no river required! An industrial boom began. **Draw** three factories- not near the river- and put smokestacks on them because the steam engines expelled nasty fumes and soot. Because many new people came to work in the factories, **add** two tenement houses next to each one for them to live. Add splotches of soot near these factories and tenements.

Round 6: Eli Whitney's cotton gin (1793) dramatically increased the availability of cotton to be made into textiles. Now, more looms could be used at the same time, and with British exports of textiles sailing around the world on ships destined for distant markets, demand soared. At the same time at home, laissez-faire working conditions were noisy and dangerous. People's clothes, hair and arms got caught in machines. People's lives were controlled by clocks and whistles. They woke up each morning in their barracks-like tenements, went to work all day and some of the night, then returned. Sunday was their only day off. They brought their kids to work to help, and they got injured and sick faster. **Draw** roads that connect all your tenements to their nearby factories. These roads are not just literal- they also symbolize the back and forth daily grind. Along each road, **place** a pub, so people can drown their sorrows on the way home.

Round 7: By 1800, early industrial growth created an entire working class of laborers, but it also created an owning class of wealthy capitalists, and an emerging middle class of managers and specialists. As these become more numerous, they begin to want services in the city. **Draw** a store, a school, and a theater.

Round 8: Robert Fulton used a steam engine on a boat, and invented the steamship. After the maiden voyage of the *Claremont* (1807), new speeds of shipping increased demand yet again for Manchester-made products. **Add** two new factories and two new tenements next to each, linking them with roads and pubs. **Cover** them with patches of soot, then add patches of soot around *all* the factories. Go ahead, we'll wait. As pollution reached critical mass, social ills increased. The culture of the pub increased drunkenness, crime and industrial poverty, **Build** a courthouse and a prison somewhere near the center of the map.

Round 9: Is your city starting to look like a riot of chaos? Now it is about to become a literal riot! It started in 1819, when a mob formed to protest the Corn Laws (tariffs on imported food), and the military (those same Redcoats of Boston Massacre fame) put it down by firing into the crowd. **Add** a police station for extra security near the prison, then **add** Manchester's famous Old Town Hall, completed in 1822.

Round 10: The next Industrial Revolution advancement rolled out in 1825- George Stephenson's locomotive, which utilized the steam engine again, this time to pull a 'train' of 'cars' along a rail line. Did you ever wonder why the second car in the choo-choo train was always a coal car? Because coal is the fuel for a steam engine! Manchester is about to became the site of the very first railroad track in the world. It linked the city's industry to the port down of Liverpool, on England's western coast. Stephenson nicknamed his locomotive, "The Rocket," because it went very fast... 27 m.p.h. "Don't stick your head out the window," people said, "or your face will burn off." **Draw** a rail line from downtown Manchester, where your cluster of public buildings are, to the *left* side of the map, and **post** a sign that says ← *To Liverpool*. **Place** a train depot station where it starts, and a train on it. Finally, **sketch** rail lines connecting the main line to each *coal mine*.

Round 11: Another agricultural advancement came next. It was Cyrus McCormick's mechanical reaper (1834), which complemented the seed drill. While the seed drill planted, the reaper mechanized the harvesting part, so fewer workers were needed to thresh grain with their scythes. The reaper's big wheel was pulled by a horse. It threshed the wheat, cutting down- get it- cutting down- the time the whole process took. Many agricultural workers gravitate to Manchester work in industry. **Build** four factories surrounded by two tenements each, **connect** them all and add pubs along the roads.

Round 12: Next up is John Lawes' chemical fertilizer (1842), which improved agriculture again, as it became understood what plants actually 'eat' through their roots (nitrogen, phosphorus and potassium). Lawes combined these into exactly the same granules found in the modern bags of fertilizer you'd get at a garden center. Thus, more people can be fed by the ever more productive farms, avoiding the Malthusian Catastrophe, and the population expands again. Britain more than doubled since Round 1, from 6 million to 16 million people. And with the rail line booming, Manchester industry is booming too. **Add** four more factories, two tenement houses around each, **connect** them together, and **place** pubs on the roads betwixt.

Round 13: Have you noticed the explosive growth of your city spiraling out of control? We are approaching the end of the *laissez-faire* era. Labor unions are forming. There is a growing public backlash against the pollution, long work hours, sicknesses, crime, and resulting social ills. Parliament passes a series of *Factory Acts* which among other things set standards for ventilation and sanitation, abolished child labor, began an inspection system for factories, and provided for a maximum 10-hour workday. But they came at the end of many people's working lives. **Add** two hospitals and two graveyards. But also **add** trees around the city, the result of a planting program to combat the pollution.

Round 14: Industrial boom! Despite the *Factory Acts*, the 1840s saw huge increases. People called the city 'Cottonopolis.' Its textiles were worn and displayed from New Zealand to New York. Good job! Plus, research is directed to finding filters for smog, and medical science is advancing to a modern understanding of germs and disease. Soap and sanitation is improving. As the city heads to the future, **look up** William Wyld's painting *Manchester* and see how your city compares to the original at this stage in its history. Imaging tilting your paper sideways and looking at it vertically- can you 'see' Wyld's painting arising? **Put** your name on it ☺

Ch. 17   INVENTIONS FLOWCHART   Tekkie _____

Hey when did that come out?

Technologies morph into new inventions as time goes on. Categorize those at the bottom into the correct eras in time. Try to keep advancements of a single technological 'thread' together:

Industrial Age **(1750-1880)**	***Machine Age*** **(1880-1945)**	***Space Age*** **(1945-1990)**	***Digital Age*** **(1990-Today)**

Above, place the following into sensible threads and locate them appropriately on the chart. Not all spots on the chart will be filled.

    Cassette Tape   *Cell Phone*   *Compact Disc*   *Desktop Computer*   *Digital Video Disc*

    Hybrid Electric Engine   *Internal Combustion Engine-Carbureted*   *Laptop Computer*

    Locomotive   *Internal Combustion Engine-Fuel Injected*   *Microwave*   *.mp3*   *.mp4*

    Operator Phone   *Phonograph*   *Push-Button Phone*   *Room-Sized Computer*

    Internet   *Rotary Phone*   *Steam engine*   *Stove/Oven*   *Toaster*   *VHS*

Based on these trends, predict five logical advancements that will succeed the most recent type of each invention stream (engines, cooking, computers, recorded sound, pictures, phone; i.e.: *tricorder*):

1)   *2)*   *3)*   *4)*   *5)*

Ch. 17   SOCIAL CRITICISM IN ART: HOGARTH   Moralizer_____

Hogarth is the Chuck Norris of Moralizers.

Image Search: **William Hogarth Beer Street and Gin Lane**. Maximize. List three 'bad things' (social vices) going on here that Hogarth believed excessive beer and liquor encouraged in society:

_____   _____   _____

URL Search: **William Hogarth A Harlot's Progress**. Moll(y) Hackabout is a country girl. She moves to the big city, London, and gets caught up in some pretty awful stuff. Look at the stages of her decline and give a brief synopsis of what happens in each:

Plate 1   *Plate 2*   *Plate 3*

Plate 4   *Plate 5*   *Plate 6*

Search: **William Hogarth A Rake's Progress**. A 'rake' in this case is a rich kid who inherited a bunch of wealth and now wants to spend away. So how does Tom Rakewell do it? Dear old dad didn't save up for this… Check out the stages of his bad decisions and give a brief synopsis of each:

Plate 1   *Plate 2*   *Plate 3*   *Plate 4*

Plate 5   *Plate 6*   *Plate 7*   *Plate 8*

Ch. 17   ARTISTS TAKE ON SUBSTANCE ABUSE   Moralizer _____

Everyone likes a good moralizer.

Just like today, people in the Industrial Age went through a lot of social changes quite rapidly. The onset of modernity separated many people from the traditional culture and morals of their ancestors, and some, well, fell into various forms of vice. This was reflected in the art of the time.

Image Search: **Nathaniel Currier The Drunkard's Progress**. Note the stages of life the drunkard will go through once they begin drinking, according to this social commentary by the Temperance Movement, the goal of which was to try to get people abusing alcohol to stop or lessen their intake:

_____

_____   _____

_____   _____

_____   _____

George Cruikshank lived a generation after Hogarth. His father was an abusive alcoholic, and he grew up to be a drinker too, until one day he determined to end the cycle. Reforming, Cruikshank turned his artistic abilities to spreading what he believed was a positive social message. **URL Search: *Cruikshank The Bottle***; click on the *Temperance Tales 1848* return. Describe the plates:

Plate 1   *Plate 2*   *Plate 3*   *Plate 4*

Plate 5   *Plate 6*   *Plate 7*   *Plate 8*

Image Search: **Cruikshank The Drunkard's Children Category Wikimedia.** Figure out the order and describe them *in chronological order.* Hint, the one with the girl is last:

Plate 1   *Plate 2*   *Plate 3*   *Plate 4*

Plate 5   *Plate 6*   *Plate 7*   *Plate 8*

Image Search: **Cruikshank Worship of Bacchus**   Image Search: **Currier Fruits of Temperance**

Message: *Message:*

How Conveyed: *How Conveyed:*

Search: **Augustus Egg Past and Present**. Here a wife is found out by her husband (it's his misfortune) to have been cheating. What does this do to the family? Describe what happens:

1- Misfortune (of the husband)   *2- Prayer (of the kids)*   *3-Dispair (of the wife)*

Search: **William Holman Hunt The Awakening Conscience**. There is a lot of 'stuff' in this room that is symbolic. What is the analysis of the objects in the room by art historians?

Object   *Meaning* | Overall, what do you think about
                                             | using art to moralize about social
                                             | values?
                                             |

Ch. 17   **TRADITIONAL OR MODERN?**   Government Pupil _____

So you think your sooooo modern do ya? Well where's your hoverboard then?

Circle those of the following which are aspects of *modern* as opposed to *traditional* society:

Gemeinschaft (small-scale community)	*Gesellschaft (anonymous, large-scale society)*
Industrial / office jobs outside the home	*Organic jobs / handicrafts in the home*
Production of goods for exchange	*Production of goods for personal use*
Gender / age roles more fluid	*Gender / age roles more strict*
Collective ownership of public space	*Personal 'bubble' within public space*
Calendar determines adulthood	*Rites of passage determine adulthood*
Exploitative use of nature	*Sustainable use of nature*
Time measured by seasons & solar cycles	*Time measured by alarms, bells and clocks*
Myth, spiritual focus	*Rational, scientific focus*
Entertainment through electronics	*Entertainment through storytelling*
Change is slow, suspicious	*Openness to change, movement, adaptation*
Opinions change via information	*Opinions set by tradition*
Status & rewards come via place in hierarchy	*Status & rewards come by merit & achievement*
Social justice by rule and law over whim	*Social justice by decision of special people*
Education by community members	*Education in state schools*
Kindness, morality and loyalty encouraged	*Professionalism, reason and equality encouraged*

Draw a line to match the educational pattern with the era that employed it:

Greco-Roman   *Apprenticeship system and eventual joining of a guild*

Medieval   *Government-run schools that everyone is expected to attend*

Modern   *Schools like the Academy and Lyceum were for 'patrician' elites*

With the advent of computers, how would *you* change the school system in the 21st century?

Ch. 17 **Great Clips: Industrial Britain** Prole _____
Video search: "CNN Millennium: 19th century" (around 1 min. in)

1. While Stephenson's *Rocket* was the first true locomotive, this previous inventor put the steam engine on rail for the first time:
    a. Fulton   b. Trevithick   c. Morse

2. The first time industrial cable was placed on the seabed of the Atlantic Ocean was in 1997 to allow Internet servers in Europe and America to be accessed by computers on the other continent:

    a. True   b. False

3. Turner's painting of the steam locomotive is a famous representation of this phase of art history:

    a. realism   b. romanticism   c. modern

4. Isambard Kingdom Brunel is best described as a great   a. artist   b. engineer   c. travel agent

5. Thomas Cook & Sons are best described as pioneers of   a. exploration   b. art   c. travel agency

6. Why do you think the world was divided into 24 time zones and not some other number?

_____

Great Clips: Industrial Working Life
Video search: "CNN Millennium: 19th century" (around 34 min. in)

7. Describe some way workers' lives were transformed by the early Industrial Revolution in Britain:

_____

8. To 'dehumanize' someone is to seemingly take away part of their humanity by treating them like a mere commodity or a number- a means to an end- instead of as an end in themselves, or else, the more important variable in the equation. Do you think laissez-faire industrial life was dehumanizing at all?

_____

9. What did the Bessemer Process (1856) involve?

10. Describe some advantages gained by nations that adopted industrial techniques of manufacturing- and provide an example.

11. While industry was hard on early workers, list 2 inventions that began to make lives better:

Ch. 17 THE POLITICAL COMPASS Politician _____
You don't get to label me! I'll do it myself.

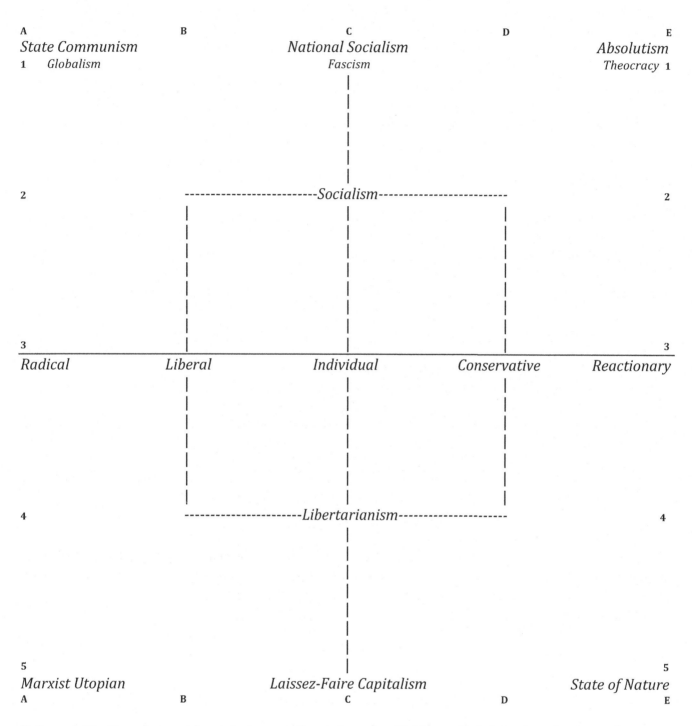

Before civilization, the world was in a state of anarchy, what Hobbes called the state of nature. There was no government, just family and kinship. Put a dot in sector 5E, label "**Prehistory**."

When civilization began, the trend was to fundamentalism and cultural conformity. The priest-kings of Mesopotamia, the pharaohs of Egypt, the Brahmins of India and the dynastic rulers of China, who ruled by the Mandate of Heaven, encouraged faith in the power of social cohesion. Put a dot in sector 2E, draw a line north to it, and label it '**Early Civilizations**."

The Greek Athenians during the Golden Age did something interesting. They encouraged free thought and individualism, and invented democracy. Put a dot at sector 3 between C and D. Free thought was still conservative, and traditional social hierarchies were still in play. Label "**Athens**"

The Romans in the 1st century were a solid 2D, because they demanded and got assimilation. They moved to the left in the centuries that followed and down toward anarchy at different times, before collapse. Put a dot at 2D and label it "**Rome.**"

Medieval states under feudalism were all rather conservative, in Europe and even more so in the Middle East. African kingdoms like Mansa Musa's, where the chieftains had power of life and death over their subjects, generally were not too much into individualism ether. Every society that was not in anarchy had fundamentalist or conservative aristocratic power structures that held it together. In Europe during the Early Modern period, we saw absolute monarchies like that of Louis XIV and Peter I, around sector 2E. Place a dot there, and label it "**Absolute Monarchies**". The constitutional monarchies like England and Holland were more liberal in their economics and social values, "nation of shopkeepers"-style. Put a dot at 2.5/C.5, label "**Georgian Britain.**"

The Enlightenment shifted the social scale west, to individualism and even liberalism and radicalism, in the case of Revolutionary France. America's Constitution adopted a libertarian stance economically and guaranteed the individual rights of every citizen. Except slaves. And women's political equality was not yet dreamt of. So, just because the document is enlightened, it doesn't mean America wasn't an Aristocratic Republic. A dot goes at 5D, labeled "**Early America**".

After the Civil War, state power grew a lot. The dot must move up, no more laissez-faire. However, the country remained very conservative compared to today. Dot at 3.5D & label: "**America 1900**".

The Federal Reserve Act of 1913 centralized the currency more, as did the income tax law of the same year. WWI increased state power too. And all that was before the New Deal! Once that came into play in the 1930s, to combat the Great Depression, capped off by WWII centralizing things even more, move the next dot to the exact center- a thoroughly mixed economy, still free to a degree and without mountains of regulations, but with a good deal more state influence than before. Next dot is at 3C. Label it "**America 1950**".

The counterculture movement of the 1960s, and the liberalizing tendencies that swept the country in that decade, shifted the social values scale to 2.5, while the Great Society programs of Lyndon Johnson moved the dot up to B. Place and label it "**America 1975**".

The Reagan years shifted the dot a little to the right again, but the general trend from the 1990s to today has been up and to the left. More state power, whether under a Republican or a Democratic president, and more liberal values in the social-cultural sphere, whether under a Clinton or Bush, or an Obama, keeps the trend apace. Place a dot at 2AB and label it "**America 2015.**"

How will Trump move the dot? It depends. If taxes are lowered and state power, such as the Patriot Act and other legal anti-privacy regulations are curtailed, the dot will move down and to the right. If state power continues to be increased, domestic surveillance and more military and 'deep state' related activity goes on at home and abroad, and if taxes are not increased but the FED offers more quantitative easing, if more people stay in more debt to government and private lenders, if more force is required to keep rioting and violence down, the dot may go up more. By the time you do this assignment, some of this may have come to pass. Ask around, place the next dot where your best educated guess thinks it should be. Label it "**America Today**".

Alternatives? Put a dot at 1.5CD and label it "**Putin's Russia.**" Put a dot a 2A and label it "**Sweden**". Put a dot at 4E and label it "**Somalia**". Put a dot at 1B and label it "**North Korea.**" Finally, dot 4.5B and label it "**Woodstock.**" If you don't know, ask your teacher or look it up. Now, what's best?

Ch. 17 THE POLITICAL COMPASS – VALUES   Politician _____

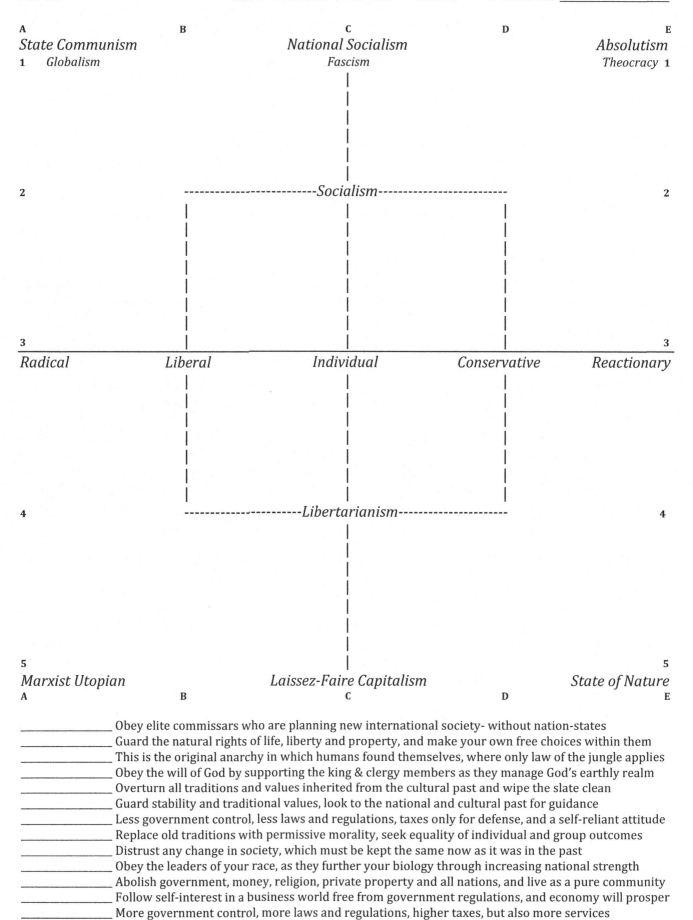

_____ Obey elite commissars who are planning new international society- without nation-states
_____ Guard the natural rights of life, liberty and property, and make your own free choices within them
_____ This is the original anarchy in which humans found themselves, where only law of the jungle applies
_____ Obey the will of God by supporting the king & clergy members as they manage God's earthly realm
_____ Overturn all traditions and values inherited from the cultural past and wipe the slate clean
_____ Guard stability and traditional values, look to the national and cultural past for guidance
_____ Less government control, less laws and regulations, taxes only for defense, and a self-reliant attitude
_____ Replace old traditions with permissive morality, seek equality of individual and group outcomes
_____ Distrust any change in society, which must be kept the same now as it was in the past
_____ Obey the leaders of your race, as they further your biology through increasing national strength
_____ Abolish government, money, religion, private property and all nations, and live as a pure community
_____ Follow self-interest in a business world free from government regulations, and economy will prosper
_____ More government control, more laws and regulations, higher taxes, but also more services

Ch. 17   **SPECTRE OF THE GUN**   O.K. _____
A trip from the future back to 1881

1. The Star Trek episode *Spectre of the Gun (S3-E6)* is a good way to look at both the culture of the Great West, and the famous gunfight in 1881 at the O.K. Corral in Tombstone, Arizona. Before watching, did you know that the gunfight at the O.K. Corral between the "Cowboys" (Billy Claiborne, Ike Claiborne, Billy Clanton, Tom McLaury and Frank McLaury) on the one side versus the "Policemen" (Town Marshall Virgil Earp, Special Deputies Morgan Earp and Wyatt Earp, and temporary deputy Doc Holliday) is perhaps the most famous in American history? Thirty shots in as many seconds? The cops won.

    a. Yeah, I knew that   *b. I heard of it, but didn't know*   *c. I never heard of it*

2. In real life, the West was an "open range" for outlaws. Sometimes a tough sheriff would try to clean up a town, but oftentimes they were kicked out themselves. Sometimes they were shot. There just were not that many police around. The Earp posse were targeted by the Cowboys because they were doing their jobs and interfering in their illegal activities, cleaning up Tombstone, AZ. Wyatt Earp. Many movies have been made about it, including *My Darling Clementine* (1946) with Henry Fonda, *Gunfight at the O.K. Corral* (1957) with Burt Lancaster and Kirk Douglas, *Doc* (1971) with Pete Hamill, which tells the story from Doc Holliday's perspective, *Tombstone* (1993) with Val Kilmer, *Wyatt Earp* (1994) with Kevin Costner, which tells the story from Wyatt Earp's perspective. If there was very little chance you would get caught, how much more likely would you be to steal, extort money from people, smuggle controlled substances and do other crimes?

    a. A lot more likely   *b. I'd definitely think about it*   *c. Not at all, crime is wrong*

3. At the beginning, what did the warning buoy left for visitors tell them to do?

4. Would you have obeyed?

5. When the crew beamed down to the planet, why specifically was it Tombstone, Arizona in 1881?

6. What makes one of the cops (Morgan Earp) especially angry at Billy Claiborne (Mr. Chekov)?

7. More than the story of the Old West, however, like usual, Star Trek has another layer of meaning. This episode is also about the emerging *empirical perspective* coming into focus in the 19th century. Science was developing quickly, and with it industry. The process of research and development (R+D) was diffusing all over the Western world and beyond. Universities became centers of scientific advancement. Knowing they are 'trapped' in the 19th century, with 19th century technology, what does Spock use the *empirical perspective* to create, that gives the crew a chance to beat the odds at the gunfight?

8. Spock's idea works: *a. True*   *b. False*

9. Mind over matter is a mystical concept, but it has a lot of historical relevance. Psychologists even tell us it has a placebo effect when employed. Spiritual gurus often speak of the same kind of real-life effect. What was the role of 'mind over matter' at the Gunfight at the O.K. Corral?

10. Who wins the gunfight?

11. In the Cold War, some leaders of small nations were wary of ties to the U.S. The big lesson: what do the Melkotians do at the very end, and why?

Ch. 18   **ABCs of IMPERIALISM**   **Future Imperialist** _____
Next time won't you sing with me?

URL: http://ufdc.ufl.edu/UF00086056/00001/4j   *Or Search: ABCs for Baby Patriots UFL*

Write what each of the letters stands for as it was taught to British kids in the Victorian Age:

A   B   C

D   E   F

G   H   I

J   K   L

M   N   O

P   Q   R

S   T   U

V   W   X

Y   Z

What do you think was the rationale for using these imperialist -and sometimes offensive to our tastes- ABCs?

Ch. 18 — VICTORIA'S EMPIRE   Player _____

Video Search: Empire Ferguson 4 Heaven's Breed (min. 1-10)

1. After the decline of the Mughal Dynasty in India, which European power moved in? _____

2. What kind of technologies helped the Victorian Britons (population 18 million in 1850) dominate the Indian subcontinent (population 284 million in 1850)?

---

3. The 'Great Game' in Central Asia, a place strategists referred to as a 'geopolitical chessboard,' was 'played' between these two powers:

   a. France and Germany   b. India and Persia   c. Russia and Britain

4. Who were the original 'James Bonds' and what did they do (besides espionage) that helped the Victorians strategically?

---

5. Describe the results of the assault on Magdala in Ethiopia by the British Indians in 1868:

6. What did the results show to the rest of the world about Britain's relationship with India?

Ch. 18 — THE SEPOY REBELLION

Video Search: Empire Ferguson 3 The Mission (~28 min – 38 min in)

7. Which two Indian practices did the British Christians *not* tolerate in their Indian colony?

a)   b)

8. Which two of the following groups did *not* constitute a warrior class from which Sepoys were obtained?

   a. Kshatriyas   b. Sikhs   c. Muslims   d. Dalit

9. What was the rumor among the Sepoys that sparked the Indian Mutiny of 1857?

---

10. Which side committed atrocities?

    a. Sepoys   b. British   c. both

11. What 'lesson' did the British learn by the Mutiny?

Ch. 18   THE DARWIN CONTROVERSY   Investigator _____

A Science Odyssey: Origins (~1 hour in)

1. What did Gregor Mendel notice about pea plants?

    a. Their heredity: that they pass down traits from one generation to the next

    b. Their tastiness: how they go with various dishes like chicken marsala and veal parmigiana

2. In 1859, Charles Darwin proposed the millions of plant and animal species we see in the world around us arose by a process of evolution by:

   _____

3. This process took place over time as _____ occurred and accumulated:

   a. Replication   b. Mutation   c. Cohesion

4. Thomas Hunt Morgan knew dog and horse breeders could make biological:

   a. whole new species   b. improvements

5. What kind of rocks are fossils found in?

   a. Igneous   b. Sedimentary   c. Metamorphic

6. Morgan was excited because Hugo de Vris noticed a new plant species that was growing right next to its parent. He believed the new plant had:

   a. Mutated   b. Replicated perfectly

7. Most fruit flies have red eyes. What color did Morgan believe was a mutation he noticed in one of his flies?

   _____

8. People are an exact mix of just their parents' traits: a. True   b. False

9. People are unique mosaics of all their ancestors: a. True   b. False

10. After Morgan found only male offspring flies inherited the new, strange eyes, he looked again at the strange spindly things in the nuclei of cells that had been discovered a few years earlier under a microscope, called

    a. Genes   b. Chromosomes   c. Elements

11. Morgan and his group of students studied millions of flies. They began to understand that genes for particular traits were passed down on particular chromosomes during cell divisions. What does he come to believe, like Darwin, about evolution?

    a. Only huge mutations make a difference   b. Small mutations over time accumulate

12. Proteins do the 'work,' they are so variable and interesting. So scientists think they are the 'secret of life.' But in 1951, Rosalind Franklin contributed to this scientific conversation by doing this:

_____

13. Describe what James Watson and Francis Crick did to seal the deal:

Ch. 18   ANNA AND THE KING OF SIAM   Teacher _____

Film: Anna and the King (first 30 min.)

Before watching: In the 1860s, while the American Civil War raged here, the British Empire was playing the Great Game with Russia and its other rivals, like France. While Russia was expanding south into Central Asia, and Britain was expanding into the Hindu Kush and Tibet, Afghanistan was chosen by the two powers as a neutral zone. The same thing is true for Siam. It was to be the buffer zone between British Burma and French Indochina. What is the name of Siam today?

    a. Myanmar   b. Singapore   c. Thailand   d. Laos   e. Philippines

Even if Siam was to be 'left alone' from imperial rule, the British Empire wanted to establish a cultural exchange with King Mongkut, which entailed sending Anna Leonowens to teach English to him, his wives, and his son. She arrives with her son Louis to Bangkok.

1) When her son asks Anna why the king of Siam needs to learn English, what does she tell him?

2) Culture shock is when you are weirded out in a new place. If you were Anna, how would you describe *your* first impressions of Siam?

3) Why were people hanging from trees near Siam's western frontier?

4) Why is King Mongkut angry when Anna meets him for the first time?

5) When Anna meets King Mongkut's family, she is surprised at how big of a family it is.

   # Wives: # Concubines:

   # Kids: # Kids 'on the way':

6) Anna agitates the king with a request for her own house. Does he agree to it?   a. Yes   b. No

7) When Anna begins teaching King Mongkut's family, it is to be done in English because:

   a. The king believes English is preferable

   b. The king believes English is necessary

8) Would you be bold like Anna's son in the classroom, or would you accept you were in a land with essential cultural differences?

9) The imperial world order is a fact of life for the Siamese government. How does the minister describe Burma, Vietnam and Cambodia?

10) Does this movie change your opinion of *monarchy*? Why or why not?

Ch. 18 EUGENICS: ALL ABOUT THE SEED DNA strand _____

Would 'superhumans' with thoroughbred genes try to turn against 'regular' humans if they had the chance?

1. The Star Trek episode *Space Seed (S1-E23)* was written to reflect the Cold War controversy surrounding whether humans should practice selective breeding- on themselves. Remember Gregor Mendel from your Bio class, and the Punnett Square? What they didn't tell you was that when his studies in heredity became known, it was linked with Darwin's evolution theory, specifically the part about 'artificial selection.' Francis Galton thought, "Hey, if farmers have been doing artificial selection for thousands of years, making wolves into all those funny dog breeds, and wildcats into domestic cats, and for that matter selecting better crop strains over time, then would the same thing work with people?" Galton believed it *could,* and called the process *eugenics* (good genes). If the theory of eugenics is true, and we can make 'better' people generation-by-generation, should we, in your opinion, try this scientifically by pairing-up eugenic people?

   a. Sure, why not?   *b. No, people should be free to mate with who they want*   *c. No, it's immoral*

2. When the *Enterprise* comes upon the *Botany Bay* adrift in space, and the away team beams over, what interesting traits about the people who are in suspended animation does the crew discover?

_____

3. The leader of the eugenic superhuman group is:

   a. Marla McGivers   *b. Joachim*   *c. Khan*   *d. Spock*

4. What was the reason these people were left adrift in space?

_____
   (If we did use eugenics and some people did become much more fit and intelligent than us, would we have to banish them?)

5. Kirk and the crew must find a way to disable the superpeople from controlling the ship. What do they try, which fails? _____

6. How does Kirk deal with Khan and his crew in the end?

_____

7. China's 'One-Child Policy' was called eugenic because they taxed second children so heavily that only 'rich and beautiful' people could have one. Do you think the government knew that and did it on purpose- or was it just a coincidence?	8. Galton knew people would not want to be set up with another by the state, so he pressed that schools teach students what eugenic qualities to look for in a future mate. Do you think this is a good or bad idea?

9. In a lot of movies, the main hero or heroes have a backstory that goes something like, "He/she came from a long line of _____ who had special qualities. These qualities he/she inherited, and that is the reason he/she are the way they are. That's why they can do this amazing stuff, or are super moral fighters for justice, or are extra smart or beautiful. Without knowing it, do you think movies like these encourage eugenics- even if it is unconsciously? Why or why not?

Ch. 19   **Great Clips: Hideyoshi and Early Modern Japan**   Daimyo_____
Video search: "CNN Millennium: 16th century" (around 20 min. in)

Before Watching

Toyotomi Hideyoshi (1536-1598) is a samurai from a famous daimyo family who is known as the unifier of Japan. He helped transition the country from a feudal society to an early modern one, equivalent to when the monarchs of Europe strengthened their power in relation to the nobility, after colonial gold increased royal wealth and the Treaty of Westphalia was implemented. Whereas Europe looked out, however, Japan remained inward-focused, rejecting contact with the outside world, and favored 'native learning' over 'Dutch learning'.

1. What does the term 'inward-focused' mean in this context? _____

After Watching

2. What was Hideyoshi's nickname? _____.

3. Where is his annual festival held?

4. "Hideyoshi loved spectacle." What kind, specifically:
_____

5. How did Korea stop Hideyoshi's invasion of their peninsula?

6. Summarize Hideyoshi's family issues:

_____

_____

7. Hideyoshi began a successful dynasty that lasted until the 19th century: True   False

_____

Hideyoshi's mixed legacy includes establishing that only samurai could bear arms in Japanese society, fixing the class system, renovating the medieval temples in Kyoto that were in disrepair, finishing the greatest Japanese castle at Osaka, restricting travel to a person's fief, and limiting Christianity's influence by executing converts. All this amounted to the political centralization of Japan, and Hideyoshi's greatest legacy- clearing the path for the Tokugawas, who would rule 300 years.

8. Does your country have a 'great unifier' like Hideyoshi? If so, who might it be? _____

Ch. 19   **Great Clips: Qing and Isolationism**   Manchu_____
Video search: "CNN Millennium: 17th century" (around 37 min. in)

Before Watching

Having overthrown the Yuan (Mongolian) dynasty in 1368, the native Ming rulers brought the resurgence of Confucian philosophy and a 'brilliant' period under Hongwu and Yongle. The latter, however, was the emperor that grounded Zheng He's treasure ships, ending Chinese exploration. He did, however, assemble a formidable encyclopedia of knowledge, of which only a portion survives.

9. Qing rulers ended Chinese exploration: **T   F**

After Watching

10. How do Chinese students practice learning all the written characters?

_____

11. What kinds of things did the Jesuit missionaries bring to the Chinese court?

    Ideas   *Instruments*

12. What became of the instruments the Jesuits brought to the Chinese court?

Ch. 19 ASIA AND THE ISLAMIC EMPIRES MATRIX Syncretist _____

Association helps people remember. Now what were we associating again? Gunpowder Empires!

	Qing	Tokugawa	Ottoman	Safavid	Mughal
Place					
Capital					
Building					
Religion					
Rulers					
Political/Cultural Issue					

Matching

China	India	Japan	Persia	Turkey
Edo (Tokyo)	Fatehpur Sikri	Isfahan	Istanbul (Constantinople)	Peking (Beijing)
Ali Qapu	Forbidden City	Taj Mahal	Topkapi	Yoshiwara Tea Quarter
Divine Faith	Neo-Confucianism	Shi'a	Shinto	Sunni

Leaders
Abbas
Akbar
Aurangzeb
Babur
Hongwu
Ismail
Jahan
Kangxi
Mehmed II
Osman Bey
Qianlong
Suleyman the Magnificent
Tokugawa Ieyasu
Toyatomo Hideyoshi
Yongle

Political/cultural issue (Choose the right letter)

A. Centralizing a country dominated by daimyo families, reconciling a 'floating worlds' culture with isolationism

B. Ruling Christian territory in Europe while battling a Shi'a empire to the east

C. Controlling a large Hindu population living under Muslim rule, battling local rajputs

D. Keeping two Sunni empires at bay, despite being situated between them

E. Practicing isolationism in a world of maritime trade, a part-foreign ruling class, becoming increasingly decadent

Ch. 19   **Great Clips: Zenith of the Qing**   Manchu_____
Video search: "CNN Millennium: 18th century" (around 36 min. in)

1. Note the ways the 18th century in China was distinctive:

   Population   *Wealth*   *Szechuan*

_____

2. The Manchu (Qing) conquest of the Ming brought about one of the most violent wars in history, with an estimated death toll of 30,000,000. From which direction did the Manchus attack China?

3. How did Kangxi reform agriculture in China? |_____

a) *Relocation of people:*   b) *New crops:*

_____   _____

4. What was found in the ship that sunk in the South China Sea?

_____

5. What did Emperor Qianlong tell the British after they asked him for greater volumes of trade?

_____

Ch. 19   **Great Clips: Opium Trade**   Manchu_____
Video search: "CNN Millennium: 19th century" (around 36 min. in)

6. For what reasons did the British grow opium and trade it with China?

_____

8. How was Lin Zexu's job comparable to Samuel Adams' role in the Boston Tea Party?

7. Thinking about the balance of trade, which country had the advantage?

   China   *Britain*

9. Why did William Gladstone not like the Opium War?

_____

_____

10. What did the British obtain from China at the end of the Opium War?

11. Is the balance of trade between China and the USA today more like that between Britain and China in the 18th or 19th centuries? Why?

_____

Ch. 19 — TO BE INDUSTRIALIZED, OR NOT TO BE?

...That is the question which preoccupies us here in 19th century Eurasia...

With the independence of the American colonies, the European powers turned their focus to Asia, the Middle East and Africa. Each power in the Eastern Hemisphere had to contend with the newly industrializing Great Powers, who maintained their balance with each other by expanding abroad.

The societies in this chapter, the Ottomans, Romanovs, Qing and Tokugawas, all faced crises internally too, as they struggled to keep up *without* enacting too much social change from above, which their autocratic leaders were uninterested in- until they got change anyway, from below!

Section I.

Match the society with 1) its major crisis and 2) reform attempt by *connecting them with lines*:

Society	Crisis Situation	Reform Movement
Ottomans	Opium War & Taipings	Self-Strengthening Mov't
Romanovs	Rice prices, taxes, isolation	Tanzimat Reforms
Qing	Territorial losses & debt	Meiji reforms & Zaibatsu
Tokugawa	Crimean War & anarchists	Zemstvos & Witte system

Section II.

Note Turkey, Russia, China or Japan in the blank:

_____ *Foreigners were targeted by the Boxers' 'Harmonious Fists.'*

_____ *Commodore Perry sailed into the bay of their capital with an 'offer you can't refuse!'*

_____ *Losing in war to Japan in 1905 came as a shock to this country and the world.*

_____ *The Young Turks demanded social and economic reforms here.*

_____ *Greece, Serbia and Egypt all defected from this empire in the 19th century.*

_____ *This country ceded Hong Kong to the British in the Treaty of Nanjing.*

_____ *Feudal serfdom was abolished here despite resistance from Boyar nobles.*

_____ *Was never governed by a Selim, Alexander, Cixi, Nikolai, Mehmed or Catherine.*

_____ *Corporatism helped this society industrialize in one generation.*

_____ *Largest empire of the time in land.*

_____ *Largest empire of the time in people.*

Ch. 20 **WWI OBJECTIVES** Recruit _____

What are we fighting for again?

The age of truly industrial warfare on a grand, terrible scale has arrived. If commanders may be forgiven for falsely believing it would be a short (though intense) war, fought in a new way with automatic weapons and mechanized units, as it dragged on and on, we might begin to sympathize with the soldier wondering, "What exactly are we fighting for?" Match the country with its war aim upon the outbreak of hostilities:

Austria-Hungary   Belgium, Bulgaria, Greece Portugal & Romania   France   Germany

Great Britain   Netherlands, Scandinavia, Spain & Switzerland   Italy

Polish Legions   Russia   Serbia   Turkey   United States

_____ Prevent the breakup of our large, landed, multinational empire; avenge the honor of the Archduke, annex all or part of Serbia.

_____ Drive the Austrians out of Bosnia and possibly annex it, remaking in part our Medieval kingdom that fought the Turks at Kosovo when they first arrived in Europe in 1389.

_____ Defend Serbia as leader of the Pan-Slavic world, aggrandize German and Austrian holdings in the Balkans and *Mitteleuropa,* wrest control of the Bosporus Straits.

_____ Recover the provinces of Alsace and Lorraine that were lost in the Franco-Prussian War of 1870-71, use Plan XVII to penetrate into the heart of enemy territory for the win.

_____ Break encirclement of the country using the Von Schlieffen Plan, annex Eastern Belgium (Antwerp and Liege), obtain some of Britain & France's colonial holdings, and exercise authority over *Mitteleuropa,* especially Russian Poland, possibly by annexing it as well.

_____ _____ _____ _____ _____ Neutral at first, then in.

_____ Honor the Treaty of London (1839) war guarantee to Belgium, retain a sense of moral superiority and imperial world hegemony, obtain colonies and financial compensation for fighting on the continent, introduce new weaponry.

_____ Survive as an empire, not lose territory to Russia, not suffer an Arab revolt.

_____ _____ _____ _____ Just let us be neutral! Thanks.

_____ Switch sides in order to gain the *irredenta* from Austria, consisting of the borderland province of South Tyrol in the Alps, something promised by the Allies upon victory.

_____ Fight *both* sides, especially Germany, Austria and Russia, because they jointly disassembled your country a century earlier, and bring it back to life after the war.

_____ Start neutral, then avenge the Lusitania and the Zimmerman Telegram, "Make the world safe for democracy," by fighting the Hun and winning the, "War to end all wars."

Ch. 20   THE GUNS OF AUGUST   Lad _____

When the Titanic sunk no one could believe it. When this happened, it was the same. In both instances, too late.

The Guns of August was historian Barbara Tuchman's great work, for which she won a Pulitzer Prize in 1962. Although she has been criticized by Niall Ferguson among others for placing too much of the blame for the war on Germany and not enough on the international factors of social-darwinism and imperialism, her book spawned a film incorporating the original footage from the pre-war moment, which, in 45 minutes, gives us an on-the-spot taste of all the factors in MANIA.

As you watch minutes 1-45 of (Video Search: *The Guns of August*), notice examples of each of the MANIA categories, the assassination and the underlying causes, and note the specific ways they factored into the opening of the war, when, at minute 45, the German Army moves into Belgium:

Specific instances of how this factor played out

M
Militarism

_____

A
Alliances

_____

N
Nationalism

_____

I
Imperialism

_____

A
Assassination

Had you lived at the time, how excited do you think you'd be about the prospect of a huge war? | What is your opinion about this 50-year-old documentary- its style and narration, vs. ours?

Ch. 20   WWI CLIPS: TRENCHES AND TECHNOLOGIES   Sapper _____

Can't nothin' break this stalemate? (Search: Tech Developments of WWI)

List each new technology as they are introduced, beginning with the machine gun:

THE CHRISTMAS TRUCE
Was it "okay" or should the soldiers be punished? (Search: Christmas Truce 1914 Sainsbury)

Who: Where:

What: Why:

When: How:

Consequences:

SINKING OF THE LUSITANIA
The first major animated movie! (Search: Sinking of the Lusitania Winsor Mackay; ~12 min)

Before watching:

    What was the Lusitania? _____

    What consequence did sinking it have? _____

After watching:

    How was it sunk and how many died? _____

    How did the movie use POV to propagandize the tragedy?

    Did you like the movie? _____

Sketch the sinking of the Lusitania as you would draw it for a comic/animation:

Ch. 20   WWI COMICS   Big fan _____

A broad stroke sketch of the war

Web Search: *AngusBurgers WWI Comic*. Click on the vertical strip in the center of the screen. Sketch the shapes Angus used to represent the antagonistic powers ready to fight at the beginning of the comic strip, in "mini-me" form:

Serbia   *Austria*   *Germany*   *France*   *Britain*

Angus makes use of some national stereotypes in the comic. Find two and identify them:

1)   2)

Near the end, there is a newspaper article announcing a big event in WWI. What and when was it?

What: *Date:*

At the end of the war, how is 'Germany's' emotional state portrayed?

Web Search: *BBC Art of War: How Comic Books Recall World War One*. In 2014, on the 100th anniversary of the 'guns of august,' comic artists commemorated the war. Scanning through, note at least three of the themes they took up, as well as three specific battles they used as background:

       Themes   *Battles*

1)

2)

3)

Web Search: *Deviantart #WWI*. Scroll through these images. Select three of the most impactful- and accurate- that you would use to illustrate the war era if you were making a website about it.

Title 1:   *Reason:*

Title 2:   *Reason:*

Title 3:   *Reason:*

Ch. 20   AMERICAN WWI POSTERS   Affected _____

Be sure you are not getting WWII posters!

In an era just before television, posters were made and put up in the towns and cities of all the belligerent powers in both WWI and WWII. They came in a few types. There were the recruitment posters, which encouraged people to join the military service. There were the propaganda posters, which employed a high degree of creativity to convey a strongly held point-of-view. Some of these reminded people why they were fighting the war in the first place, usually by depicting the enemy powers in a dangerous or otherwise negative light. Still others simply conveyed information the government wanted people to see. Many advertised ways ordinary people could help their nation's war effort.

Directions: Image search <u>WWI propaganda posters</u> along with the <u>type</u> below. Scan posters of each type. Consider the purpose and POV of the posters, what kind of imagery the artists use to get their point across, and if they have a specific audience (civilians, youngsters, kids, soldiers, etc. in mind):

Poster Type 1: War Bonds

In an era when taxes were much lower and some of the currency was backed in gold and silver, why did the government encourage people to buy bonds?	What kinds of messages did they use in the posters to convince people to buy the bonds?

Poster Type 2: Enlistment and the Soldier's Life

For which services did the government need people?	What kinds of advertising lures did they use to attract enlistees?

Poster Type 3: Women's Roles   *Poster Type 4: Kids, Schools & Homefront Work*

List jobs and activities the government advertised that were specifically directed toward women:	How could people on the homefront contribute to food security?

Poster Type 5: Charity and Giving   *Poster Type 6: Propaganda*

Which organizations/places/countries were advertised by charitable organizations as in need of help?	Propaganda can be easy or difficult to detect, depending on the intentions and abilities of the propagandists in question. Note an obvious- or not so obvious- propaganda aspect in one or more poster(s):

Ch. 20 WOMEN'S ROLES IN WORLD WAR I Nightingale _____

Image Search: WWI propaganda poster women

Florence Nightingale *founded* the art and science of nursing on the battlefields of the Crimean War in the 1840s. She became a hero to Victorian Britain, and nurses soon enlisted in the British service whenever there was a conflict in which they might be needed. Soon, women in other nations did the same. Nurses aided soldiers on both sides of the U.S. Civil War, saving many lives, and they played a key role in WWI.

Directions: Click the *Women in WWI* Link in the Upper Right of the website. Of the 60, select 6 that illustrate *different things/roles* women had doing during the war. Do not discriminate against posters in other languages (a translation appears below the poster). Judge each on its overall merit, then, in the following space, state 1) what the role is, and 2) what sort of imagery the poster uses to get its point across:

POSTER #1

Role:

Imagery:

POSTER #2

Role:

Imagery:

POSTER #3

Role:

Imagery:

POSTER #4

Role:

Imagery:

POSTER #5

Role:

Imagery:

POSTER #6

Role:

Imagery:

(Circle the one you'd have preferred if you had to pick)

Ch. 20   BATTLES OF WORLD WAR I   _____

Allied Powers vs. Central Powers: Fight! Finish the one-line summary of the following by searching: Battle of ____x____

1914:   The Frontiers   Heligoland Bight   Liege   Marne   Masurian Lakes   Tannenburg

1. _____. **1914.** In this first battle of WWI, Belgian defenders used a series of forts and cut rail lines to slow the German advance into France, giving the French more time to prepare.

2. _____. Plan XVII and the Schlieffen Plan collide with simultaneous attacks on fortresses along the border.

3. _____. The first major battle on the Eastern Front was a German victory that stopped the Russian advance into East Prussia. Paul von Hindenburg came out of retirement to lead the Germans, while Russian commander Samsonov shot himself at the battle's conclusion.

4. _____. The first naval battle of the war saw the British sink a few German cruisers and command the coastline.

5. _____. After this battle, in which the French trenches were dug and the German advance to Paris stopped, the famous 'race to the sea' meant the whole Western front was made into trench stalemate.

6. _____. This second huge victory of the Germans over the Russians on the Eastern Front ensured Hindenburg and Ludendorff command the East for the duration of the war.

1915:   Armenian Genocide   Gallipoli   Isonzo   R.M.S. Lusitania   Sandfontein   Ypres

7. _____. **1915.** The German territory of South-West Africa fell to the British colony of South Africa after this battle, stripping Germany of its most important African holding.

8. _____. Terrible trench combat took place here, pronounced Ee-pray, and just saying you fought here was enough. People knew you went through a serious battle, chlorine gas attacks, and much misery. But that nothing was gained, and nothing lost.

9. _____. This campaign meant the opening of a Southern (Italian) Front after Italy switch to the Allies. Austrian forces were tied up in Tyrol and could not be used elsewhere. Heavy casualties.

10. _____. Following failed attempts to take Scimitar Hill and others in the Dardanelles, the British ordered a fighting retreat of its largely Australian contingent that became the Ottoman's greatest victory in the war.

11. _____. Behind Ottoman lines, around a million Christian Armenians were massacred in what some consider the first modern genocidal campaign, in what is now Eastern Turkey.

12. _____. The sinking of this ship with over a thousand people on board helped turn American public opinion against the Central Powers during the war.

1916:   Brusilov Offensive (Lutsk)   Great Retreat   Jutland   Siege of Kut   The Somme   Verdun

13. _____. **1916.** The Russian high command called for an enormous pullback which lowered morale considerably and sparked protests within the country.

14. _____. The longest battle of the war saw a ring of forts on the Western Front assaulted with trench fighting after Falkenhayn wrote to the Kaiser that if France were 'bled white' and knocked out, Britain would leave the war too. Huge casualties, little accomplished.

15. _____. This largest naval battle of the war and the greatest dreadnaught-battleship campaign ever fought, this struggle ended in a partial British victory, but ultimately disappointed the empire that still believed it ruled the waves.

16. _____. Called the greatest humiliation ever to have befallen the British army, the siege of this Ottoman city near Baghdad could not be sustained.

17. _____. Russian counterattack that made up the most powerful thrust into Austrian controlled territory, but at a gigantic loss of life. While considered Russia's greatest victory in the war, it had simultaneously sown the seeds of its own demise.

18. _____. This terrible battle saw the largest one-day loss of British life in history. German trench fighter Corporal Adolf Hitler was wounded in this battle.

1917: *Balfour Declaration   Baghdad   Cambrai   Jerusalem   Kerensky Offensive*
Nivelle Offensive   Passchendaele   Russian Revolution   Zimmerman Telegram

19. _____. **1917.** This coordinated British-French attack, culminating at Vimy Ridge, penetrated further into German trench lines than had yet been accomplished. But its losses and sustained heavy casualties led to a mutiny in the French military.

20. _____. When the British took this city, the modern capital of Iraq, from the Ottomans, it opened the way to Jerusalem.

21. _____. After the February Revolution in Russia in the shadow of the Winter Palace, and the protests of masses of people calling for bread and peace, Czar Nikolai II abdicated (abandoned) the throne. A provisional government was formed but amazingly, it did not suspend action in the war and called for this new offensive, which failed miserably.

22. _____. In October (Russian calendar), Lenin and the Bolshevik communists overthrew the government, declared the Soviet Union, and signed the Treaty of Brest-Litovsk.

23. _____. A note decoded by British intelligence on the way to Mexico, this document spurred anger on the part of Americans and heightened resolution to enter the war.

24. _____. This agreement between Jewish leaders and the British saw Britain endorse the Zionist concept of a Jewish state in Palestine in exchange for the community's support.

25. _____. British General Allenby marched into this Holy City, which set the stage for the Mandate System (British control over the Middle East) begun after the war.

26. _____. Winding up totally bombed out, this city played host to the British Mark IV tank's main action in the war, but was ultimately ineffective.

27. _____. Featuring the worst loss of life day in New Zealand history, this British attack to help the French recover from Nivelle & mutiny was tough fighting in bad weather.

1918:   *Amiens   Argonne Forest   Belleau Wood   Chateau-Thierry*
Friedensturm (2nd Marne)   St. Quintin Canal   Vittorio Veneto

28. _____. **1918.** Fresh American Marines shown forth in this battle in France.

29. _____. Americans snuck up on German positions without artillery barrages.

30. _____. Opening battle of the *Hundred Days* offensive that would end the war.

31. _____. Allied victory on the Italian front that bumped Austria out of the war.

32. _____. Final German offensive in the spring. Covered old ground, defeated by the Hundred Days offensive that began at Amiens.

33. _____. Allied forces spearhead the Hindenburg Line and break through, convince German high command continued war was hopeless.

34. _____. Largest battle in history of the USA, 1,200,000 Americans compel the surrender of Germany on 11/11/1918.

Ch. 20 **TRENCH WAR - SIMULATION** **Frontswine** _____

Never before, never again: The trench was its own version of terrible

After machine guns but before dive-bombers, in WWI and in WWI only, the trench ruled. Today we are going to write a letter home describing life in the trenches. To get an idea of what life really is like, we're first going to go through a simulation:

URL: Warmuseum.ca/overthetop/

1) What is morning like for a trench soldier?

2) Note the various kinds of dangers faced by trench soldiers:

3) Sketch a drawing for your letter home- it can be how the trench looks, or another scene from the war:

4) What kinds of tasks did you have to *do* in the trench?

5) Did you die in the trench?   Yes   No

6) How did you die? _____

7) Play the game again until you live to the end of the war. What happens on Armistice Day?

Ch. 20   **WWI DEAD**   **Willy McBride** _____

Makes you want to mutiny against war- like the French Army did during the Nivelle Offensive in 1917

Ethnic groups which lost lives in the First World War:

Make a horizontal bar chart using boxes for each 100,000 dead. The boxes should be small enough for Russia's 36!

Group	Dead	|1	|10	|20	|30
Russian	3,654 k				
German	2,424 k				
French	1,800 k				
Armenian	1,500 k				
Polish	1,100 k				
Turkish/Arab	771 k				
Romanian	748 k				
British	702 k				
Greek	676 k				
Italian	651 k				
Serbian	505 k				
Hungarian	385 k				
Croat-Slovene	320 k				
French African	265 k				
Czechoslovak	185 k				
Austrian	175 k				
Belgian-Congolese	155 k				
British African	141 k				
German African	118 k				
American	116 k				
Jewish	100 k	|1	|10	|20	|30
Bulgarian	87 k				
Portuguese	82 k				
British Indian	73 k				
Australian	62 k				
Canadian	61 k				
Belgian	59 k				
Portuguese African	52 k				
Irish	45 k				
British Nepalese	20 k				
New Zealander	18 k				
Montenegrin	13 k				
Estonian	10 k				
Brit. South African	10 k				
Japanese	5 k				
Nor/Swede/Dane	4 k				
British Rhodesian	1 k				

For those lucky countries where less than 100,000 died, try to categorize them into Allied or Central Powers supporters:

Allied   *Central Powers*

Dividing the death tolls by ethnicity into death tolls by alliance, and recalling many of the above were in the Central or Allied Powers via imperial tie, add up the tolls for each. *Other* includes Polish (fought for and against both sides), Armenian (massacred in the Ottoman Empire), and Jewish (fought for and against both sides). Oh, and put Italy's on the Allies- almost all died vs. CP.

Central Powers: *Allied Powers:*   *Other/Nonaligned:*

Ch. 20 THE EDGE OF FOREVER   Soup kitchen volunteer _____
Would you fire?

1. The Star Trek episode *The City on the Edge of Forever (S1-E29)* was written to reflect the idea that an individual's destiny is his own, but that it may be vital in altering the course of history. There is an argument called the Butterfly Effect, which says that if you went back in time and appeared for 2 seconds only, saw no one, but twacked a butterfly with your finger, setting it off the course it was on, then future history would change from what it would have been had you not been there. Because that butterfly would not have pushed air the way it would have, or would not have flitted to sit later on a windowsill, where a girl looking out would not have said "Aww," and then paused to watch it, and had not seen a boy walking by who wouldn't have waved and said, "Hey, aren't you the new girl in school?" They never would have met and got married and had a family etc. History might change at the turn of a butterfly's wing. Or it may take more than that. What do you think?

---

2. In *Back to the Future,* Marty could interact with people without changing the future, but he had to make one particular meeting take place in order for the future to be 'right.' That's the same problem facing Captain Kirk and Mr. Spock in this episode. *How* do they get from the 23rd century to the 20th century, specifically, 1930s New York during the Depression?

3. *Why* did they have to do it?

---

4. Describe the clothes people wear in the 1930s.

Men's: Women's:

5. What is different about people's manners 80 years ago?

---

6. A moral choice confronts Kirk and Spock. What is the choice, and why is the choice so difficult for Kirk especially?

---

7. What did Edith Keeler tell the people from the future she believed the future would be like?

8. What would Edith Keeler have done if McCoy had stopped her from being hit?

---

9. This episode is about destiny. Do you think you have a kind of destiny? That what you do in this life will echo somehow in eternity? Why or why not?

Ch. 20   GERM THEORY OF DISEASE   Epidemiologist_____

GROSS. GERMS AGAIN.

1. Warm up: Make a list of as many elements on the periodic table as you can. If you know the atomic number, so much the better, but it's not necessary. No cheating now (this isn't a test):

2. Video: *Daniel Radcliffe sings the Elements*
How long do you think it took him to memorize all of those names?
_____

3. How long would you take to memorize all the periodic table elements like Harry Potter did?

Video Search: ***A Science Odyssey Matters of Life and Death (min. 1-25)***

4. Before viewing: Think of one of each of the following categories of U.S. president:

    Assassinated   *Died in Office*   *Shot but Lived*

_____   _____   _____

5. After viewing the first five minutes, categorize William McKinley: _____

6. Note three things the doctors operating on McKinley did that would be medical fails today:

a)   *b)*   *c)*

7. Quick! Before getting further into the video, name three diseases off the top of your head, like 'the flu' and identify them as being *caused* by either: *bacteria, virus,* or *nutrient deficiency:*

Disease	*Cause*
a)	
b)	
c)	

8. A virus like the flu is   *more simple*   *more complex*   than a bacterium like Bubonic Plague.

After the Civil War, the reunited USA set itself to the task of building a Transcontinental Railroad from "sea to shining sea." Four years later it was completed, the last golden spike having been driven into the track at Promontory Point, Utah, connecting the eastern and western railroads as one. Today, the golden spike is a museum piece at Stanford University in California. As labor was short (~600,000 young men died in the Civil War) and therefore expensive, the government and rail companies brought back the indentured servitude system, but this time the laborers who came to work in exchange for payment of their voyage to America were not from England, but from China. They came to work on the railroad. After a public backlash and anti-Chinese riots in some western cities, the program was ceased.

9. Why did people in San Francisco become concerned about the Chinatown neighborhood around 1900?

10. Why did 'posses' of exterminators go around spraying Chinatown's dwellings?

11. What were the exterminators- despite success in preventing the spread of the disease- wrong about?

        a. the deadliness of the disease   *b. the vector of the disease*

12. After the 1906 San Francisco earthquake struck, the reaction of medical officials was different than during the 1900 plague scare. What did they consider that revolutionized their approach?

      a. the Germ Theory of disease   *b. the poor-sanitation theory of disease*

13. Around 1900, would you have been excited to go into the medical field with the knowledge that you might be able to apply the new understanding of how disease works?

14. When Dr. Goldberger investigate the mysterious disease *pellagra*, which caused skin blisters and insanity, which region did he have to visit?

15. What was the major breakthrough Goldberger made in investigating the cause of pellagra?

16. "Eat a healthy, balanced diet!" our parents and advisors tell us. Even the little cereal characters brag that their cereals are, "part of a balanced breakfast," *part* being the operable term. Why was there so much negativity towards Goldberger's thesis that a *deficiency of vitamins* caused pellagra?

*In an experiment, the experimental group is the group to which the variable being tested is administered. The control group gets a placebo to test whether the variable given to the other group is really a possible cause or effect on the experimental group.

17. The *variable* in the experiment, the thing given to the experimental group, was:

a. corn and fatback   *b. a balanced diet*   *c. a high-five each day for self-esteem*

18. Would you have volunteered for this or stayed on the chain-gang?

19. What was the conclusion of the experiment?

20. In sum, how conscious are YOU about checking whether you are getting all the vitamins and minerals you need- like niacin- that are, "part of a healthy diet?"

Ch. 20   **THE MESSAGES OF MODERNISM**   **Judge** _____

Nudity is okay if it's in art, especially if it's Cubism

http://www.pptpalooza.net/ and download **#48, Early 20th Century Art,** in the central column.

What are the 5 themes in post-WWI art?   I am comfortable/uncomfortable with this theme

1 _____   a. totally fine with it   b. a little disturbing

2 _____   a. totally fine with it   b. a little disturbing

3 _____   a. totally fine with it   b. a little disturbing

4 _____   a. totally fine with it   b. a little disturbing

5 _____   a. totally fine with it   b. a little disturbing

Painter	*Name of Painting*	*Theme*	*My rating:* 1-blah, 2-okay, 3-like it!
1			
2			
3			
4			
5			
6			
7			
8			
9			
10			
11			
12			
13			
14			
15			

16 _____

17 _____

18 _____

19 _____

20 _____

21 _____

22 _____

23 _____

24 _____

25 _____

26 _____

27 _____

Architecture

Draw the Walter Gropius House below (be sure to keep the windows in the right spot)!

Search: bauhaus final .ppt (click on first return).

Do you like Bauhaus style school architecture?

_____

What's basic idea- the philosophy- of Bauhaus schools?

1

2

3

4

_____

Draw a Bauhaus style chair below:

Find the Bauhaus lamp. Do you like the design? _____

Draw a Bauhaus picture:

Ch. 20 TARIFFS: TARIFFYING OR TARIFFIC? Fair Trader _____

Whatever you do, do not Youtube: Ferris Buller Hawley-Smoot

70%

60

50

40

30

20

10

0

    1900 1910 1920 1930 1940 1950 1960 1970 1980 1990 2000 2010 2020

This chart displays the average rate at which tariffed goods were taxed. However, the number and type of goods has fluctuated over time as well, which should be borne in mind. At the height of the Hawley-Smoot Tariff after 1930, about twenty percent of imported goods were taxed, the highest rate of the century. In 2016, less than 2 percent of goods were tariffed- and those goods were tariffed at 1.5 percent- historic lows on both counts.

On the chart above, place a dot at each of the following points:

1) From the 1860s to 1900, the Morrill Tariff and others kept the average rate of taxation on imported goods at about 45%, so place an appropriate dot over 1900.

2) During the first decade of the 20th century, the rate was dropping in general, despite certain new imports being taxed by the Payne-Aldrich Tariff of 1909. In 1913, the Underwood Tariff Act lowered taxes further, to zero on many products, and instituted a federal income tax to cover the lost income. Then, WWI placed a hold on tariff collection. Place a dot at 15% in the year 1918.

3) Tariffs began going up after WWI. European countries raised them on farm products and the U.S. did as well, with the Emergency Tariff Act of 1921. A year later, the passage of Fordney-McCumber raised tariffs on manufactured goods to protect American industry. Meanwhile, Europeans who bought from U.S. banks used some of the loaned money to buy American goods, which was good for the U.S. economy and contributed to the boom of the Roaring '20s. Put a dot at 35% above 1922.

4) Following the circular-loan disaster, whereby Germans borrowed money to pay reparations to France and Britain, who then turned around and used it to pay Americans back for loans in WWI, as well as for speculation-marginal stocks- the bubble of which burst on Black Thursday in 1929, the Smoot-Hawley Tariff was passed to protect American industries during the Great Depression. Put a dot at 60% over 1930.

Sketch a circular-loan disaster graphic here:

5) Four years later- at the height of the Great Depression- the Reciprocal Tariff Act rewrote the rules. It gave Congress incentives to lower tariffs, unlike earlier, when individual members were under pressure from their constituents (who wanted them to lobby for more protection for their small businesses). Now, if a simple majority of Congress voted for a certain level of tariff, it stuck. Separate interests could be overruled more easily, and tariffs were lowered from the Smoot-Hawley high due to bilateral tariff reduction treaties, which based on the concept of reciprocity. Place the 1934 level at 40 percent- still a high figure.

6) During the 1940s, two agents acted to lower tariffs dramatically. First, more and more Reciprocal Act treaties were negotiated. Second, WWII changed the game. The Lend-Lease Act and others made it possible to sell, loan and give items made in the U.S. to the Allies and vice-versa, which brought about a suspension of some charging of tariffs. Place a dot over 1947 at 15 percent.

7) The postwar General Agreement on Tariffs and Trade (GATT) signatories- the U.S. included among them- met at Geneva, then Annecy, then Torquay. Employing a new, internationalist free trade philosophy, they made '50,000 concessions,' lowering tariffs 25 percent worldwide from their already historic low. Place a dot at 12 percent above 1950.

8) GATT signatories met at Geneva and again at Dillon to negotiate more tariff cuts. Place a dot at 10 percent over 1960.

9) GATT signatories met at Geneva and again at Tokyo (the Geneva round was nicknamed the 'Kennedy' round to honor the recently slain-president, and perhaps to give more credibility to the conference (after all, who would oppose an expansion of free trade named after Kennedy?). Place a dot above 1980 at 5 percent.

10) GATT met again in 1986 at the Uruguay Round, with the goal of reducing subsidies to agriculture, increasing foreign direct investment opportunities, and lowering tariffs and other trade barriers. It concluded in 1994 and announced the creation of the World Trade Organization (WTO). Textile and related tariffs were completely abolished, and most of the American clothing manufactures outsourced to lower-cost labor markets. Mark a dot at 5 percent above 1990.

11) The North American Free Trade Agreement (NAFTA), signed in 1994 by Bill Clinton, marked a major step. Mark a dot 7 percent above the year 2000. Since the number of goods tariffed was dramatically lowered, it had the effect of making it seem like tariffs went up a little since there were fewer goods to tax as a whole, and the ones that remained carried slightly higher tariffs.

12) The WTO is currently involved in the 'Doha Round,' focusing on lowering barriers further in industrial goods. Many meetings have taken place in Doha, Cancun, Paris, Potsdam and Geneva. Talks broke down in 2008 but place the 1.5% percent current rate over 2015.

*13) Place a **question mark** over 2020 at 35 percent, as the Trump Administration is considering raising tariffs on select goods for the first time in a while. This is considered the extreme high figure.*

Connect the dots!

What do you think are some advantages countries gain from placing tariffs on imports?	What do you think are some things countries lose out by placing tariffs in imported goods?

Ch. 20 RISE OF THE DICTATORS: STALIN

*Search: **Stalin's Paranoia, the Great Purge and the Cult of Personality.***

1. Who won in the contest for power after Lenin died?   *a. Leon Trotsky   b. Josef Stalin*

2. What might happen to someone targeted in the Great Purge? | 3. What is a GULAG?

4. What kind of trials took place during the Great Purge?   *a. fair and legal   b. kangaroo court*

MUSSOLINI'S MARCH ON ROME - 1922

*I always wanted to visit Rome! Search: **Mussolini March on Rome 20th century almanac***

5. Was Mussolini from the political right or the political left?   *a. the Right   b. the Left*

6. What kinds of things did Mussolini do that inspired Hitler in Germany? | 7. What kind of symbols did Mussolini use to represent himself and his fascist movement?

THE FIRST TRUE TELEVISION BROADCAST – 1936 OLYMPICS

*The very first transmission space aliens will get from earth is... seriously? Search: **1936 Olympics Opening Ceremony***

8. TV signals had been transmitted before, but none with the power to escape the Earth's ionosphere. That changed with the 1936 Olympics Opening Ceremony, which was broadcast on the most powerful carrier in the world to a record-setting audience. Name an element the director used to convey a feeling of grandeur in the opening sequences of the ceremony:

9. In the 'parade of nations' procession, as the Greeks, Brits, Japanese, Americans and others march by, the fans welcome them with the infamous Hitler salute. Do the Americans salute back? | 10. The German fans' reaction when Third Reich flag appears is best described as:

     a. ashamed   b. subdued   c. excited

11. When Hitler speaks, he's announcing:

a. the opening of the games   b. the end

| 12. Knowing that the concept of the life-giving sun is powerful in Aryan mythology, how did the director link it artistically with the Olympic flame at the end, making sure Nazi propaganda got into the telecast?

Ch. 20 — RISE OF JAPAN
Wakon, Yosai

Recruit _____

Place the historically significant places Nara, Kyoto, Sapporo, Nagasaki, Edo/Tokyo, Hiroshima and Osaka on the map on the back, along with the islands, and then answer the questions below:

1) How did the concept of *Yamato-Damashii* help Japan able to keep its unique culture but modernize its industry and military so quickly?

_____

2) What are *ziabatsu*, and how did they influence Japanese policy during the Meiji era?

_____

3) Clip (1-5 min in): How does the U.S. Government Orientation briefing for soldiers in WWII depict Japanese culture and values?

_____

4) Clip 2 (6 min. in): Who actually rules Japan- and how does the U.S. government briefing describe Japan's political system?

_____

5) What was Japan's vision for the future of Asia embodied in the term *Hakko Ichiu* (15 min in.)? | 6) Why do you think Japan would ally with Nazi Germany and its *Lebensraum* policy in WWII?

_____

7) 19:00 min in: Note Japan's social and cultural norms, at least according to the U.S. government:

Social Pyramid   *Cultural Norms*

Ch. 34   THE NAZI OLYMPICS   Athlete _____

As the first major TV broadcast in world history, if there are space aliens, this is the first image they will get of Earth.

Video search: *Jesse Owens Returns to the 1936 Olympics*

1896 Athens	
1900 Paris	
1904 St. Louis	
1908 London	
1912 Stockholm	
1916 Cancelled	
1920 Antwerp	
1924 Chamonix	
1928 Amsterdam	
1932 Los Angeles	
1936 Berlin	
1940 Cancelled	
1944 Cancelled	
1948 London	
1952 Helsinki	
1956 Melbourne	
1960 Rome	
1964 Tokyo	
1968 Mexico City	
1972 Munich	
1976 Montreal	
1980 Moscow	
1984 Los Angeles	
1988 Seoul	
1992 Barcelona	
1996 Atlanta	
2000 Sydney	
2004 Athens	
2008 Beijing	
2012 London	
2016 Rio de Janeiro	
2020 Tokyo	

1. The modern Olympics were resurrected in 1896, why might it not be surprising that they were held in Athens first?

_____

2. When were the modern Olympics cancelled, and *why*, do you think?

_____

3. Which *city* and *country* have hosted the most modern Olympiads?

_____ / _____

4. What benefit is a city likely go get from hosting the Olympics?

_____

5. If your city was chosen to host an Olympiad, what kinds of changes and preparations do you think would have to be done?

_____

6. Jesse Owens is a famous athlete of the 1930s. He was a patriotic African-American runner, despite the social discrimination he faced in his home country. What about 1930s Germany might give him the idea he might face discrimination there as well?

_____

7. **Video clip.** During the Opening Ceremonies of the '36 Olympics, some countries gave Hitler the 'Hail' salute and some not.

Did: *Did not:*

8. Did Hitler stand and salute the American flag after Jesse Owen won the gold or did he spurn America? | 9. Why was Hitler reprimanded by the Olympic Committee at one point?

10. Which events did Jesse Owens win a medal in? | Bonus: these Olympics were the first TV signal strong enough to reach other stars in the galaxy. What do you think aliens might think about Earth after seeing this broadcast?

Ch. 20   CARTOONS GO TO WAR!   Loony Toon _____

Today we could use a 3D printer to print out 1,000 Donald Ducks and send them into a real war? Seriously? Sweet.

You might remember *author's purpose* from English class, when you analyze a text, art, or film with an eye towards figuring out why it was produced, the context, the message, and intended effect. During the rise of the dictators in Europe and Asia, the new medium of cartoons were used to influence the way people saw world events and personalities. As we view the following selections, ask yourself the following:

Video Search: *Donald Duck Der Führer's Face* | **Video Search: *Loony Tunes The Ducktators***

Describe what happens in this cartoon: | *Describe what happens in this cartoon:*

For what possible purpose was this made? | *Why do you think this cartoon was made?*

Video Search: *Private SNAFU Spies* | **Video Search: *Disney Education for Death***

Describe what happens in this cartoon: | *Describe what happens in this cartoon:*

For what possible purpose was this made? | *Why do you think this cartoon was made?*

Hold up, people didn't have TVs till the 1950s. So how did people watch cartoons? People went to the movies once or twice a week, and the cartoons were played as a preview, or a pre-preview to the news, which was shown as well. It was a 3-4 hour burden to go see a movie! What kind of psychological effect do you think cartoons like these had on people at the time? | When is the last time you saw something on TV that you definitely knew was propaganda? And what was it?

Ch. 20   NEW ALLIANCES: ALLIES AND AXIS   Ally _____

The following countries all had certain objectives on the eve of war in 1939. 1) Match them up into the right categories on the bottom, *Status Quo*, *Revisionist* and *Neutral*, depending on where it was at the beginning. Countries like Bulgaria and Greece who were 'drafted' or invaded by a belligerent power- classify 'status quo.'

Austria's branch of the Nazi Party, angry about the Treaty of St. Germain, advocated and held a referendum on *Anschluss* (unification), after which this land of Hitler's birth was unified with the German Reich.

The Baltic States became independent after WWI, declared neutrality, then were annexed by the Soviet Union in 1940. When Germany invaded the USSR, they were German until 1944. After the war they would revert to the USSR.

Belgium, Denmark, Netherlands and **Norway** all declared neutrality but were invaded and conquered by Germany.

Bulgaria joined the Axis and helped in its invasion of Greece and Yugoslavia, but later switched to the Allies.

Czechoslovakia was neutral until it was absorbed into the German Reich after Sudetenland & the Munich Conference.

Finland started neutral, then was invaded by the Soviet Union in the Winter War of 1939-1940. After that, it supported Germany militarily against the USSR, but otherwise never joined either the Axis or Allies.

France sought to keep the peace, rebuild flattened cities from WWI, fortify the Maginot Line along the German border, contain or minimize expansionism in the League of Nations, & solidify ties to its colonies in Africa and Indochina.

Germany wanted to expand east (*Lebensraum*), revise or discard the Versailles Treaty, unite all the German-speaking peoples into the Reich, and build a new order in Europe with itself holding superpower status.

Great Britain sought to contain or minimize expansionism with diplomatic pressure, build infrastructure in the Middle East under the Mandate system, issue a war guarantee to Poland.

Greece joined the Allies after being invaded by Italy and later Germany.

Hungary, angry about the Treaty of Trianon, sought to gain its *irredenta* territories (ethnic Hungarians living in Transylvania, parts of Yugoslavia and Czechoslovakia). Joined the Axis.

Ireland, having achieved Home Rule from the British Empire in 1920, stays out of the fray.

Italy, having adopted a fascist government after reconciling with king and pope, sought to expand in Ethiopia and Libya, and is building power on the Roman example. Signed the Pact of Steel.

Poland was wary of Nazis & Soviets. Having driven back Lenin's armies in 1920, who were looking to spread communism, they now won't negotiate on Danzig or their 'Corridor' to the sea.

Romania, despite problems with Hungary, joined the Axis under the fascist Iron Guard. The Transylvania issue was touchy, but Romania switched sides at the end of the war and kept it.

Soviet Union signs a nonaggression pact with Germany and invades Poland, Finland and the Baltic States. When it is attacked by Germany in 1941, it joins the Grand Alliance of USA, Britain and USSR.

Spain was embroiled in a civil war between fascists and democrats in the 1930s, and would remain neutral in WWII while its political order is sorted out under the victorious General Franco.

Switzerland and **Sweden** are able to maintain their neutrality throughout the whole war.

Yugoslavia- led by Serbs- fought with the Allies, although many Croats and Slovenes favored the Axis and after Axis conquest, Yugoslavia descended into civil war for the rest of WWII.

Status Quo / Appeasement   *Revisionism / Expansionism*   *Neutral*

Ch. 20   DEAR PROFESSOR...   Recruit _____

We'd like a word with you.

The AP program is known worldwide. Tests are taken in many countries. So what if government officials in one country objected to the way their country was portrayed in the AP World History curriculum? It happened. The textbook *Traditions & Encounters* has three authors, Jerry Bentley, who passed away recently, Herbert Ziegler and Heather Streets-Salter. Then one day, while he had office hours at the university, Professor Ziegler got a visit from a Japanese official. They wanted to talk about the way he wrote about Japan, because textbooks influence so many students' understanding about places in the world. Ziegler has a lot of power in that respect- and his opinion becomes a meme, multiplied in many minds around the world. So, what was it the Japanese government was upset about?

Article Search: **U.S. academics condemn Japanese efforts to revise history of 'comfort women.'**

Read this *Washington Post* story, and answer the following questions:

1) First off, how influenced are you by what you see in textbooks or on other multimedia in your history class?   1=not at all   5=I think about it   10=It is my main source of understanding:

_____ If you put something other than 10, what are your other sources of understating the world and the past?
_____

2) Briefly describe what the Japanese official objected to in Ziegler's textbook:
_____

3) What was Professor Ziegler's opinion about his conversation with the Japanese officials?
_____

4) Who is the author of *this* article? _____ Does he or she have a POV on the matter?
_____

5) The term 'academic freedom' was thrown out there. What does 'academic freedom' mean to you?
_____

6) Should 'academic freedom' be extended to politically sensitive or offensive topics? This topic was offensive to the Japanese government. Should that part of the curriculum be censored? Why or why not?
_____

7) If you were Ziegler, would you have changed the passages in the textbook if a bribe of a thousand dollars had been offered? Why or why not- and if not- how much would it take?

Ch. 20   **MASSACRE OF THE INNOCENTS: WWII DEAD**   Civilian _____

Maybe it's time to mutiny against war?

All countries study WWII. Guess the language of the terms on the right. You may choose from the following: English, French, German, Italian, Japanese, Polish, Russian, Spanish:

WWII dead (Allies *, Axis +, Neutral -)

Russian*	22,000 k
Chinese*	11,000 k
German+	8,100 k
Jewish*	5,100 k
Polish*	3,200 k
Indonesian*	3,100 k
Japanese+	2,900 k
Indian*	1,900 k
Yugoslavian*	1,400 k
Vietnamese*	1,300 k
Romanian+	800 k
Hungarian+	580 k
Philippine*	557 k
French*	550 k
Italian+	454 k
British*	450 k
American*	420 k
Greek*	415 k
Korean+	410 k
Lithuanian-	350 k
Czechoslovak+	325 k
Dutch*	301 k
African*	300 k
Burmese*	272 k
Latvian-	230 k
Austrian+	120 k
Ethiopian+	100 k
Malayan*	100 k
Finnish+	100 k
Belgian*	88 k
South Pacific*	57 k
Estonian-	50 k
Singaporean*	48 k
Canadian*	45 k
Australian*	41 k
Albanian+	30 k
Bulgarian+	25 k
New Zealander*	12 k
South African*	12 k
Norwegian*	10 k
Thai+	8 k
Danish-	4 k
Swedish-	1 k

Secunda Guerra Mundial _____

Vtoraya Mirovaya Voyna _____

Seconda Guerra Mondiale _____

World War Two _____

Dainijisekaitaisen _____

Zweiter Weltkreig _____

Drugi Wojna Swiatowa _____

Seconde Guerre Mondiale _____

1. Add up the total number who died in WWII of all causes, including in battle, as civilians, of famine and disease:

   Axis Powers: *Allied Powers:*

2. Indonesia, India and Vietnam had huge famines during the war years. What was their combined death toll?

   _____

3. Why do you think Spanish *WWII* casualties are so few?

   _____

4. Evaluate American casualty figures vis-à-vis the others:

   _____

5. In sum, what most surprises you most about these figures?

Ch. 21 **20th CENTURY IDEOLOGIES SIMPLIFIED** "Owner"_____

You can't make this stuff up. No, not this worksheet- the actual ways all these crazy ideas have been applied in the real world!

FEUDALISM: You have two cows. Your local lord takes some of the milk in exchange for protecting the village where you and your cows live and letting you continue to reside there.

SOCIALISM: You have two cows. The government takes them and puts them in a barn with everyone else's cows. Your job is to take care of all of the cows along with all the other owners, together. The government distributes to you as much milk as it thinks you need, and as much of the milk of "your" cows to others as it thinks they need.

BUREAUCRATIC SOCIALISM: You have two cows. The government takes them and sticks them in a barn with everyone else's cows, where they are cared for by chicken farmers. Meanwhile, you are told to take care of the chickens the government took from the chicken farmers. The government gives you as much milk and eggs as the regulations say you need, and gives as much milk and eggs to the others as the regulations say they need. At first the government regulates what the cows can be fed and when you can milk them. Sometimes it pays you not to milk them. Then it takes both, shoots one, milks the other and pours the milk down the drain. Then it requires you to fill out forms accounting for the missing milk.

COMMUNISM: You have two cows. Your neighbors agree property rights do not exist, so everyone joins a collective farm and helps take care of all the cows. You all share the milk while singing campfire songs.

SOVIET COMMUNISM: You have two cows. A collective farm is formed. You and the others take care of the cows by force, and Stalin takes almost all the milk. Half the farmers starve, including your family.

FASCISM: You have two cows. The government takes both and A) either hires you to take care of them and sells you the milk, or B) expels you if you don't fit the profile of the type of citizen they want in their *Volkstaat*.

DEMOCRACY: You have two cows. Your neighbors decide who gets the milk by popular vote.

REPRESENTATIVE DEMOCRACY: You have two cows. You and your neighbors elect someone with the best face for TV to lecture you on how you should take care of your cows.

ANARCHY: You have two cows. You put a security cordon around your cows. Either you barter the milk in a way that makes the people around you happy, or roving gangs and syndicates try to take the cows away.

POLITICAL CORRECTNESS: You are associated with (the concept of 'ownership' is a leftover from our hateful, sexist, ethnocentric, intolerant, classist and warmongering past) two differently-abled and aged (but no less valuable to society) bovines of non-specific gender, breed, or religious or other affiliation. They graze while you wonder what happened to your culture.

SURREALISM: You have two dancing pandas. The government requires you to take harmonica lessons.

CAPITALISM: You have two cows. You sell one and buy a bull.

1. As a RULER, I would most like to live under | 2. As a COMMONER, I would most like to live under

_____ | _____

3. What's the reasoning behind your answer to #2?

Ch. 21   **ANIMAL FARM**   **Comrade** _____
                        Four legs good... two legs bad

1. What is the original name of the farm?

_____

2. Who does Old Major declare to be the enemy of all animals? | 3. Who did Marx say was the
                                                              | enemy in real life?
                                                              |
_____

4. List two reasons why the animals rebelled | 5. List a reason why peasants and workers in
against Farmer Jones: | Russia started resenting the Czar:
                                                 |
   1) |
                                                 |
   2) |
                                                 |
_____

6. Note two of the seven rules Old Major makes for the animals:

1)   2)

_____

7. How does Napoleon (Lenin) take control of | 8. What does Napoleon use the TV for?
the farm? |
                                              |
                                              |
_____

9. Who gets the milk and the apples? _____

10. Find two examples of Napoleon's propaganda:

1)   2)

11. How is Boxer like a real life Russian peasant | 12. What kind of slogans do Squealer and the
or even GULAG prisoner? | other commissars come up with?
                                                  |
                                                  |
                                                  |
                                                  |
                                                  |
_____

13. What happens to Napoleon at the end of the movie? | 14. What happened that was similar in
                                                      | 1989?
                                                      |
                                                      |
                                                      |

Ch. 21   ANIMAL FARM   Comrade _____

At some point, "Four legs good… two legs bad!" became, "Some animals are more equal than others."

In America, we believe this country was founded as a great experiment in politics based on Enlightenment values like individual rights to life, liberty and property. The American Republic built itself up during the 19th century, and by the time of the communist revolution in Russia in 1917, was already a prosperous counterweight to socialism. At the time *Animal Farm* was written by George Orwell in 1945, the revolution in Russia was already 28 years in the making. It was another kind of experiment in politics and order, one that wasn't honoring- in Orwell's mind- the sovereignty of the individual. Instead, as communism comes from community, it subsumed the individual to the state, which under Lenin and Stalin was supposed to "guide the people to full communism," then wither away. It was also tasked, under Lenin, with spreading communism to other countries. In *Animal Farm*, the animals and people mirror real life people and events. **Your job is to figure out what in the movie occurs that mirrors these real life people and events!**

What was the feeling many in the Eastern Bloc had when communism finally ended (1989-1991)? Narrator: *"For years we had been hiding under oppression. Hiding from Napoleon's spies. But now nature was washing away the disease. I always knew, as with all things built on the wrong foundations, the farm would one day crumble. At last the wait was over. The poisonous cement which held Napoleon's evil dream together was being washed away. I could taste it in the water. I was old, I was almost blind, but I could still remember."*

Situation in Real Life   *Situation in the Movie*

1. European royals and industrialists are noted for allegedly mistreating workers and peasants, giving rise to a class consciousness in some intellectuals who sense it as oppression.

2. Karl Marx has a dream of universal brotherhood where all people are equal. He identifies the feudal lords of old and the capitalist owners of his own day as enemies. He writes the *Communist Manifesto*, outlining the idea that private property should be abolished and the capitalist order overthrown.

3. European royal families are related, but still competitive with each other. As one country gains in power, the others must keep up. With various bad harvests, and in order to support the foundation of society, workers and may have to work harder, and leaders borrow money.

4. The bourgeois classes have parties and live a life of relative prosperity and increasing decadence, oblivious to the idea that a class consciousness is forming among the workers and peasants, especially in Russia.

5. *The Internationale* is a song written to express the Marxist dream of capitalist overthrow, where the proletarians gain 'freedom,' by taking control of the means of production, getting rid of the rich, and living the dream.

6. In 1905, the Czar's troops fired into a crowd on 'Bloody Sunday,' which sparked a socialist revolution that led to reforms, but a decade of uncertainty followed, where the wealthy bourgeois classes didn't know what to expect.

7. During WWI, people increasingly believe the Czar is neglecting the country. They hold up signs for 'Land, Bread and Peace.' These signs are ignored, and people are seeing WWI as the "Czar's war." Peasants are hungry.

8. The Czar takes a trip to visit the front, and the *February Revolution* occurs. He returns to St. Petersburg to find himself out of a job (and a throne). A Provisional government under Kerensky forms to "feed the people."

9. They fail. The *October Revolution* sees Lenin's armed Bolsheviks storm the Winter Palace, take over the government, and exile the Czar and leaders. _____

10. Other European leaders fear communism might spread to their countries too, just as their ancestors once feared the Enlightenment/French Revolution. _____

11. Dedicated communists look to Lenin, Trotsky and Stalin to guide them to a new ideological life. Old Russia is abolished, country's name is changed to the Soviet Union, which is a name meaning 'Union of Councils.' _____

12. The Red Terror begins, as peasants raid the homes of the former rich 'to see how they lived,' and looted and killed many of their owners, a depicted *Dr. Zhivago,* a movie about the time from a book by Boris Pasternak. _____

13. The communists unveil a new symbol: the Hammer & Sickle. _____

14. The communists start realizing how to use propaganda to indoctrinate young people to serve as loyalists, secret police, and enforcers of their will. _____

15. The Russian Civil War breaks out, as the 'Reds' (communists) fight and defeat the 'Whites' (anti-communists) who are backed by neighboring countries. Bolshevik leaders debate international revolution vs. socialism in one country. _____

16. After Lenin died, Stalin ruled, exiled Trotsky, instituted policies such as Five Year Plans, work quotas, and began the repressions associated with the Cheka and later NKVD- secret police forces. _____

17. Communist Party members give themselves privileges denied to ordinary people in a society that is supposed to have equality as its primary aim. The police root out dissenters and send them to gulag prison camps in Siberia. _____

18. Lenin's body is embalmed and displayed in Red Square in Moscow, while Stalin and the commissars bend Marxist principles to their own will. Commissar for Foreign Affairs (Maxim Litvinov) works out Anglo-Soviet trade. _____

19. Hitler criticizes Britain for trading with the Soviets, arguing Stalin will steal the goods from ordinary people to trade to the British, embezzle the money, and export communism to other European countries. _____

20. A new anthem is written to replace *The Internationale,* glorifying the Soviet Union and its leaders, containing the line: "As great Lenin illuminated our path; So we are raised by Stalin to be true to the people." _____

21. In the *Great Purge,* Stalin has 'traitors' arrested, even from his own party, and put on trial in kangaroo courts. Most were executed or sent to Siberia to die mining minerals in gulag prison camps. The people suffered. _____

22. Even believers in communism could now see that the Soviet Union was a totalitarian state. Of the hard workers, the ordinary people who already suffered so long, millions were sent to certain slaughter in gulag prisons or the army. _____

23. The British and Americans pay Stalin to keep fighting WWII, and provide him weapons. The Allies eventually do win. They meet at Tehran, Yalta & Potsdam. _____

24. Stalin dies. Decades pass, and in 1991, the USSR also died. Russians begin rebuilding their culture after 70 years of state-sponsored socialist terror. _____

Ch. 21   TOTALITARIAN GOVERNMENT   Person _____

So... should we burn books advocating censorship?

Absolute monarchs of the past, like Louis XIV or Peter the Great, would have blushed at the degree to which modern dictators and party leaders are able to control their societies. The rulers of the past had no access to modern forms of communication (to spread propaganda) or surveillance (to monitor their subjects). Even though they are different in their goals, the fascism of the far right and the communism of the far left had some similarities in the sense that they evolved *totalitarian* forms of government that emphasized state control over more aspects of society and the life of individual citizens than is usual in democratic countries like the United States or Great Britain. Examine the choices below, and match the form of government with the item in question by drawing a line from one to the other:

Form of Government   **Concept / Goal**

1) What is the goal of society?

Communism---   ---Form a strong national community that can compete in the world-jungle

Democracy----   ---Form a classless society in which all people are equal and work together

Fascism--------   ---Allow people to vote for representatives who will guard their natural rights

2) What are the symbols of society?

Communism---   ---Hammer and sickle representing the workers and peasants, red stars

Democracy----   ---Roman eagle, fasces, swastika, Viking runes, Nordic crosses

Fascism--------   ---Statue of Liberty, American eagle, Union Jack, red, white and blue

3) Who 'loses out' under this form of government?

Communism---   ---People whose opinions are in the minority, if their rights are not protected

Democracy----   ---Ethnic and religious minority groups since they are seen as disruptive to unity

Fascism--------   ---People 'against the revolution' who favor individual rights and a free market

4) Who are the historical leaders of this type of government?

Communism---   ---Cleisthenes of Athens, John Locke, Thomas Jefferson, Franklin Roosevelt

Democracy----   ---Karl Marx, Vladimir Lenin, Josef Stalin, Mao Zedong, Fidel Castro

Fascism--------   ---Benito Mussolini, Adolf Hitler, Francisco Franco, Eugene Térre'blanche

5) Relationship of radio, TV, news and other media to the state:

Communism---   ---Limited exchange of ideas, monitored by the state, burning of decadent books

Democracy----   ---Free exchange of ideas in the press and in public life, right to criticize

Fascism--------   ---Limited exchange of ideas, monitored by the state, burning of decadent books

6) What are the classic slogans of this form of government?

Communism---   ---One People, One State, One Leader! / Blood and Soil!

Democracy----   ---Workers of the world, unite! / From each according to ability, to each according to need

Fascism--------   ---No taxation without representation! / Give me liberty, or give me death!

7) What is human nature?

Communism---   ---Everyone is due the natural rights of life, liberty and the pursuit of happiness

Democracy----   ---Races & self-interested ethnoreligious divisions exist, build nations / cultures

Fascism--------   ---All people are equal, so class, race, wealth and national divisions are irrelevant

8) What is the role of the nation in people's lives?

Communism---   ---It is a collection of individuals who vote for their own and the common good

Democracy----   ---It is the very embodiment of the collective will of the ethnic group that made it

Fascism--------   --- It has no relevance, all countries should be abolished and humanity made one

So far, what is *similar* about fascism and communism? _____

9) What are key elements that inform this type of government?

Communism---   ---Nationalism, social-darwinist outlook, meritocracy, gender roles, militarism

Democracy----   ---No private property, collectivism, shared ownership of means of production

Fascism--------   ---Free market economics, free speech and exchange of ideas, individualism

10) What is the relationship of religious and spiritual life to the government?

Communism---   ---State enforced atheism, organized religion banned as "opiate of the masses"

Democracy----   ---Freedom of religion and belief, emphasis on secular humanism in public space

Fascism--------   ---Government support of a national religion with a focus on civic pride

11) Major are the major literary works explaining this form of government?

Communism---   ---*Treatise on Government* (Locke), *Wealth of Nations* (Smith), *On Liberty* (Mill)

Democracy----   ---*Mein Kampf* (Hitler), *Myth of the 20th Century* (Rosenberg), *Lightning and Sun* (Devi)

Fascism--------   ---*Communist Manifesto* (Marx), *Capital* (Marx), *Eros and Civilization* (Marcuse)

Do you think today's 'democratic' governments are getting more or less totalitarian as time goes on? Why?

Video Search: *Should We Fight Mein Kampf?* | Do you think *Mein Kampf* should be banned? If so, what
                                                               | other books should be banned?

What is the controversy surrounding *Mein Kampf* today? |

Ch. 21   RUSSIAN SECURITY TERMS   Translator_____
This seems Orwellian

Cosmonaut   *Agitprop*   *Duma*   *Nomenklatura*   *KGB*   *NKVD*   *FSB*

Okhrana   *Oprichnina*   *Politburo*   *Kolkhoz*   *Cheka*   *NEP*   *Samizdat*   *Kulak*   *Gulag*

Perestroika & Glasnost   *Spetsnaz*   *Commissar*   *Bolshevik*   *Apparatchik*   *Gavlit*

_____ Propaganda that is generated and delivered to agitate (effect) a social belief

_____ An astronaut in Russian, Yuri Gagarin was one, the first person in space

_____ Abolished by the communists, it was and now is again the Russian parliament house

_____ From 'Bolshinstvo,' meaning 'majority,' this was the communist party of Lenin

_____ From 'apparatus,' this was someone involved in the Soviet state machinery

_____ First communist political police, the *Commission for Combating Counter-Revolution*

_____ An official of the communist regime, responsible for political education

_____ *Federalnaya Sluzhba Bezopasnosti*, the modern day Federal Security Service

_____ *Komitet Gosudarstvennoy Bezopasnosti*, the Committee for State Security in USSR

_____ Term for a collective farm

_____ Prosperous peasants in czarist times, were liquidated under the Bolsheviks (Holodomor)

_____ *Novaya Ekonomicheskaya Politika*, the New Economic Policy enacted by Lenin in '21

_____ *Narodniy Komissariat Vnetrennikh Del*, the People's Commissariat for Internal Affairs

_____ Meaning 'List of Names' this was the Soviet elite who occupied the positions of power

_____ Czarist secret police, called *Protection Section*, which guarded the Czar & staff

_____ The domestic policy and security force of Ivan the Terrible, enforced his reign

_____ "Restructuring" and "Openness" the Gorbachev reforms of the 1980s _____

_____ The policymaking committee in the USSR, "Political Bureau". Unelected.

_____ 'Special Purpose Regiments' similar to Einsatzgruppen or Afrikaner Kommandos

_____ District or provincial assemblies under the later czars, were converted into soviets

_____ Notorious prison for political or criminal prisoners in cold and difficult regions

_____ Illegal publication against the regime or its ideology, you got in a lot of trouble for this

_____ Main Administration for the Protection of **Literary** & State Secrets, Orwellian

Ch. 21 — **LYRICS OF THE COMMUNIST LEFT** — Worker _____
The Интернационал

THE INTERNATIONALE

Stand up, damned of the Earth
Stand up, prisoners of starvation
Reason thunders in its volcano
This is the eruption of the end.
Of the past, let's make a clean slate
Enslaved masses, stand up, stand up!
The world is about to change its foundation
We are nothing, let us be all.
This is the final struggle
Let us group together, and tomorrow
The Internationale
Will be the human race.

There are no supreme saviors
Neither God, nor Caesar, nor tribune.
Producers, let us save ourselves,
Decree the common salvation.
So that the thief expires,
So that the spirit be pulled from its prison,
Let us fan our forge ourselves
And strike the iron while it is hot.
This is the final struggle
Let us group together, and tomorrow
The Internationale
Will be the human race.

Workers, peasants, we are
The great party of laborers.
The earth belongs only to men;
The idle will go to reside elsewhere.
How much of our flesh have they consumed?

After the Reds won the Russian Civil War and the Soviet system became entrenched, Lenin looked outward to spread the communist revolution to all the workers of the world.

After the failed invasion of Poland and Germany in 1920, however, the Soviets adopted a policy of "Socialism in One Country," postponing the worldwide revolution for a later date.

1) In the lyrics to the *Internationale*, written by a member of the Paris Commune in 1871, what is "the *Internationale*" as a movement?

_____

2) What did the *Internationale* as a movement think about religion and freedom of religion?

_____

3) Check the lyrics for at least five direct actions the song encourages its followers to take, to further the cause of the *Internationale*:

a)

b)

c)

Ch. 21 — HOW TO BE A GOOD COLLECTIVIST

Oh boy an old Soviet cartoon! There wouldn't be any weird stuff in something like that, right? I mean, It's for kids, right?
Search: **Propaganda Result of the XII party congress Russian cartoon**

4. What kind of propaganda messages do you see in this Soviet cartoon? How are capitalists portrayed and what are people encouraged to do?

5. If you saw cartoons played on TV with a political message, would you want your own kids watching it?

Ch. 21 COMPARING CHINESE & SOVIET COMMUNISM

Introducing the new boss, same as the old. Or worse.

Soviet and Chinese communism shared some similarities but were also quite different. Figure out 'which was which' using the following word bank:

1917 & 1949   *Alexander Solzhenitsyn & Harry Wu*   *Collectivization & Great Leap Forward*

Cultural Revolution & Great Purge   *Great Chinese Famine & Holodomor*   *'Guomindang' & 'Whites'*

Laogai & Gulag   *Lenin & Mao*   *Puyi & Nikolai II*   *Perestroika & Glasnost & Open Door Policy*

Socialism with a Human Face & Socialism with Chinese Characteristics   *Tiananmen Square & Berlin Wall*

_____ 1. The October Revolution brought communism to Russia in this year, while the victory of Mao's forces over Chinese nationalists occurred four years after WWII.

_____ 2. This was China's anti-communist opposition under Sun Yat-sen and Chiang Kai-shek, while these were Russian anti-communists under Alexander Kolchak and Lavr Kornilov.

_____ 3. Revolutionary leaders who established Soviet / Chinese communism.

_____ 4. Deposed and imprisoned Qing ruler, the 'Last Emperor' of China, vs. the dethroned Czar of Russia, last of the Romanov Dynasty, who was executed with his family.

_____ 5. Soviet order to eliminate privately held peasant farms and unite them into 'kolkhozes' in the late-1920s, similar to this movement in Mao's China in the 1950s and early-1960s.

_____ 6. 10 million or so Soviets died in this state-sponsored forced famine in 1933, while 15 million or more died in this event following collectivization in 1959 in China.

_____ 7. Stalin enforced ideological conformity and had 'enemies of the revolution' arrested and sent to Siberia or killed, including a wave of arrests of suspected traitors to his rule. Similarly, China had a forced indoctrination program in the 1960s, resulting in summary executions.

_____ 8. Chinese re-education and labor camps strewn throughout the country vs. Soviet prison camp archipelago in which millions of people were worked, starved or frozen to death.

_____ 9. Famous dissident against the communist system's excesses, wrote *One Day in the Life of Ivan Denisovich* vs. he who daringly exposed China's prison system in *Bitter Winds*.

_____ 10. Slogan for reform in Czechoslovakia in 1968, which hoped Stalinist-style repression could give way to a 'kinder' political situation, vs. Chinese economic reform under Deng Xiaoping in which elements of market economics were grafted onto China to increase prosperity.

_____ 11. Terms for 'Restructuring' and 'Openness' in the Soviet Union of the 1980s vs. Deng's policy of allowing foreign companies to invest in China and build factories there.

_____ 12. 'Moment of truth' in China in 1989, when the government ran over protesters and students with tanks, killing a few hundred but showing everyone 'The System' would not fall, as it did in Eastern Europe when this barrier between East and West Germany was bashed down.

Ch. 21 **DECADE BY DECADE** Reaper _____
DEATH TOLLS OF THE 20TH CENTURY

Conflicts and disasters of 20th Earth: *Make a horizontal bar chart using boxes for each million dead- .1 = 100,000, 1 = a million:*

		.1	1	5	10	15	20
Russo-Japanese War	40,000						
Greek Massacre	500,000						
Armenian Massacre	1,500,000						
World War I – military	11,000,000						
World War I – civilian	7,000,000						
Russian Civil War	3,500,000						
Russian Famine of 1921	6,000,000						
Ukrainian Holodomor	5,000,000						
Soviet Great Purge	1,600,000						
Spanish Civil War	1,000,000						
World War II – military	21,000,000						
World War II – civilian	20,000,000						
Vietnamese Famine	2,000,000						
Bengalese Famine	3,000,000						
Indonesian Famine	2,000,000						
Jewish Holocaust*	5,100,000						
Polish non-Jewish losses*	2,900,000						
German Repatriation*	2,000,000						
Chinese Civil War	2,000,000						
Korean War	1,500,000						
Soviet Gulags	1,900,000						
Great Leap Forward	22,000,000						
Vietnam War	1,500,000						
Nigerian Civil War	2,000,000						
Bangladesh War	1,000,000						
Cambodian Genocide	2,000,000						
Soviet-Afghan War	3,000,000						
Ethiopian Famine	1,000,000						
Iran-Iraq War	1,000,000						
Sudanese Civil War	1,500,000						
Rwandan Genocide	800,000						
Congolese Civil War	4,000,000						
September 11 attacks	3,000						
War on Terror	600,000 +						

*Subtracted out from other WWII deaths

The costliest **decade** of the 20th century in terms of preventable loss of life was _____

Democide (literally 'extermination of people') is when your own government murders you and it's *not* based on race. If it is based on race, it's *genocide*. If another government murders you in times of peace, it's called assassination. In times of war it's, well, war, and you're an enemy (combatant or civilian). But if a cop or hitman shows up at night and shoots you because his boss in the government told him to, because you're of a certain class, did something they object to, or are just *you*, it's democide. A few of the above slaughters are democides. Can you identify one or more (hint: 43 million died under Stalin- many by democide):

Ch. 21 **EVERY ATOMIC BOMB** _____

Search: Time Lapse Atomic Bomb. Watch the 14 min. time-lapse video first all the way through, then the second, 3 minute one to answer the questions

1. The Manhattan Project was finally successful on July 16, 1945, when the first atomic bomb was exploded by scientists in this U.S. state:

_____

2. In August, the U.S. dropped *Little Boy* and then *Fat Man* on these two Japanese cities, killing perhaps 200,000 people but obtaining surrender

_____

3. After the war, bombs continued to be tested in places like Bikini Atoll, in this ocean:

_____

4. In 1949, this other Cold War superpower became the second country to obtain the bomb:

_____

5. Now atomic testing really picks up, and this third power gets in on the action: _____

6. Over Eniwetok atoll in the Pacific, the U.S. blasted this new kind of bomb in 1952: _____

7. For the rest of the 1950s, atomic tests by the nuclear powers continued. Rounding to the nearest hundred, about how many total nukes were exploded in the fifteen years since WWII? ____

8. Why would France explode its first atomic bomb in the Sahara Desert and not somewhere else?

_____

9. What still remains unique about the 1961 detonation of *Tsar Bomba*, the Soviet super bomb?

_____

10. The closest the world probably ever came to nuclear armageddon was during the Cuban Missile Crisis of the early-1960s. By the end of it in 1964, the total count in the arms race skyrocketed to 600 detonations. At this time the Nuclear Test-Ban Treaty came into effect, as scientists demanded governments not launch bombs into space and blow them up there. Ever heard of an EMP? That is how they are caused. Why is it good that they did it over the Pacific?

_____

11. Was the political ideology of the 5th country to achieve atomic status closer to that of the USA or the USSR?

_____

12. In 1974, this country detonated "Smiling Buddha":

_____

13. The Cold War officially ended in 1991. Note the five countries in order of how many they detonated in total:

1) _____ 2) _____ 3) _____ 4) _____ 5) _____

14. The "Islamic Bomb" was obtained when this became the first Muslim country to get it _____

15. Note the nuclear status of these other countries:

Israel   *South Africa*   *Ukraine*   *North Korea*   *Iran*

Ch. 21   PRESIDENTS AND PREMIERS OF THE COLD WAR

The following people led their respective superpowers

Place the nine Cold War presidents in correct chronological order according to the clues:

George H.W. Bush   Jimmy Carter   Dwight D. Eisenhower   Gerald Ford
Lyndon B. Johnson   John F. Kennedy   Richard Nixon   Ronald Reagan
Harry S. Truman

1. _____ *Decided to drop the atomic bomb & won reelection during Berlin Airlift*

2. _____ *Two-term war hero who dealt with Suez Crisis in the halcyonic 1950s*

3. _____ *Inspired mission to land on the Moon, faced down Soviets in Cuba*

4. _____ *Promoted 'Great Society' programs at home, Vietnam War abroad*

5. _____ *Visited Mao's China during Cold War, infamous for Watergate scandal*

6. _____ *Pardoned predecessor, was not elected president, presided over Détente*

7. _____ *Peanut farmer, focused on Mideast Peace and government programs*

8. _____ *Popular actor-president whose hardline stance helped end the Cold War*

9. _____ *Sent U.S. troops to Iraq in Gulf War, inaugurated 'New World Order'*

Place the six Soviet premiers in correct chronological order according to the clues:

Yuri Andropov   Lenoid Brezhnev   Konstantin Chernenko
Mikhail Gorbachev   Nikita Khrushchev   Josef Stalin

1. _____ *Led Soviets in WWII, sent people to Gulags, infamous strategist*

2. _____ *Led Soviets in Space Race, faced Kennedy during Cuban Missile Crisis*

3. _____ *Presided Soviet Union during Détente, but continued totalitarian state*

4. _____ *Hardliner 'butcher of Budapest' who only led 15 months before dying*

5. _____ *Continued Afghanistan war, died of alcohol and smoking 11 months in*

6. _____ *Presided over Perestroika and Glasnost, popular but losing ground...*

Crash Course World History #39. Watch and identify the following:

7. What was in the Secret Compartment:

8. What the open letter was about:

9. What the 'big lesson' was at the end:

Ch. 21 COLD WAR MAP
The places to match the events

A. 1946 – Churchill's **'Iron Curtain'** speech warns of Europe dividing into East and West. Draw it.

B. 1947 – Truman Doctrine proclaimed, aid sent to Greece and Turkey. Put weapons in **Turkey**.

C. 1948 – **Berlin** Blockade triggers airlift to supply Berliners with food. Later wall is built. Label it.

D. 1949 – NATO is formed with the U.S. as its leader. Mark the **U.S.** and write NATO there.

E. 1949 – Mao Zedong declares the foundation of the PRC. Mark **China** communist.

F. 1949 – Soviets declare their zone of Germany to be the **GDR**, a communist state. Split n' mark.

G. 1950 – ROC (Republic of China) flees to **Taiwan** and considers itself legitimate Chinese gov't.

H. 1950 – Korean War begins, which splits **Korea** into communist north and free market south.

I. 1953 – CIA and MI6 overthrows **Iran's** PM Mosaddeq because they nationalized its oil industry.

J. 1955 – **India** declares itself 'nonaligned' in the Cold War, along with Indonesia, Egypt & Ghana.

K. 1955 – Soviets declare Warsaw Pact alliance. Mark the **USSR** and write 'Warsaw Pact' there.

L. 1956 – Anti-communist uprising in **Hungary** is crushed by Soviet tanks.

M. 1957 – Sputnik launched from Baikonur Cosmodrome in Soviet **Kazakhstan**, starts Space Race.

N. 1962 – Soviets send nuclear weapons to **Cuba**- standoff is known as Cuban Missile Crisis.

O. 1964 – Gulf of Tonkin incident leads to Johnson announcing U.S. 'involvement' in **Vietnam**.

P. 1967 – **Israel** fights Arab States in the Six-Day War, occupied West Bank, Golan and Gaza.

Q. 1968 – Prague Spring tries to liberalize **Czechoslovakia** and is crushed by Soviet tanks.

R. 1969 – Apollo 11 launches from Cape Canaveral, **Florida** and lands on the Moon on July 20th.

S. 1972 – Ferdinand Marcos declares martial law in **Philippines** and confiscates all firearms.

T. 1974 – Pro-West dictator of **Ethiopia** Haile Selassie is ousted by Marxist junta.

U. 1978 – Soviets invade **Afghanistan** and communize it, then fight Osama bin Laden's forces.

V. 1981 – Martial law declared in **Poland** to stop Solidarity Trade Union's popularity.

W. 1981 – CIA supports anti-Sandinista Contras in **Nicaragua** using 'black ops' Iranian sales.

X. 1986 – Chernobyl nuclear reactor in **Ukraine** melts down, worst accident in history.

Y. 1986 – Reykjavik Summit in **Iceland** sees Reagan and Gorbachev agree to cooperate.

Z. 1991 – Yeltsin and other leaders meet in Minsk, **Belarus** and declare CIS. Gorbachev resigns.

Ch. 21 **BALANCE OF TERROR** Brinksman _____
Would you fire?

1. The Star Trek episode *Balance of Terror (S1-E15)* was written to reflect Cold War paranoia about the kind of *brinksmanship* that led to the Cuban Missile Crisis and events beyond. The episode was written in 1966, only four years after the missile crisis, and despite the White House-Kremlin direct phone line, people were still very paranoid about the possibility of a nuclear world war. Additionally, this TV show about humanity's future in space was being aired in prime time at the height of the Apollo Moon program, so reality mirrored it. People connected the events of the day in space as the first steps toward the realization of the world depicted on *Star Trek*. Do you think humanity will ever become a multi-planet species? If so, about what decade?

_____

2. What happens to break up the nice wedding ceremony happening on board the Enterprise?

a. The ship was attacked

b. The bride said, "on second thought, forget this"

c. A red alert claxon signaled an emergency

3. Kirk taking the Enterprise into the Romulan neutral zone is most like:

a. The Soviet Union sending advisors to Angola

b. An American sub surfacing near Murmansk

c. A proxy war in Nicaragua won by the socialists

4. Technological advancement in arms and equipment was a major area of Cold War competition. Who can build the best fighter jet? Missile sub? Battleship? Radar jamming equipment? Stealth aircraft? What was the big technological breakthrough the Romulans made that gave them a big advantage?

5. Romulans look like:

    a. Klingons

    b. Vulcans

6. What clever trick does the Romulan captain play on the Enterprise?

7. To save the day, what clever trick does Kirk play in return on the Romulan ship?

8. "Sportsmanship" is becoming an old-fashioned concept. A troll or a cyberbully is not someone who will stand up against another person or team face-to-face in competition. Cheating in sports or games is not sportsmanlike either. To be a true sportsman, one must value the integrity of the game itself even above the outcome of the game. It is to congratulate the better team, even if the loss was bitter or even heartbreaking. The ultimate is even if it is one's last game. Describe the Romulan captain's sportsmanship at the end:

_____

Ch. 21   WHO WON THE SPACE RACE?   First person _____
...to finish this assignment?

Technically, the first Space Race began in 1957 when the Soviets launched the Sputnik satellite, opening the Space Age, and ended in 1975 when the Americans and Soviets declared a truce. They symbolized this truce by sending an Apollo spacecraft into orbit where it docked with a Soyuz spacecraft, and the astronauts opened the hatch and shook hands with the cosmonauts in a spirit of friendship. So who 'won' the 'Space Race'? Below, determine by the name who accomplished what, then shade Soviet accomplishments in *red* and American in *blue.* Finally, count them up!

Year	Accomplishment	Who/What		
1957	first satellite	*Sputnik I*	→ __**Red**__	← shade/write
1957	first dog in space	Laika, on *Sputnik 2*	_____	
1958	first scientific discovery	*Explorer I* found Van Allen Belts	_____	
1959	first Moon flyby	*Luna I*	_____	
1960	first return of living things	Belka and Strelka on *Sputnik 2*	_____	
1961	first primate in space	Ham, on *Mercury 5*	_____	
1961	first man in space	Yuri Gagarin, on *Vostok I*	_____	
1961	first piloted spacecraft	Alan Shepherd on *Freedom 7*	_____	
1961	first Venus flyby	*Venera I*	_____	
1963	first woman in space	Valentina Tereshkova on *Vostok 6*	_____	
1964	first crew in space	*Voskhod I*	_____	
1965	first spacewalk	Alexei Leonov on *Voskhod 2*	_____	
1965	first Mars flyby	*Mariner 4*	_____	
1965	first orbital rendezvous	*Gemini 6* and *7*	_____	
1966	first Moon lander	*Luna 9*	_____	
1966	first orbital docking	*Gemini 8* and *Agena Target Vehicle*	_____	
1966	first Moon orbiter	*Luna 10*	_____	
1968	first ultraviolet observatory	NASA-*OAO-2*	_____	
1969	first crew exchange	*Soyuz 4* and *5*	_____	
1968	first men to circle Moon	*Apollo 8*	_____	
1969	first man on the Moon	Neil Armstrong on *Apollo 11*	_____	
1970	first rescue mission	*Apollo 13*	_____	
1970	first Moon sample return	*Luna 16*	_____	
1970	first Moon rover	*Lunokhod 1*	_____	
1970	first X-ray observatory	NASA-*Uhuru*	_____	
1970	first Venus lander	*Venera 7*	_____	
1971	first space station	*Salyut 1*	_____	
1971	first car driven on Moon	*Apollo 15*	_____	
1971	first Mars orbiter	*Mariner 9*	_____	
1972	first gamma-ray observatory	NASA-*SAS 2*	_____	
1973	first Jupiter flyby	*Pioneer 10*	_____	
1974	first Mercury flyby	*Mariner 10*	_____	
1975	first USA-USSR rendezvous	*Apollo-Soyuz*	_____	

Technically, at this point, the first Space Race ends. At this point, not only does the focus shift to cooperation instead of competition, but new space agencies appear in other countries. Presently, the following space agencies all operate satellites: Australia (ASA), China (CNSA), Europe (ESA), India (IRSO), Israel (ISA), Iran (ISA), Japan (JAXA), North Korea (NADA), South Korea (KARI), and Ukraine (NSAU.

1. Which country had the most 'first' accomplishments?   *a. USA*   *b. USSR*   *c. Tie*

2. What accomplishment do you think was the most amazing of all of them, and why?

1975	first Venus orbiter	*Venera 9*
1976	first Sun flyby	*Helios 2*
1976	first Mars lander	*Viking 1*
1979	first Saturn flyby	*Pioneer 11*
1981	first space shuttle	*Columbia*
1983	first infrared observatory	NASA-*IRAS*
1984	first free-floating spacewalk	McCandless, *STS-41*
1986	first Uranus flyby	*Voyager 2*
1986	first long-term space station	*Mir*
1986	first comet flyby	Roscosmos-*Vega 1*
1989	first Neptune flyby	*Voyager 2*
1989	first microwave telescope	NASA-*COBE*
1990	first optical observatory	*Hubble ST*
1991	first asteroid flyby	*Galileo*
1992	first Sun orbiter	*Ulysses*
1995	first Jupiter orbiter	*Galileo*
1997	first radio observatory	JAXA-*HALCA*
1997	first Mars rover	*Pathfinder*
1998	first international station	*ISS*
2000	first asteroid orbiter	ESA-*Shoemaker*
2001	first asteroid lander	ESA-*Shoemaker*
2001	first tourist in space	Mark Shuttleworth
2004	first Saturn orbiter	ESA-*Cassini*
2004	first Titan lander	ESA-*Huygens*
2006	first comet sample return	NASA-*Stardust*
2009	first exoplanet observatory	*Kepler Telescope*
2010	first asteroid sample return	JAXA-*Hayabusa*
2011	first Mercury orbiter	*Messenger*
2012	first interstellar probe	*Voyager 1*
2014	first comet lander	ESA-*Rosetta*
2015	first Ceres orbiter	*Dawn*
2015	first Pluto flyby	*New Horizons*
2015	first soft landing of rockets	SpaceX *Falcon-9*
2015	first food grown in space	NASA/JAXA on *ISS*
2018	first asteroid rover	JAXA-*Hayabusa 2*
2019	first food grown on Moon	CNSA-*Chang'e 4*

3. From the beginning till today, go back and find all the planets and objects that have been visited to varying degrees:

a. *Flyby:*

_____

b. *Orbited:*

_____

c. *Landed on:*

_____

d. *Rover:*

_____

e. *Sample Return:*

_____

f. *Visited by people:*

_____

4. Below is the Electromagnetic Spectrum. The shortest wavelengths are on the left and they get bigger to the right. Put a check into the areas we can observe:

Gamma Rays	*X-Rays*	*UV Rays*	*Optical-Visible*	*Infrared*	*Microwave*	*Radio*

5. Which part of the EM spectrum gives people sunburns?

_____

6. Which part heats up food and carries cell phone signals?

_____

7. The shorter the wave, the more dangerous to people. Which is the most dangerous wave in the universe?

_____

8. Which waves are all around us, invisible, yet completely harmless

_____

9. If you were advising NASA, what would you suggest to them we should do next?

Ch. 21   **THE WORST GAME OF CHICKEN. EVER.**   Duck _____
Don't flinch. Unless doing so would keep the world from being destroyed.

1. What kinds of school 'threats' do people worry about and practice drills for today? List some:

_____

During the Cold War, it was the threat of nuclear war that freaked people out. In fact, some of the very first school documentaries were actually training videos on what to do if you saw a mushroom cloud nearby (if possible, see a quick clip of the *Tsar Bomba*, the biggest nuke ever).

Clip 1: Duck and Cover (1951).

2. What advice does the video give to students?	3. Was this good advice in your considered opinion? Why or why not?

Clip 2: U.S. Office of Civil Defense Fallout *When and How to Protect Yourself.*

4. What is 'fallout' and what does the government tell you to do if some is around?	5. Do you think videos like these were made to calm people, or scare them?

On a 1-10 scale, people during the 1950s were at nuclear scare level 7. People in the 1960s during the Cuban Missile Crisis were at scare level 10, while in the 1970s during détente they were at scale level 5. In the 1980s it heated up again to scare level 7, then the Cold War ended.

6. Where would you rate *your* scare level today?

   1   2   3   4   5   6   7   8   9   10

7. In the movie *Sum of All Fears*, released just after Sept. 11, 2001, an American city is nuked. What city?

   a. Washington   b. Baltimore   c. Miami

This came closest to actually happening during the Cuban Missile Crisis in 1963. When Fidel Castro and his communist revolutionaries overthrew the Cuban government in 1957, Moscow couldn't have been happier. Khrushchev rolled out the red carpet (get it, red?) for Castro, and the two struck a deal. The Soviets were aiming (get it, aiming?) to put nukes close to America, and what better place than Cuba, only 90 miles from Key West? This would have most likely been bad for world security, but the Americans were not innocent in all this. Most Americans didn't know, but the U.S. had places nukes of its own near the Soviet border, just across the Black Sea in Turkey! In fact, from his Yalta dacha, Premier Khrushchev could point into the sea and say to his friends, "You can't see them, but they (the American nukes) are pointed right at us".

Clip 3: TED Cuban Missile Crisis Jordan. | Clip 4: CNN Cuban Missile Crisis Counterfactual.

8. How is Vasily Arkhipov an 'unsung hero'?	9. What were the (unrealized) U.S. plans for war?

Ch. 21 TEAR DOWN THIS WALL!
Reagan and the End of the Cold War

Clip 1: **Hungarian Tragedy 1956.** When Hungarian communist leader Imre Nagy criticized the Soviets for being too rigid, and announced the withdrawal of Hungary from the Warsaw Pact alliance, what did Khrushchev do to stop them?

_____

Clip 2: **Prague the Sad City 1968.** Filmed in the happy days of relative prosperity before the tanks rolled in, the narrator forebodingly compares the Medieval Karlstejn Castle and Franz Ferdinand's residence to the communist system then in Czechoslovakia. How are these things related- from the Czech perspective- as in, what are they symbols of?

_____

Budapest and Prague are good examples of Brezhnev Doctrine-style interventions: **T   F**

Clip 4: **Reagan tells Soviet Jokes.** Rate Reagan's jokes (1=not funny, 2=don't get it, 3=like it!)

   1)   2)   3)   4)   5)   6)

Clip 5: **Naked Gun Opening Scene.** This world leader was *not* at the Beirut, Lebanon summit:

a. Ayatollah Khomeini   b. Yasser Arafat   c. Mikhail Gorbachev   d. Ronald Reagan   e. Momar Gaddafi   f. Idi Amin

Clip 6: **Let Poland be Poland Solidarity 2.**

What did the workers protesting in the Gdansk shipyard strikes want?	The government responded with martial law. What's that?

Clip 7: **Let Poland be Poland John Paul II.** What values and atmosphere did the pope promote in Poland that worried the communist authorities who had declared martial law?

_____

Clip 8: **Reagan Evil Empire Speech excerpt.** The controversial thing in this speech is that Reagan said:

        a. the Russian people are evil   b. the Soviet government is evil

_____

Clip 9: **American Artifacts Reagan Assassination Attempt Rawhide Down.** Tally which of the six bullets hit where:

Secret service / cops: *Stuff in the background:*   *Reagan:*

Clip 10: **Top Gun Dogfight Scene MiG-28**. Which country (or system?) was able to produce both advanced military equipment like that shown here *and* consumer good for the population in the 1980s?

        a. Soviet communism   *b. American capitalism*

Clip 11: **The Hunt for Red October (1990) - Submarine anthem:** What does Captain Ramius say to the crew that bolsters the argument that, "A rogue sub commander is one of the most dangerous people on the face of the earth?"

Clip 12: **'Soviet March' from 'Command and Conquer'.** What kinds of symbols of communism are present in this display of the military equipment the Soviets were spending state money on?

Clip 13: **Reagan Tear Down this Wall speech at Berlin Wall.** What is the monument in the background of this speech:

    a. Big Ben   *b. Eiffel Tower*   *c. Coliseum*   *d. Brandenburg Gate*

Clip 14: **SDI Strategic Defence Initiative Star Wars.** What was the goal of the SDI program?

Clip 15: **Fall of the Berlin Wall.** Note some motivations on the part of the following during the scenes shown here?

    East Germans: *West Germans:*

Clip 16: **McDonalds in Moscow MPEG**. Globalization and the influences of global capitalism preceded the collapse of the USSR. This clip looks at how McDonald's was able to open in Moscow, a propaganda coup if nothing else. The authorities didn't want it, but people did. As they take you through the McDonald's, note ways it is different than in McDonald's in America:

Clip 17: **Collapse of the Soviet Union 1991.** After the allowance of free elections in Poland and the fall of the Berlin Wall, other countries like Czechoslovakia and Hungary had free elections too. Then Soviet republics started breaking away from the country. What was the final straw in the Soviet Union that ensured its demise and ended the Cold War?

Ch. 22 — INDIA'S POLITICAL ORDER

If some of these seems familiar, you might have been reincarnated. Or you just remember it from a few months ago.

Place the following South Asian political entities in chronological order:

British Crown Colony   *British East India Company Rule*   *Delhi Sultanate & Vijayanagar*

Gupta Dynasty   *Harappa & Mohenjo-Daro*   *Harsha & Chola*   *Mughal Dynasty*

Mauryan Dynasty   *Independent India & Pakistan*   *Vedic Age*

1. These two city-states were the oldest Indus civilizations _____

2. The Aryan migrations brought a new culture to South Asia _____

3. Under Asoka and others, Northern India was united _____

4. This classical dynasty made breakthroughs in mathematics _____

5. Postclassical kingdoms in the subcontinent's north & south _____

6. First Muslim rule in the north, Hindu rule in the south _____

7. Central Asian dynasty under Babur, Akbar, Jahan and others _____

8. 'Corporate conquest,' province by province in 18th century _____

9. The new order following the 1857 Sepoy Rebellion _____

10. Gandhi's dream gave way to those of Nehru & Jinnah _____

Place the following events towards self-rule in South Asia into chronological order 1-10:

____ Bandung Conference is attended by India, a Cold War policy of non-alignment is adopted

____ Day of Direct Action in 1946 sees Muslim riots in favor of a 'vivisection' in which 6,000 die

____ India Act of 1937 doesn't work because 600 princes don't find common ground

____ Indian National Congress (Nehru) and Muslim League (Jinnah) stir for self-rule

____ Mass migration of 10,000,000 in the largest population transfer/ethnic cleansing in history

____ By the end, a million die on the roads from Pakistan to India, and vice-versa

____ Vivisection partitions India, against Gandhi's wishes, into India, Pakistan and East Pakistan

____ Wilson's 14 Points and their lack of realization in India give support to the self-rule coalitions

____ WWI battles show Indians that the 'British bleed too'

____ WWII casts doubt on European imperial rule as a general principle and weakens the British Empire

Ch. 22 DECOLONIZATION IN INDIA & AFRICA

Britain left peacefully. Sort of.

Clip 1: *1947 Indian Independence color.* India set the stage for the *'end of empire.'* While Gandhi desired a united India but was assassinated by a Hindu fundamentalist, Nehru and Jinnah struck a deal.

What was the deal? | What happened on the day of freedom?'

How many people died in the largest population transfer in history? _____

Clip 2: *Ghana's independence 6th March 1957 (~5:54).* The year 1960 is known as the "Year of Africa." The British backed off on the imperial idea, and many African colonies became new nations that year.

Which representatives from the United States came to observe the independence of the Gold Coast colony? | Was the transfer of power from Britain to Kwame Nkrumah peaceful or not?

Sketch the new nation of Ghana's flag at right → → → →

Kwame Nkrumah had a greater vision for Africa, what was it?

Clip 3: *Jomo Kenyatta and the Mau Mau Oath (~9:20).*

Nkrumah and Ghana inspired other African leaders to demand independence. The issue with Kenya was a lot of white settlers from Europe moved there. They built farms and businesses, employing African labor, and saw the colony as a legitimate place for them to live.

What were Kenyatta's Mau Mau group's goals? | What were some ways the British dealt with the Mau Mau Uprising?

Clip 4: *Verwoerd Defines Apartheid.* | **Clip 5: *Report on Rhodesia (~14:47).***

How did the 'architect of apartheid' define the term? | Summarize Ian Smith's, the British and the African Rhodesians' desire in all this:

| 1)   2)   3)

Ch. 22   POSTCOLONIAL CONFLICTS   _____

The fighting never really ends. Is it still on right now? Yup. Are there any signs of it letting up? Nah.

DIRECTIONS: SELECT TWO POSTCOLONIAL CONFLICTS AND RESEARCH THEM ONLINE OR IN AN ENCYCLOPEDIA. SPEND ABOUT 10 MIN. BRIEFING YOURSELF ON EACH ONE.

1. Conflict Name & Timeframe:	2. Conflict Name & Timeframe:
_____	_____
Side 1 vs. *Side 2*	*Side 1* vs. *Side 2*
Political goals *Political goals*	*Political goals* *Political goals*
What were the results of the conflict and what did this result mean for the country/region?	What were the results of the conflict and what did this result mean for the country/region?
Below, sketch a map of the battle zone and label the flashpoint areas relevant in the postcolonial conflict:	Below, sketch a map of the battle zone and label the flashpoint areas relevant in the postcolonial conflict:

ASIA
1946	Day of Direct Action (India)
1947	Partition of India Population Transfer Now
1949	Chinese Civil War
1950	Korean War
1954	Dien Bien Phu
1965	Vietnam War
1971	Bangladesh Liberation
1984	Sikh Uprising (Punjab)

MIDDLE EAST
1948	Israeli War of Independence
1954	Algerian War of Independence
1956	Suez Crisis
1967	Six-Day War
1973	Yom Kippur War
1975	Lebanon Civil War
1977	Libyan-Egyptian War
1979	Soviet-Afghan War
1980	Iran-Iraq War
1981	Iran Hostage Crisis
1987	First Intifada
1990	Gulf War
2000	Second Intifada
2001	9/11/2001
2001	War in Afghanistan
2003	Iraq War
2010	Arab Spring

LATIN AMERICA
1957	Castro Revolution
1961	Bay of Pigs Incident
1962	Cuban Missile Crisis
1967	Guevara Bolivian Revolution
1973	Chilean Coup d'état
1978	Nicaraguan Revolution
1979	Salvadoran Civil War
1982	Falkland Islands War
1983	Guatemalan Civil War
1983	Shining Path of Peru
1984	Nicaragua-Contra War
1984	Anti-Duvalier protest movement
1994	Chiapas Conflict
Now	Mexican Drug War
Now	2014-2017 Venezuelan Protests

POSTCOLONIAL CONFLICTS
(Select two)

AFRICA
1952	Mau Mau Uprising
1960	Congolese Civil War
1970	Biafra-Nigeria Civil War
1974	Ethiopian Civil War
1976	Angolan Socialist War
1976	Soweto Uprising
1977	Mozambique Civil War
1978	Congo-Shaba Wars
1979	Rhodesian Bush War
1990	South African Border War
1990	Namibia Independence
1990	First Liberian Civil War
1991	Eritrea-Ethiopia War
1991	Sierra Leone Civil War
1993	Somali (Black Hawk Down) conflict
1994	Rwandan Genocide
1997	First Congo War
2000	Second Liberian Civil War
2002	Uganda Civil War
2002	Angolan Civil War
2002	Azawed-Niger Insurgency
2003	Darfur Genocide
2003	Second Congo War
2004	Itaba/Gatumba
2005	Sudanese Civil War 2
2010	Chad Civil War
2011	Ivorian Civil War
2012	Tuareg Rebellion

EUROPE
1992	Yugoslav Wars (Serb-Croat / Bosnian)
1996	Chechen War (first, second)
1999	Kosovo War (Serb-KLA)

List is ever-changing. Best idea it to search *List of Ongoing Armed Conflicts* for the latest

Ch. 22 — MATCHING POLITICAL LEADERS AND THEIR GOALS

The following politicians and writers are well known in their countries and to experts... how about to you?

1. _____ **Franz Fanon** a. Iraqi dictator who fought Iran then the U.S. in the Gulf War

2. _____ **Ho Chi Minh** b. Founder of Chinese communism and the *Great Leap Forward*

3. _____ **Gamal Abdel Nasser** c. Shah of Iran overthrown during Iranian Revolution of 1979

4. _____ **Mohandas Gandhi** d. Argued for violent attack on Europeans in colonial territories

5. _____ **Kwame Nkrumah** e. Supported the Day of Direct Action and partition of India

6. _____ **Mao Zedong** f. Leaders of transition of South Africa from white to black rule

7. _____ **Indira Gandhi** g. Signed British statement supporting Jewish state in Palestine

8. _____ **Mohammed R. Pahlavi** h. Anti-French communist independence leader in Vietnam

9. _____ **Muhammad Ali Jinnah** i. Anticolonial Ghanaian who went from jail to president

10. _____ **Saddam Hussein** j. U.S. supported Nicaraguan militarist, replaced by communist

11. _____ **Raul Prebisch** k. Arab nationalist who gained prestige during Suez Crisis

12. _____ **Arafat / Rabin** l. Argued India should be "nonaligned" during Cold War

13. _____ **Lord Balfour** m. Desired British Empire remain intact but was overruled

14. _____ **De Klerk / Mandela** n. Iranian Islamist who fought the Shah and took U.S. hostages

15. _____ **Winston Churchill** o. Backed *Negritude* and black overthrow of Rhodesia in music

16. _____ **Deng Xioping** p. Popular Argentine leaders whose militarism led to ouster

17. _____ **Queen Elizabeth II** q. Supported independence from Britain and Indian unity

18. _____ **Bob Marley** r. Guatemalan socialist overthrown by CIA, for a militarist ally

19. _____ **Jawaharlal Nehru** s. Congolese dictator who stole for 30 years before overthrown

20. _____ **Somozas/Sandinistas** t. Indian leader who used sterilization to promote birth control

21. _____ **Mobutu Sese Seko** u. Opened China to U.S. and other foreign investment in 1981

22. _____ **Ayatollah Khomeini** v. British monarch who presided over the 'end of empire'

23. _____ **Juan and Eva Peron** w. Argued wealthy countries keep poorer ones in 'dependence'

24. _____ **Arbenz/Armas** x. Palestinian and Israeli leaders who won Nobel Peace Prize

Ch. 22   REGIME CHANGE   Intervener _____

Hey, look, what's that up in the sky? "Oh, stop droning on about UFOs again."

YEAR	PLACE	AGAINST
1893	Hawaii	Liliuokalani
1898	Cuba	Spain
1898	Puerto Rico	Spain
1899	Philippines	Aguinaldo
1903	Panama	Colombia
1907	Honduras	Nic. Rebels
1912	Nicaragua	Zelaya
1915	Haiti	Cacos
1916	Dominican	Jimenes
1918	Russia	Lenin
1941	Panama	Arias
1943	Italy	Mussolini
1944	Greece	NLF
1944	Philippines	Communists
1944	Belgium	Grohe
1944	Netherlands	Seyss-Inquart
1944	France	Petain
1945	Germany	Hitler
1945	Japan	Meiji
1945	China	Mao
1949	Syria	Quwatli
1950	Korea	PRK
1952	Egypt	Farouk
1953	Iran	Mosaddegh
1954	Guatemala	Arbenz
1960	Congo	Lumumba
1960	Laos	Le
1961	Dominican	Trujillo
1961	Cuba	Castro
1961	Brazil	Goulart
1963	Vietnam	Ngo Din Diem
1965	Vietnam	Viet Cong
1965	Dominican	Cabral
1965	Indonesia	Sukarno
1967	Greece	Papandreou
1971	Bolivia	Torres
1972	Iraq	Saddam
1973	Chile	Allende
1979	Afghanistan	Soviet puppet
1980	El Salvador	FMLN
1981	Nicaragua	Sandinista
1981	Ecuador	Roldos
1981	Panama	Torrijos
1983	Grenada	Marxists
1989	Panama	Noriega
1991	Iraq	Saddam
1997	Indonesia	Suharto
2000	Yugoslavia	Milosevic
2002	Afghanistan	Taliban
2003	Iraq	Saddam
2005	Syria	Assad
2006	Palestine	Haniyeh
2011	Libya	Gaddafi
2015	Yemen	Saleh
2017	Syria	Assad
2019	Venezuela	Maduro
2020	Iran	Khamenei

Whether we like it or not, regime change via CIA, direct military attack, support of a proxy ally, or by other black ops has been a fact of life for America for over 100 years.

Regime change was also a big issue in the 2020 election, where candidates like Tulsi Gabbard and to an extent Bernie Sanders argued against aggressive intervention.

Wikipedia: *United States Involvement in Regime Change*.

Pick two regime changes, and note the following:

1) Year: *2) Place:*

3) What was the geopolitical goal of U.S. invervention?

_____

4) By what method was this intervention undertaken? For example, was it direct military attack, support of a proxy, or something else?

_____

5) Who did the U.S. support and ultimately help put into power?

_____

1) Year: *2) Place:*

3) What was the geopolitical goal of U.S. invervention?

_____

4) By what method was this intervention undertaken? For example, was it direct military attack, support of a proxy, or something else?

_____

5) Who did the U.S. support and ultimately help put into power?

What is your opinion of an <u>interventionist</u> foreign policy? <u>Isolationism</u> often gets a bad rap and is called 'appeasement,' as in, we 'could have stopped Hitler (or Stalin, Mao, Pol Pot, Saddam, bin Laden, Assad, Putin, Kim, etc.) from doing something.' What should our role be?

Ch. 22   ELAAN OF TROYIUS   Diplomat _____
Don't cry

1. The Star Trek episode *Elaan of Troyius (S3-E13)* is a good way to look at the misunderstanding American diplomats had, and the impatience ordinary people had, at not being able to comprehend 'the other' (people not like them, of a different culture) while simultaneously courting them for an alliance. The crew visits a star system that is in a strategic location near Klingon space and is mineral-rich. Could be the "Middle East" of the galaxy so to speak. Could be South America. Could be a lot of places. Both the Federation and the Klingons (America and the Soviets) want to gain the star system and its resources into their alliance. But there is a bit of a curve ball. The Enterprise has to ferry one planet's queen to the other planet in the same system, so she can marry the ruler of that other planet, end the local mini-war that's been going on, and united the system to join an alliance. No problem, right? Both planets will be happy, and both will be allies of the United States (err, sorry, the Federation). Except, the lack of understanding of and respect for the ins and outs of the local situation, the local history, the local culture- something the Americans were notoriously bad at- means there's going to have to be some learning on everyone's part. If you went to another country for two weeks, would you expect to live by 'your rules' or 'their rules'? Why?

_____

2. What is the task the ambassador from Troyius (Petri, the green guy) is on the ship to accomplish while the Enterprise transports the Dohlman of Elas (Elaan) from her planet to his to marry the planet's king?

3. Is he successful in his attempts?

4. This situation is most like:

a. The Soviet and American MAD situation.

b. The Israelis and Palestinians trying to work out the things that drastically divide them

c. The civil war in Guatemala.

5. The issue here is primarily:

   a. religious   b. economic   c. cultural

6. Why does the Dohlman listen to Captain Kirk more so than the ambassador from Troyius?

7. What happens to bring Kirk under the spell of Elaan? _____

8. Remember when the West Africans during Mansa Musa's time had all that gold but didn't place as great a value on it as we do, because it was so common? How is Elaan's necklace similar to that?

9. Elaan give Kirk a gift at the end. What was it, and more importantly, what was her reasoning behind giving it to him (i.e.: what did she learn?):

10. Elaan is certainly a 'reluctant bride'. But we've seen that marriage for something other than 'love' was and is actually very common. Psychologists say we want to be with people for a few reasons: *eros* (attraction- think *Pretty Woman*), *ludus* (gaming- think *Cruel Intentions*), *storge* (companionate friendship- think *When Harry Met Sally*), *mania* (obsession- think *Misery*) *agape* (actual deep, selfless love- think *Titanic*) and/or *pragma* (rationality- think *Pride and Prejudice*). Which was Elaan marrying for? And would you marry to bring peace to your people?

Ch. 22   IRANIAN REVOLUTION   _____
Crash Course World History 226: Iran

Today there is a lot of political discontent between the U.S. and Israel on the one hand, and Iran on the other. George Bush referred to Iran as a member of the "Axis of Evil." Probably not many Iranian civilians slept well that night. Note the events in Iran in the 20th and 21st century:

What the Safavids did:

What the Qajars did:

Shi'a Muslims believe that   a. Abu Bakr   b. Ali   should have been the first prophet.

1906:

What is the primary language in Persia? _____

1921:

1935:

Why is Reza Shah Pahlavi compared to Mustafa Kemal Ataturk?

_____

WWII (1941):

1951:

1953:

1963:

1975:

What did Ayatollah Khomeini argue was bad about the Shah's government?

_____

1978:

1979:

_____

In what sense is Iran a democratic country? | In what sense is Iran not a democratic country?

Ch. 23 **POPULATION THROUGH TIME** **Demographer**_____
Image Search: World Population Growth Graph

Video Search: **Population growth dot map (5:47).**

1. Pause at the year 500. In which three regions is world population clustered?

_____

2. What happens around the years 1240 in Asia and 1345 in Europe to lower population?

_____ and _____

3. About how many millions (dots) were in the Americas on the eve of Columbus' voyage in 1492?

North: _____   Mexico/Central: _____   South: _____

4. Which essential change made population begin growing so rapidly around the year 1800, first in Europe and later in the rest of the world?
_____

5. While debilitating for Europe, describe the total effect of the two world wars on world population:	6. From now until 2030, what does the future hold for world population?

On the graph below, sketch in the historical population in billions of people.

```
9
8
7
6
5
4
3
2
1
0
  1 AD     500      1000         1500       1800      2000  2030
  Rome         Middle Ages    Plague  Exploration  Industry   Modernity
```

Ch. 23   EARTH: COSMIC PARADISE OR... OTHER?
What does the last chapter say?

The last chapter in our book is upon us- a book about the course of human history upon the face of a single, blue world, floating in the great cosmic dark around its star, our bright yellow sun.

Upon the following issues in Ch. 23, summarize the book's assessment on the present and future of state of mankind in our century, as well as whether you agree or disagree with the assessment.

Issue	*Book's Assessment*	*My Assessment*
GLOBALIZATION Will all economies be connected and places be made more similar through 'Mcdonaldization?'		Is a standardization of culture and habits a good thing?
HOMOGENIZATION Will traditional nations and borders be abolished in favor of the world becoming a blended, multicultural political unit?		Is there a best balance between ethnocentrism & multiculturalism?
POPULATION Will the Malthusian dilemma return to annihilate millions due to high human birthrates in lesser developed countries?		How do you think we can best avoid mass famine and social chaos?
POPULATION CONTROL Will 3 billion more people damage local or worldwide ecosystems or even cause runaway greenhouse effect?		Many human societies tend to be r-selected as opposed to K-selected. Should they use population control?
CLIMATE CHANGE Do human activities contribute to the natural cycles of cooling and warming?		Should America force all countries to control CO_2 emissions?

POVERTY
With 8 billion people, there is more poverty than since the modern age began. What can be done?

Should tax rates on wealthy and middle class people go up to help out those in poverty?

TRAFFICKING
Which specific kind of human being is most likely to be trafficked against their will and why?

Drugs and people are trafficked every day. What do you think can be done to help?

EPIDEMICS
Will medical science continue to be able to stave off 21st century epidemics? Why or why not?

Should cancers and heart disease take priority in medical science, or behavioral diseases like HIV/AIDS, or contagions like ebola? Why?

FUNDAMENTALISM
Will non-state political actors massively disrupt civilization enough to effect its collapse?

How should the U.S. mix up its strategy to fight non-state forces as opposed to countries?

FEMINISM
What issues have women's groups made the focus of their public campaigns?

Are 'women' and 'men' even meaningful concepts anymore?

MIGRATION
Which regions of the world are great numbers of people migrating from, and which regions are they migrating to?

How many immigrants from poverty or war torn countries should wealthier countries be obligated to accept per year?

URBANIZATION
What kinds of social consequences are occurring with the great movement to cities around the world?

Should city and national governments be allowed to destroy slum areas? What happens to the residents?

Ch. 23   CIVS AND DYNASTIES @ A GLANCE _____

Categorize the dynasty or civilizational phase into the right period of time – but write small, because some of these have six to a box!

Era	Timeframe	Middle East	Africa	South/SE Asia	East Asia	Meso/Latin Am.	Europe/U.S. (West)

THE GEOGRAPHY OF DISNEY   Animator _____

Where do Disney movies actually take place? Use the geography clues to find out!

How many Disney movies on the *Clues Sheet* have you seen? Circle them and tally up: _____
_{Total}

An important concept in Human Geography is regionalization. Your job is to use the clues to categorize the Disney movies by the cultural regions used by geographers:

North America (you might need two columns!)	**Europe (identify the country if you can)**
	Snow White (Germany)

Latin America	Middle East / North Africa	Sub-Saharan Africa	South Asia
			East Asia
			Southeast Asia

Down Under in Oceania	Out in or 'Under the Sea'	Prehistory or the Future -Specify (P) or (F)-	Other Worlds/ Places Out There...

THE GEOGRAPHY OF DISNEY: CLUES SHEET

1930s
Snow White – Original dwarfs: *Chef, Brummbar, Glucklich, Schlafmutz, Pimpel, Hatschi,* and *Seppl*

1940s
Pinocchio – Mastro Gapetto's cottage was in the land of the Apennine Mts. and the Po River
Fantasia – Mozart and Beethoven helped make 18th century Vienna the world capital of music
Dumbo – Disney was prophetic- Dumbo was born where Disney World was built 30 years later!
Bambi – White-tailed deer like Bambi live where caribou do but reindeer don't
The Three Caballeros – Donald is joined by ducks from Rio, Buenos Aires and Cuidad de Mexico
Song of the South – Uncle Remus lives near the city burned down on Sherman's march to the sea
Ichabod Crane – Sleepy Hollow is a real village in the state where the capital is Albany
Peter and the Wolf – The names of the animals are *Sasha, Ivan, Sonia, Misha, Yasha* and *Vladimir*

1950s
Cinderella – She lived near Joan of Arc, the Duc de Barry and the Three Musketeers
Treasure Island – Long John Silver left Buckinghamshire to search for the treasure
Alice in Wonderland – The cat is a "Cheshire cat"- so where are counties called 'shires' again?
Robin Hood – The Merry Men operate out of Sherwood Forest against the Sheriff of Nottingham
20,000 Leagues Under the Sea – Captain Nemo docks the Nautilus at Port Moresby, New Guinea
Peter Pan – They fly over London town on the way to Neverland
Davy Crockett – The King of the Wild Frontier fought at the Alamo in 1836
Lady and the Tramp – They celebrated the 4th of July and ate at a colonial-style 18th century café
Johnny Tremain – He joined the Sons of Liberty
Sleeping Beauty – *Fleur de lis* decorated her quarters and she sang the song *La Marseillaise*
Man in Space – Disney personally shows us how astronauts will leave Earth and enter into orbit
Man and the Moon – Astronauts travel to the moon like in Jules Verne's famous story
Mars and Beyond – Astronauts venture all the way to Mars and give us hope for the future

1960s
101 Dalmatians – Cruella's name might make us think of Cadillac but she drove a Jaguar!
The Sword in the Stone – King Arthur and the Excalibur legend
Mary Poppins – Her Edwardian Age antics made this London nanny famous
The Jungle Book – Kipling was born in Bombay, British Empire, and Mowgli gets lost near there

1970s
Aristocats – They live in a fancy *chateau*
Winnie the Pooh – Ashdown Forest, a medieval hunting ground, was Henry VIII's favorite place
The Rescuers – They operate out of Bayou Country near Lake Pontchartrain
Pete's Dragon – Northeastern lighthouse for fishermen on the Grand Banks

1980s
The Fox and the Hound – Appalachian scenery
Oliver & Company – Ellis Island and the Statue of Liberty figure here
The Great Mouse Detective – Big Ben and Windsor Castle are in this film
The Little Mermaid – Singing in Caribbean accents, they call a storm a hurricane, not a typhoon
The Black Cauldron – It's based on the *Chronicles of Prydain*, a tale from medieval Wales
The Brave Little Toaster – In an U.S. junkyard, a bunch of different machines help each other

1990s
Aladdin – One of the 1,001 Arabian Nights stories told by Scheherazade to the Shah of Persia
Duck Tales – Uncle Scrooge searches for the treasure of Collie Baba in a pyramid
Beauty and the Beast – The main characters are *Belle, Gaston, Maurice* and *Lumiere*
The Lion King – Takes place on the *Serengeti* on foothills of Mt. Kilimanjaro
Pocahontas – She was romantically involved with John Smith of the Jamestown colony
Hunchback of Notre Dame – The cathedral of Notre Dame is on the *Il de la Cite* in Paris.
Toy Story – A college sports team banner is in the room, and the winter is a lot like Cleveland's
Hercules – In mythology he was son of Zeus and a human woman who accomplished 12 labors
Mulan – The Huns assaulted the Great Wall in Mulan's time.
A Bug's Life – The bugs migrate from lake to lake seasonally in cowboy country
Tarzan – The local wildlife is a lot like that found in the Congo River basin
Rescuers Down Under – If it has 'down under' in the title, you better guess right!
James and the Giant Peach – Taking off from the White Cliffs of Dover, James heads to the Azores

2000s
Dinosaur – The supercontinent Pangaea is the scene…
Emperor's New Groove – The Incan rulers dominated the Andes Mountains
Atlantis – In mythology, it's an amazing city that lies at the bottom of the Mediterranean Sea
Monsters Inc. – This one's way out there!
Return to Neverland – Starts during the London Blitz during WWII
Treasure Planet – This thing is far, far, far, far, far, far away
Lilo & Stitch – They greet each other saying, "Aloha!"
Finding Nemo – They live in the Great Barrier Reef
Spirited Away – Chihiro adventures among Shinto spirits
Wreck-It Ralph – Symbolic of suburbanization, they live everywhere and nowhere
The Incredibles – An elevated train in a Midwestern city? Bet it starts with a C
Brother Bear – The tribes are Inuit-Eskimos of the far north
Teacher's Pet – A dog named Spot travels to the Everglades
Home on the Range – The cattle ranch featured is in sight of natural rock arches
Chicken Little – The farm is on the cornfields of the Great Plains
The Wild – Animals at the Central Park Zoo are able to leave their cages
Cars – The place they drive is off the famous highway Route 66
Bolt – The iconic Hollywood sign is seen in the background

2010s
Up – They travel to the Amazon to get away from it all
Tangled – Rapunzel's story was written by the Brothers Grimm near Sachsen Wald
Ponyo – The goldfish befriends a boy named Sosuke
Big Hero Six – Features kabuki masks, wasabi sauce and karate moves
Princess and the Frog – Alligators in Bayou country during Mardi Gras
Arjun – From the old Hindu epic called the Mahabharata
Brave – Tartan-clad highlanders
Wall-E – In the far future of earth, cool robots explore their emotions
Planes – Dilapidated crop-dusters compete at JFK Airport in an airshow
Frozen – The fjords of the far north are the Kingdom of Arendelle
Inside Out – Has the Golden Gate Bridge in the bay in the background
Zootopia – Means, literally, "the zoo that is a place," so good luck on this one
Moana – Polynesian navigators explore the islands of the largest ocean on earth
Gigantic – Jack is scared when the giant says, "Fe, fi, fo, fum, I smell the blood of an _____!"
Newest One? Add your own movies and clues here:

Musical Journey #1: Medieval → Renaissance → Baroque → Classical

Ready for the festival?

Artist	Composition	Heard / Like?	Notes
Guillaume Dufay	Ave Maris Stella	_____/_____	In mystical connection we 'hail the sea of stars'
Alfonso X	Rosa das Rosas	_____/_____	Demonstrates the rise of the lute
Francois Couperin	Baricades Misterieuses	_____/_____	Harpsicord is like a proto-piano
William Byrd	The Battell	_____/_____	Another harpsicord- who wins Byrd vs. Couperin?
Henry Purcell	Funeral March	_____/_____	Queen (Mary) died, this is the first funeral march
Claudio Monteverdi	L'Orfeo	_____/_____	Overture to the first great opera
Jacques Offenbach	Infernal	_____/_____	Can the pace be picked up? Yes, it can can!
Johann Pachelbel	Canon in D	_____/_____	The 'greatest hit' of 1734 started the Baroque Era
Johann Sebastian Bach	Toccata & Fugue in D-	_____/_____	No, it's not from a haunted house
	Brandenburg Concerto	_____/_____	The *Kapellmeister* wrote it about his homeland
George F. Handel	Fireworks Music	_____/_____	Music specifically for a royal parade and party
	Zadok the Priest	_____/_____	Still England's coronation anthem
	Messiah (Hallelujah)	_____/_____	Perhaps the most famous 'winter holiday' chorus
Antonio Vivaldi	Four Seasons - Spring	_____/_____	Evocative of the season- did you think of spring?
Josef Haydn	Symphony 94 Surprise	_____/_____	Started Classical era with a real surprise- wake up!
	Trumpet Concerto	_____/_____	Less flighty than Baroque, more perfectly flowing
Gioachino Rossini	The Barber of Seville	_____/_____	Classical opera definitely was lighthearted
	La Donna e Mobile	_____/_____	More humor from Rossini, master of comic opera
	William Tell Overture	_____/_____	Now this is Classically smooth- and pointed
Antonio Salieri	Meeting with the Emperor	_____/_____	Salieri was Mozart's musical competitor…
Wolfgang A. Mozart	Marriage of Figaro	_____/_____	Remember Figaro from Rossini's opera? Same dude.
	Eine Kline Nachtmusik	_____/_____	Please say you know this one. Please.
	Symphony 40	_____/_____	It's elegance itself
	Sonata 16	_____/_____	More famous than Sonata 15 and 17 put together…
Niccolo Paganini	Caprice 5	_____/_____	He was a sheer virtuoso. Good luck playing this.
Luigi Boccherini	Sailing Fugue	_____/_____	Did they play it on the Titanic? Maybe…
Gaetano Donizetti	Luccia di Lamarmoor	_____/_____	A wide range of emotions in opera
Carl Maria von Weber	Oberon	_____/_____	A long shot, but you might be that one person…

Musical Journey #2: Romantic & Opulent   Illusionist _____
Put the candle away. It's a fire hazard

Artist	Composition	Heard / Like?	Notes
Ludwig van Beethoven	Fur Elise	_____/_____	Beethoven started in the Classical era with this
	Symphony 3 Eroica	_____/_____	Dedicated this to Napoleon then almost threw it out
	Symphony 5	_____/_____	Thunderous transition to the Romantic era
	Symphony 6 Pastoral	_____/_____	Romantic brings back the feeling of nature's power
	Turkish March	_____/_____	Nationalist military forces aligning in Europe
	Sonata 23 Appassionata	_____/_____	A favorite among piano players to actually play
	Fidelio Prisoner's Chorus	_____/_____	The great hymn to freedom
	Symphony 9 Ode to Joy	_____/_____	Well, what can one say? The highest peak of music?
Hector Berlioz	Les Troyens	_____/_____	The 'Hunt and Storm' from the myth of the Iliad
Christoph von Gluck	Orfeo and Eurydice	_____/_____	He will overcome Hades and Elysium for her
Fryderyk Chopin	Minute Waltz	_____/_____	Because "1:33 Waltz" is nowhere near as catchy
	Nocturne 2	_____/_____	Actually found to put people to sleep
	Funeral March	_____/_____	It was the funeral not of a person, but of a country
	Revolutionary Etude	_____/_____	"Guns hidden in fields of flowers"- are you listening?
Franz Schubert	Serenade	_____/_____	If trees could talk they'd say, "Quit serenading me?"
Robert Schumann	Traumerei	_____/_____	Traumerei is a dreamscape- so let the images flow
Georges Bizet	Carmen	_____/_____	Romantic era opera- whoa!
	Habanera	_____/_____	One of the famous operatic vocals
	Gypsy Song	_____/_____	Makes you want to go cross country camping
Gabriel Faure	Pavane	_____/_____	Great feeling of accomplishment
Anton Bruckner	Symphony 6	_____/_____	Romantic power
Giacomo Puccini	La Boheme – O Mio	_____/_____	The Bohemians were a bunch of artistic roommates
	Nessun Dorma	_____/_____	Longest note in opera- wait till the very end!
Camille Saint-Saens	Carnival of the Animals	_____/_____	More wonder of nature kind of stuff, with critters
	Danse Macabre	_____/_____	Ain't afraid of no ghosts, but skeletons freak me out!
	Symphony 3 Organ	_____/_____	Famous because of the unexpected notes
Johann Strauss II	Tritch-Tratch Polka	_____/_____	Time to get fancy
	The Blue Danube	_____/_____	Do NOT look up "Simpsons Blue Danube."

Musical Journey #3: Rites of Passage & National   Idealist _____
I declare- this is an official person

Artist	Composition	Heard / Like?	Notes
Sir Edward Elgar	Pomp & Circumstance	_____ / _____	Rites of passage must include this graduation song
Felix Mendelssohn	Wedding March	_____ / _____	First Pachelbel's Canon, now this?
Richard Wagner	Bridal Chorus	_____ / _____	TV shows and movies... love this...
Johannes Brahms	Cradle Song	_____ / _____	When babies in the crib are trying to sleep, play this
	Academic Festival	_____ / _____	Eventually they grow up and go off to school
Emile Waldteufel	Skater's Waltz	_____ / _____	Figure skating is mostly just CGI, isn't it?
Leo Arnaud	Olympic Theme	_____ / _____	Some are just great at sports, workin' hard to win
Aaron Copeland	Fanfare for Common Man	_____ / _____	Whoa- America finally gets onto the musical map
	Rodeo Hoedown	_____ / _____	Fueled world's imagination of the American west
John Philip Sousa	Stars & Stripes Forever	_____ / _____	The classic parade song
Charles Ives	Variations on America	_____ / _____	Medley of American tunes put into classical form
Traditional British	Fantasia on Sea Songs	_____ / _____	Medley from when Britain 'ruled the waves'
Isaac Albeniz	Asturias	_____ / _____	Spain's great composer's contribution
Franz von Suppe	Light Cavalry	_____ / _____	If you get up and run out of class, we understand
Giuseppe Verdi	Anvil Chorus	_____ / _____	Italian national composer's famous chorus
Josef Haydn	Das Deutschlandlied	_____ / _____	The organ version without words might be best...
Franz Liszt	Hungarian Dance #2	_____ / _____	Translating folk dances into classical style began
Johannes Brahms	Hungarian Dances	_____ / _____	Brahms was Austrian, but we're one happy empire!
Bela Bartok	Romanian Dances	_____ / _____	Bartok's Hungarian, but the one big empire thing...
Antonin Dvorak	Slavonic Dances	_____ / _____	Dvorak was... okay he was actually Czech, so fine
Bedrich Smetana	Ma Vlast – Moldau	_____ / _____	A 'symphonic poem' to his homeland & River Vltava
Modest Mussorgsky	Pictures at an Exhibition	_____ / _____	Walk down the promenade and see them
	The Great Gate of Kiev	_____ / _____	Where Russian culture began- still a big thing today
	Night on Bald Mountain	_____ / _____	Next time you go camping, think of the possibilities
Alexander Borodin	Steppes of Central Asia	_____ / _____	The empire extended into this fascinating region
Nikolai Ippolitov-Ivanov	Caucasian Sketches	_____ / _____	The empire extended into the Caucasus area too
Armin Khachaturian	Sabre Dance	_____ / _____	Armenia's celebrated national composer

Musical Journey #4: Fantasian, Impressionist & Modernist
So, they, like, got this from Disney, right?   _____

Artist	Composition	Heard / Like?	Notes
Piotr I. Tchaikovsky	Piano Concerto 1	_____/_____	We just crossed into Fantasy- Disney's favorite
	The Sugar Plum Fairies	_____/_____	Has anyone actually ever eaten a sugar plum?
	Nutcracker - Trepak	_____/_____	Winter holidays-time favorite
	Swan Lake	_____/_____	Everyone loves Swan Lake
	1812 Overture	_____/_____	It must have the cannons in it
Paul Dukas	Sorcerer's Apprentice	_____/_____	Is Mickey the sorcerer or the apprentice?
Edvard Grieg	Hall of the Mountain King	_____/_____	Norway's great composer lives in the hall
	Morning Mood	_____/_____	Time to use this as your alarm sound
	Piano Concerto	_____/_____	Grieg rivals Tchaikovsky in Fantasy with this
Ralph Vaughn-Williams	Fantasia on Tallis	_____/_____	Crossing the seas, under the stars, nothing like it
Gustav Holst	The Planets – Mars	_____/_____	Bringer of war brings the first scifi-style piece
	The Planets – Jupiter	_____/_____	Bringer of joviality lent to Britain's 'I Vow to Thee'
Richard Strauss	Thus Spake Zarathustra	_____/_____	Perhaps the most epic
Richard Wagner	Ride of the Valkyries	_____/_____	Romantic fantasy at its height, see you in Valhalla!
Nikolai Rimsky-Korsakov	Flight of the Bumblebee	_____/_____	It's like an onomatopoeia written as music
Claude Debussy	Clair de Lune	_____/_____	Sitting in a Paris café looking at a Monet painting…
Erik Satie	Gymnopedie 1	_____/_____	Is this your impression of modernity?
Maurice Ravel	Bolero	_____/_____	Impressionists can make powerful music too
Arnold Schoenberg	Variations for Orchestra	_____/_____	Atonality agitated many- Nazi censors banned it
	Pierrot Lunaire	_____/_____	Coming to grips with the possibility of no meaning
Igor Stravinsky	Rite of Spring	_____/_____	Not Vivaldi's Spring; carnal, wild nature blooms
	The Firebird	_____/_____	More Primitivism in music, troubling, like the age
George Gershwin	Rhapsody in Blue	_____/_____	1920s New York, the Big Apple, modernity in blue
Sergei Rachmaninov	Rhapsody on Paganini	_____/_____	Neoromantic, he carries the mantle of 19th century
Samuel Barber	Adagio for Strings	_____/_____	Neoromantic take on senseless agony of total war
Sergei Prokofiev	Battle on the Ice	_____/_____	Social realism in Soviet music, Eisenstein movie
	Peter and the Wolf	_____/_____	Social realist take on classic Russian story
Dmitri Shostakovich	Sym. 11 – The Year 1905	_____/_____	Haunting reminder of the day the people awoke

Musical Journey #5: Postwar & Postmodern   All _____

Take do your own thing to the next level

Artist	Composition	Heard / Like?	Notes
Henryk Gorecki	Sym. 3 – Sorrowful Songs	_____/_____	Auschwitz prisoners wrote the poems used in this
Karl Jenkins	Palladio	_____/_____	Perhaps the most famous postwar classical piece
Carl Orff	O Fortuna	_____/_____	Modernist on a grand scale
Philip Glass	The Hours	_____/_____	Minimalism in music, poignancy of lost modernism
John Cage	The Dream	_____/_____	Postmodernity in music means whatever you like
John Adams	Nixon in China	_____/_____	Politically themed opera? Ooh, fun.
Karlheinz Stockhausen	Helicopter String Quartet	_____/_____	The sky's the limit in postmodernity
Harrison Birtwistle	Panic	_____/_____	And some people actually panicked at this music
John Cage	4'33"	_____/_____	Beginning of the end, or the end of the beginning
Vangelis	Heaven and Hell	_____/_____	Cuts through nihilism to a grand, cosmic vision
2Cellos	Thunderstruck	_____/_____	A rebirth?

Classical lives on! It does? Where? In epic movie scores and video games!

Artist	Composition	Heard / Like?	Notes
Harold Arlen	The Wizard of Oz	_____/_____	Somewhere over the rainbow, skies are blue
Maurice Jarre	Lawrence of Arabia	_____/_____	Helped turn the Arabs against the Ottomans
	Dr. Zhivago- Lara's Theme	_____/_____	When life gets turned upside down and inside out
Vangelis	Chariots of Fire	_____/_____	Score depicting the drive to win the Olympics
Jerry Goldsmith	Star Trek	_____/_____	The Final Frontier is out there for us to explore
John Williams	Jaws	_____/_____	Most famous movie score composer's first big hit
	Superman	_____/_____	The other Man of Steel (besides Stalin)
	Star Wars	_____/_____	Perhaps the best known epic movie score
	ET	_____/_____	Somewhere over the Moon, skies are dark…?
	Indiana Jones	_____/_____	Based on a real guy named Roy Chapman Adams
	Jurassic Park	_____/_____	They came, they saw, they destroyed the whole park
James Horner	Titanic	_____/_____	"Houston, we have a problem." Dude, they can't hear us.
Hans Zimmer	Interstellar	_____/_____	We can't keep all our eggs in one basket forever…
Kojo Kondo	Legend of Zelda	_____/_____	Classical tradition continues in video game scores!
Nobuo Uematsu	Final Fantasy	_____/_____	Voted the number one video game musical score

INFO CRASH COURSE – STRAYER 4th EDITION CORRELATION CHART

TOPIC IN STRAYER 4	CRASH COURSE 1 EPISODES	CRASH COURSE 2 EPISODES
1 Before History	1 – Agriculture Revolution	201 - Civilization
2 Early Southwest Asia	3 – Mesopotamia	205 – War, 211 – Bronze
3 Early African Societies	4 – Ancient Egypt	---
4 Early South Asia	2 – Indus Valley	---
5 Early East Asia	7 – 2,000 Years of China (part)	---
6 Early Americas and Oceania	---	---
7 Empires of Persia	5 – Persians (part)	---
8 Unification of China	7 – 2,000 Years of China (part)	---
9 Quest for Salvation in India	6 – Buddha & Ashoka	---
10 The Greek Phase	5 – Greeks (part), 8 - Alexander	---
11 The Roman Phase	10 – Rome, 11 – Christianity	---
12 Silk Roads	9 – Silk Road	---
13 Resurgence in East Asia	---	227 – Heian Japan
14 Expansive Realm of Islam	13 – Islam	216 – Islam and Politics
15 Indian Ocean Basin	18 – Int'l Commerce	---
16 Two Worlds of Christendom	12 – Byzantium, 14 – Dark Ages	224 – Vikings
17 Nomadic Empires	17 – Mongols!	---
18 Sub-Saharan Africa	16 – Mansa Musa	---
19 Late Medieval Europe	15 – Crusades	---
20 Worlds Apart	---	222 – Water
21 Expanding Horizons	20 – Russia, 22 – Renaissance	203 – Disease, 206 - Climate
22 Transoceanic Encounters	21 – Columbus, 23 – Exchange	229 – Capitalism and VOC
	26 – Seven Years', 27 – Cook	---
23 Transformation of Europe	---	204 – War, 212 – Rise
	---	218 – Luther, 219 – Charles
24 New Worlds	25 – Spanish Empire	---
25 Africa and the Atlantic	24 – Atlantic Slavery	---
26 Early Modern East Asia	---	---
27 The Islamic Empires	19 – Venice & Ottomans	217 – Mughals
28 Revolutions and Nationalism	28 – American, 29 – French	---
	30 – Haitian, 31 – Latin Rev.	---
29 Industrial Society	32 – Coal, Steam, 33 – Capitalism	202 – Money, 214 – RR
	---	215 – Population
30 Independent Americas	---	225 – Latin nation building
31 Societies at Crossroads	34 – Samurai and Nationalism	213 – Asian responses
32 Building of Global Empires	35 – Imperialism	208 – Famine
33 The Great War	36 – Archdukes & World War	209 – WWI, 210 – WWI #2
34 An Age of Anxiety	---	---
35 Nationalism and Identities	37 – China's Revolutions	---
36 New Conflagrations	38 – WWII, 39 – Cold War	220 – WWII
37 The End of Empire	40 – Decolonization	221 – Congo, 223 – Israel
	---	226 – Iran, 228 - Peace
38 A World without Borders	41 & 42 – Globalization	207 – Energy, 230 – Gov't

INFO   CNN MILLENNIUM SERIES – STRAYER 4th EDITION CORRELATION CHART

TOPIC IN STRAYER 3RD	CNN MILLENNIUM
1 Before History	
2 Early Southwest Asia	
3 Early African Societies	
4 Early South Asia	
5 Early East Asia	
6 Early Americas and Oceania	12th century #1: American Indians / #5: Aboriginal Australia
7 Empires of Persia	
8 Unification of China	
9 Quest for Salvation in India	
10 The Greek Phase	
11 The Roman Phase	
12 Silk Roads	
13 Resurgence in East Asia	11th century #1: China and Nomads / 11th #4: Heian court
14 Expansive Realm of Islam	11th century #2: Abbasids and Cordoba / 13th cent. #4: Egypt
15 Indian Ocean Basin	11th century #3: Postclassical India / 14th #4: Spice Islands
16 Two Worlds of Christendom	11th century #5: Great Schism
17 Nomadic Empires	13th century #1: Genghis' conquests / #2: Pax Mongolica
	13th century #3: Kubilai & Marco Polo / 14th #3: Tamerlane
18 Sub-Saharan Africa	12th century #3: Lalibela's churches / 14th #2: Mansa Musa
19 Late Medieval Europe	12th century #2: Gothic / #4 Scholastic Italy
	13th century #5: Venice / 14th #5: Classes
20 Worlds Apart	15th century #3: Aztecs
21 Expanding Horizons	14th century #1: Plague / 15th #1 Zheng He
	15th century #2: Renaissance / 15th #5: Henry the Navigator
22 Transoceanic Encounters	16th century #2: Ivan's Russia
23 Transformation of Europe	16th century #5: Curiosities / 17th #1: Newton & Science
	18th century #1: Measuring the Earth
	17th century #4: Dutch Republic
24 New Worlds	16th century #1: Spanish America / 17th #2: Jamestown
25 Africa and the Atlantic	17th century #3: Sugar and Brazilian slavery
26 Early Modern East Asia	16th century #3: Hideyoshi's Japan / 17th #5: Qing science
27 The Islamic Empires	15th century #4: Ottoman conquests / 16th #4: Mughal India
28 Revolutions and Nationalism	18th century #2: Enlightenment / 18th #3: Age of Revolutions
29 Industrial Society	19th century #1: British industry / #5: Industrial society
30 Independent Americas	19th century #3: American West
31 Societies at Crossroads	18th century #5: Zenith of the Qing/19th century #4:Opium War
32 Building of Global Empires	18th century #4: Tipu & British India / 19th #2: Darwinian ideas
33 The Great War	20th century #2: A century of war
34 An Age of Anxiety	20th century #1: Social uncertainty, Freud
35 Nationalism and Identities	
36 New Conflagrations	
37 The End of Empire	
38 A World without Borders	20th century #3: Migration / #4: Communications / #5: Japan

(The ones most relevant to the class curriculum are found throughout this workbook)

INFO

EVERY FRQ EVER

What are their topics and where do they fall in the AP World curriculum?

	YEAR	THEME/TOPIC
UNIT 1 ANCIENT	2019	SAQ on how Neolithic Revolution changed lifestyles
UNIT 2 CLASSICAL	2004 A	Diffusion of Buddhism in China
	2006 B	C/C in cultural and political changes in Han, Gupta or Rome
	2007 A	Han vs. Roman attitudes towards technology
	2009 B	C/C interactions along Silk Rd. 200-1450
	2010 C	S/D in political control in Han, India and/or Rome
	2012 B	C/C in trade between AF and Eurasia 300-1450
	2013 B	C/C in culture of Mediterranean region due to political change
	2018	LEQ on factors that lead to diffusion of new religious ideas
	2019	LEQ on rise of classical empires and trans-regional trade
UNIT 3 POSTCLASSICAL	2002 A	Attitude of Christianity and Islam to merchant class
	2003 B	C/C cultural, econ and political Islam on AF, South Asia or EU
	2005 C	S/D effects of Mongols on China, Mideast and/or Russia
	2008 B	C/C commerce in Indian Ocean basin 650 to 1750
	2011 C	S/D rise of African, Aztec and/or Mongol empires
	2014 C	S/D religion and politics in Byz, Islam and/or India
	2015 C	S/D exchanges on two major trade routes
	2016 B	C/C in trade networks of Afro-Eurasia, 600-1450
	2017	SAQ on Chinese relations with nomadic groups
	2017	DBQ on religious responses to wealth accumulation 600-1500
	2018	SAQ on sedentary vs. nomadic societies in this era
	2019	SAQ on cultural exchanges between nomadic and sedentary
	2019	LEQ on tech changes and the effects on trans-regional trade
UNIT 4 EXPLORATION	2003 A	Causes and consequences of indentured servitude
	2005 B	C/C transformations in Atlantic basin due to triangle trade
	2006 A	Social and economic effects of the global flow of silver
	2007 C	S/D empire building in Spain vs. Ottoman or Russian
	2009 C	S/D in racial ideologies in NA vs. LA
	2010 B	C/C in religion in Africa or Latin America 1450-present
	2011 B	C/C in Migration in two different world regions
	2012 C	S/D in Columbian Exchange btw. Americas and AF, Asia or EU
	2013 A	European colonial competition in mid-18th century
	2014 B	C/C interregional trade in LA, AF or SE Asia
	2015 B	C/C labor systems in Latin or North America
	2017	SAQ on how population shifts affected environment
	2017	LEQ on labor migration continuity and change
	2018	LEQ on how Columbian Exchange affected native Americans
	2019	SAQ on role of Portugal in changing Indian Ocean trade

UNIT 5 **REVOLUTIONARY**	2002 B	C/C global trade patters in two world regions, 1750 to present
	2002 C	S/D in differing responses of China and Japan to Rise of West
	2003 C	S/D women's roles in East Asia, LA, AF and/or EU
	2004 B	C/C labor systems in LA, Russia and/or AF
	2008 A	Factors that shaped modern Olympics
	2008 C	S/D nation-state dev. in LA and AF or ME
	2009 A	African responses to Berlin Conference
	2010 A	Mechanization of cotton industry in Japan and India
	2012 A	Cricket and politics in South Asia
	2013 C	S/D Japanese econ dev. vs. China, Ottoman or Russia
	2016 C	S/D in causes of two revolutions
	2017	SAQ on how industrialization was social, political & economic
	2018	SAQ on British India relations, British East India Company
	2018	DBQ on effect of railroads during imperial age
	2019	SAQ on economic changes and effects on social hierarchies
UNIT 6 **CONTEMPORARY**	2004 C	S/D how WWI affected East Asia, ME and/or South Asia
	2005 A	National leaders and issues in South Asia and North Africa
	2006 C	S/D goals and outcomes of revolutions in Mexico, China, Russia
	2007 B	C/C formation of national identity in ME, SE Asia, or AF
	2011 A	Green revolution and new technology
	2014 A	China from republic to people's republic
	2015 A	Influenza outbreak
	2016 A	Gender & politics in Latin America
	2017	SAQ on technologies that encourage process of globalization
	2017	LEQ on global changes in balance of power 1900 to today
	2018	SAQ on totalitarianism vs. democracy
	2018	SAQ on Agricultural vs. Green Revolution
	2018	LEQ on how 20th century ideologies challenged status quo
	2019	SAQ on life expectancy vs. per capita GDP in modern times
	2019	LEQ on ways states have controlled/managed their economies

Crash Course* Guide

Reviewer _____

It's Review Time!

Topic of today's episode _____

Why was "Me From the Past's" question silly (or smart)?

_____

What topic did "Thought Bubble" portray in this episode?

_____

What did Mr. Green find in the "Secret Compartment?" _____

Who (or what) was the "Open Letter" directed to? _____

How did that item tie in to the material in the chapter?

_____

_____

_____

What was the 'deep' lesson at the very end of the episode?

_____

Any further notes about this episode you think are important:

*The producers of Crash Course were not involved in the production of this review worksheet.

Answer Key

Chapter 1: First Peoples, First Farmers

Big History
Big bang, reality, gravity, light, star, supernovas, heavy elements, terrestrial planets, Sun, Solar System, Jupiter, Earth, Theia, Moon, magnetic shield, comets / ice, atmosphere, save haven, 'alive', 'body', sex, planets, oxygen, land animals, lungs/amphibian, reptile, P/T catastrophe, dinosaurs, medulla, comet annihilation, mammal, cerebrum & cerebellum / family, continents drift, consciousness, tools, Ice Ages, Cro-Magnon, civilizations, writing, ancestors, periods, family, meeting, future of life.

Generations
C. 1918, 4 in the average century, a. true, 80 generations (minus you, parents and grandparents = 77). Cave art done for luck in the hunt and in the gathering of food. Venus figurines for good luck in childbirth and child survival. Sheep, goats, dogs, cats, pigs, cows, horses, basically any of the common farm animals. Wheat, rice, maize, barley, sorghum, yams etc.

Prehistoric Art Show
Students will do their own sketches of the hall of the bulls etc. All the artists will be unknown. Ratings should be based on skill and theme both. Subject will be an interpretation as well, but it should be emphasized that art historians believe cave art was an imaginative connection with a metaphysical world, a world of the spirit, wherein the hunting of an animal had meaning for the hunted as well as for the hunter. That the Venus was a good luck charm for childbirth and successful family life.

Chapter 2: First Civilizations

Mansplainin' World History?
Answers will vary, some will keep the name of the class, others will change it to something else, as long as they have a rationale it is subjective. Answers will vary for whether to use mankind or humankind, and on whether to use BC/AD, BCE/CE or something else.

His-Story?
Each letter will have a different number of men and women underneath it, but in no case will the women equal or exceed the number of men.

Ancient Law
Most students will pick 'liberal freedoms,' though some might pick 'tradition respected.'
Most will say a happy medium is a mix of respect for traditions along with freedom of individuality. However, they should also indicate what it means on a personal level for them, hopefully with an example to back it up.
Retribution means evenly getting back at someone.
Unequal societies have always had leniency on the noble class or royals, or clergy, vis a vis the peasants.
1 monotheism, 2 idolization, 3 words, 4 more to life, 5 family and nation, 6 life and death, 7 honor marriage, 8 property rights, 9 speak the truth, 10 jealousy.
If someone, according to Kohlberg, does good and not bad only because they might get caught doing the bad thing, that isn't morality- its fear. If they do something good not bad only because the bad thing is illegal, they may be a good person only because of legislation. If they do the good thing because of a higher ethical principle that they have internalized, that is the truly moral person— if morality exists.

Pyramid!
Ma'at is important because it is both object and cause of the Egyptians' social stability. Their society is directed to maintaining it that it might do its job of keeping the society in balance. Therefore, whether it metaphysically exists or not is less important than the effect the concept itself had in encouraging social stability. The pharaoh's key role in its maintenance encouraged political stability and continuity.
A, R, E, R, P, G.
Answers will vary between "yes, I think conscripted labor is a form of slavery" to "no, it's duty to the state."
Answers will vary on rating the movie

Chapter 3: State and Empire

The Oracle
1. Everything underlined should be within quotation marks, spoken by the Oracle to the person.
2. Lycurgus, Solon, Croesus, Lionidas, Chaerephon, Lysander, Philip of Macedon, Alexander the Great, Zeno, Cicero, Nero.
3) The Oracle was always right.
4) When the Oracle pronounces something, the people go out and expect it to happen, so they act like is a given fact, and by doing so, encourage that fact to come into being in the material world.

Greek Terms Used in English
Both, old, against, self, book, life, time, universe/order, hidden/below, circle/cycle, people, give, power, human type, good, marriage, writing, earth, family, different, same, water, over, under, word, beyond, measure, form, new, nerve, law/science, view, all, suffering, sound, light, city, before, first, false, mind/soul, fire, wisdom, with, art, god/divine, heat, arrangement, animal.

Latin Terms in English
Answers will vary depending on how many of these the student has used or heard used before.

Emperors' Matrix
Julius Caesar, Augustus Caesar, Tiberius, Caligula, Nero, Vespasian, Trajan, Hadrian, Marcus Aurelius, Commodus, Septimus Severus, Valerian, Diocletian, Constantine, Valens, Theodosius, Honorius, Valentinian III, Romulus Augustalus.

Conrad-Demarest Model:
1) Han, Rome, Gupta   2) Han, Gupta, Rome   3) Rome, Gupta, Han   4) Han, Gupta, Rome

The Cycle of Empire:

	Buildings	Lifestyle	Conrad-Demarest stage
I	hovels, teepees	simple, natural	n/a or 1
II	temple building, homes	building virtues	2
III	administration, temples, grand public buildings, technology	glorious, wealthy, decadent	3
IV	buildings being destroyed	war, barbarian invasion	4
V	back to nature, ruins	simple, natural, with a twist	n/a or 4

Chapter 4: Culture and Religion

The Tao of Pooh
1. Compassion, 2. Humility, 3. Moderation.
4. Finding balance in yourself and nature.
5. Finding joy and laughter.
6. Letting go of stress and worry and forget about things that make you sad.
7. Eeyore frets, Piglet hesitates, Rabbit calculates, Owl pontificates, Tigger boasts, and Pooh just is.
8) **Piglet** is loyal, not center of attention, think of others first, needs pats on the back, wants approval, prefers one good friend to many, worries a lot. **Tigger** is energetic, physical, fun, impulsive, loud, doesn't sit still, emotional, erratic, likes noise, music, sports. **Eeyore** is cynical, expects bad will happen, focuses on problems, complains, loses things, forgetful, shy, tired, sad, but loveable and loves his friends and family. **Rabbit** likes to be in charge, is detail-oriented, clever, good at planning, can be counted on, organized, neat, likes everything in its place, doesn't like mess, makes a schedule and follows it. **Owl** is academic, scholarly, well-educated, good problem-solver, thoughtful, common sense, reads a lot, shows off how smart he is. Wise. **Kanga** is sweet and nurturing, loves children, wants everyone to be safe and fed, loving, gentle, like a cozy home and quiet moments. **Christopher Robin** is imaginative, clever, artsy, has good ideas, likes to act, and write, loves being around friends and daydreams and plays. **Pooh** is clueless, maybe a bit of an airhead, almost always happy, wanders through life happy, no goals, but no disappointments, simple pleasure, likes cake, balloons and a full belly. Yum. Honey.
9. Answers will vary.
10. Piglet, Eeyore and Kanga are more yin, Tigger is more Yang, perhaps Owl and Rabbit too, Pooh and to an extent Christopher Robin are wuwei, and Owl and Rabbit are Confucian (active role in the world, building a better society through fostering interpersonal relationships within the framework of set-understanding of one's role in each.

Secret Knowledge: Metaphors
Box 1: b, c, a. Box 2: a, c, b. Box 3: c, a, b. Box 4: a, b, c. Short answers will vary. Answers will vary for the *aletheia* answer as well.

Who Mourns for Adonais?
C. A hand made of energy. Apollo. E. B. He explains how our progress is measured in our cultural advancement and social evolution, and while our ancestors had a need for the Olympians thousands of years ago, we no longer did. Freedom is an important human value now, living as a captive is not for us. Kirk at the end says the gods inspired us to do great deeds, gave us something to aspire to, and were a key reason in our cultural youth that drove our progress. Answers will vary.

Hellenic Philosophy: The Beginning of Reason
Thales way of questioning was new because he was looking at natural phenomena as being caused by other natural phenomena.
Inductive reasoning is from specific to general.
Answers will vary, but a good one will say either you name a river, it is the same river in essence today and tomorrow, so you can, OR, a river is never the same because the moving water will always be different water. Everything is changing.
The plant life example would support Parmenides because the molecules and atoms of the plant life were reordered in the ground and yet- are still there.
The Empedocles' argument was for four primordial elements governed by love and strife, while Anaxagoras' arguments was for very tiny seeds being constantly reordered by a grand, transcendent mind.
Answers will vary on if good is an absolute or relative concept.
Democritus was more right because he correctly figured out that cosmic space is a void in which atoms move eternally into different forms.
Answers will vary, some will say the divine created reason and mathematics, a deist or theist concept. Others will say they cannot because supernatural divinity is based on faith, which may in fact be true, but whether it is or is not, is different than reason.

Hellenic Philosophy: Socrates
Socrates' outlook is optimistic because he said regular, humble people can be molded into good people.
Achievements are elucidating the logical argument, the appeal to reason, and the cross-examination technique of dialogue.
Virtue is knowledge of the good, and vice is ignorance of it.
He was wiser in the sense that he knew he was not. "All I know is that I don't know."
The essence of justice is a very difficult question to answer. But it is a very good question to think about. We know one thing though, it is not giving back something you owe, and being given something owed to you. It must be something deeper than that.
To the Sophists, like to Machiavelli 1,910 years later, justice would be whatever got you ahead, without regard to an absolute concept, because "justice is relative."
Happiness is self-knowledge.
Answers will vary.

Weeks and Days
Mercury, Venus, Earth, Mars, Jupiter, Saturn, Uranus, Neptune, Pluto.
Janus, Februa, Mars, Aphrodite, Maya, Juno, Julius, Augustus, 7th, 8th, 9th, 10th.
D, B, E, C, A, F, G.

Chapter 5: Society and Inequality

A Socialist Emperor?
1) Each box will be differently divided, depending on the whims of the student-emperor.
2) Ask if anyone has a perfect division without anyone including themselves having a larger plot. There's your socialist ☺. If others have divvied up larger plots to their friends, that's rather elitist, and if they did something like "It's all mine," well, there's your authoritarian megalomaniac. All in jest, of course. But Wang Mang really did use sheer authoritarianism to break up landed noble estates.
3) depends.
4) depends on 3. But if you were elitist, you might not feel to happy about having the land redistributed. The concept of political alliances is key now. Usually, royals will ally with the noble class, warriors, etc. Brahmins and Kshatriyas in India, for example. But sometimes a ruler will go against this class, and right to the people. That's what Wang Mang did. How about Trump? Many of his supporters felt by circumventing the establishment (the landed elite) he 'allied' with the common person too.

5) Here's the rub. The socialist emperor used state control and authoritarianism next on those same common people he allied with.
6) Answers will vary, but these issues of state power, socialist vs. elite dynamic, new elite within a new social system, etc., are recurring themes.

Roman City!
Verbonia, France, Gaul.
Acco favored assimilation after the bloody conquest by Caesar's legions, one that would favor both peoples economically and socially. Aiden and the Druids, a mystical Celtic sect, favored fighting the Romans back from Gaul.
P, S, E.
Theater, amphitheater, temples, forum, bathhouse, aqueducts.
Answers will vary.

Arranged Marriages – Pro and Con
Answers will vary as to recent behaviors.
Self esteem, Safety, Physiological, Belonging, Self-actualization, Self-transcendence
Answers will vary but should be reflective
Top row – ludus, eros, mania. Bottom row – pragma, agape, storge.
Answers will vary on what kind of love someone is likely to seek.

Media: Roman Places
D
It should look like arches next to each other and connected, rather the same as in an aqueduct.
B
B
There are many comics of modern politicians 'fiddling' while something in their society 'burns', answers will vary.
Manger / stable
B
Some people are aghast/screaming, others are trying to run away, others seem to be praying
Answers will vary
Any number of Trajan's victories can be found on the column
Dome, Jerusalem
Images mostly, of Jesus and the apostles
Jesus was crucified on a cross
The fish come from the bible story where Jesus multiplied them, and became a symbol of Christians in Rome when was a banned religion, in the dust and dirt people would draw half a fish with their foot, and if the other person was Christian he'd draw the other half.
The beginning and the end, from John I-I
Jesus was a good shepherd to his flock, who were lost sheep, but now are found
Symbol of the Holy Spirit is a dove, which came to rest on Jesus' shoulders
Patrick used the shamrock (three leaf clover) to teach people about the Trinity, three leaves, one clover.

Chapter 6: Commonalities and Variations: Africa, the Americas and Oceania

African Terms in English
Swahili, banjo, gumbo, ebony, mumbo-jumbo, chimpanzee, jazz, jive, jumbo, kwanzaa, jenga, voodoo, impala, mojo, goober, tsetse, zebra, zombie, mamba, vuvuzela, bwana.

Great Clips: Lalibela / Mansa Musa
They were built in large holes in the ground, out of material that was part of the hole itself.
In the legend, bees came to announce his importance.
Ethiopians say the Ten Commandments are there, inside the Ark of the Covenant.
He saw them in the seventh heaven, and knew how the holy buildings ought to be built.
He used religion as a way to united his people against the forces around him, mostly Muslims.
> Arid desert with the Niger River as main source of water.
> Camel.
> Hippopotamus.
> As an elite chieftain, he was too important to speak to commoners.
> 5,000 slaves.
> Gold was made into decorative jewelry, inlaid into textiles, and used to ornament buildings.
> He is portrayed holding a gold nugget and wearing a lot of gold items.

America Before Columbus
By land bridge across the Bering Strait.
Magnetic field repelling solar wind.
Seal, caribou, also bear etc.
Yes, people live on Greenland (It is the world's largest island, so it is appropriate to say *on* Greenland).
Leif Erickson, 1000.
Britain, France, Spain, Russia.
Ohio.
Cherokee, Navajo, Cree, Sioux, Chippewa.
55,000.
Seminole.
Red and black.
Cahokia, St. Louis.
A meeting place for Southwest tribes such as the Anasazi.
Olmec.
Tula, Chichen Itza.
Pyramidal.
F.
The Dead.
Answers will vary.
Tikal.
Mayans.
No.
It kept the sun coming up in the sky the next morning.
Chocolate.
Pierce herself.
Tenochtitlan.
Special farms made of dredged silt from the bottom of Lake Texcoco.
Similar.
Drawings will vary.
The causeways and monumental structures.
A kiva-type ceremonial center.
Chimu left irrigation canals.
Collected trophy heads.
It is in high in the Andes Mountains, embedded on the tops and sides.
Maize, potatoes.
A system of record keeping- some go so far as to say a form of writing- but certainly kept time.

Chapter 7: Commerce and Culture, 600-1450

Silk Road Trip
Chang'an, Xi'an, Lanzhou, Mati Si – Han Chinese
Dunhuang, Crescent lake – Chinese Buddhists
Turfan, Bezeklik, Urunqi, Kazil, Kashgar, Lake Karakul – Uyghurs
Almaty - Kazakhs
Bishkek - Kyrgyz
Dushanbe - Tajiks
Tashkent, Samarkand, Bukhara - Uzbeks
Ashkhabat - Turkmens
Bactra - Afghans
Qom, Ecbatana, Ctesiphon - Persians
Baghdad, Palmyra - Arabs
Edessa, Antioch - Turks

Diseases in History:
The three worst are Black Death, Spanish Flu and Plague of Justinian.
Student should have circles and squares appropriately
Cholera and AIDS are good examples
Endemic means they are part of the regular environment of the place, like malaria in some tropical regions

Revenge of Phase 1?
Bacteriological: Sepsis, Tuberculosis, Meningitis, Typhoid, Cholera.
Viral: Pneumonia, HIV, Flu, Hepatitis, Norovirus
Parasitical: Malaria, Schistosomiasis, African Sleeping Sickness
Making a comeback for two reasons. One is biological- because new strains appear, more resistant. The other is cultural-environmental. More people means more hosts, less sanitation in many places contributes to spread, mass migration, globalization (inc. mass tourism) bring people around the world.

Chapter 8: China and the World

Dynasties of China
Xia, Shang, Zhou, Qin, Han, Sui, Tang, Song, Yuan, Ming, Qing, Republic, People's Republic
Philosophies are: Confucianism, Daoism, Legalism.

Chinese Provinces
1. Calm emblem, 2. Northern capital, 3. Ultimate purity, 4. Happy, 5. Big eastern land, 6. Pleasant, 7. Big western land, 8. Noble, 9. Southern sea, 10. Great northern river, 11. Black dragon river, 12. Great southern river, 13. Spice harbor, 14. Northern lake, 15. River awakening, 16. Western river, 17. Lucky forest, 18. Distant peace, 19. Inner Mongolia, 20. Peaceful summer, 21. Pure blue sea, 22. Western mountain(s), 23. Same as Shanxi but in a different dialect, 24. Eastern waters, 25. Upon the sea, 26. Four corners, 27. Gulf island 28. Tibet, 29. Heavenly gateway, 30. New frontier, 32. Southern clouds, 33. Winding river

Chapter 9: The Worlds of Islam

Arabic Terms in English
Admiral, ghoul, alchemy, elixir, alcohol, apricot, arsenal, assassin, azimuth, algebra, candy, caravan, cheque, crimson, gerbil, algorithm, giraffe, adobe, jar, average, hazard.
Jasmine, tariff, sugar, hummus, lemon, lime, lute, magazine, mattress, mummy, macabre, nadir, orange, ream, serendipity, sofa, harem, sultan, sheik, syrup, zenith, hookah, zero.

Largest Empires in History
The largest should be the British Empire in 1920. They tend to get bigger over time, but the duration is variable.

The Hajj (1 pg., 30 min.)
The ABC correspondent converted to Islam, so he was allowed to make the Hajj.
Mecca is along the western coast
Plain towel dress makes everyone equal
Road checkpoints make sure only Muslims visit the Great Mosque
Prayer in public encourages community feeling
Seven circuits in counterclockwise direction means to put god at the center of one's life
Zamzam well reenacts thirst and ordeal of Ishmael and Hagar
Tent city is to meet others and sleep on the way to the cave
Plains of Arafat is to meditate on belief, values and look forward in life
Gathering of 49 pebbles is because they will be symbolically thrown at a pillar representing the devil

Star Names
Roman, greek, greek, greek, greek, Arabic, roman, Arabic, roman, Arabic, Arabic, Arabic, Arabic, roman, Arabic, greek, roman, greek, Arabic, Arabic, roman, roman, Arabic, Arabic, greek.
Greek: 7   Roman: 7   Arabic: 11
Secret symbols are: no italics on Roman ones, = signs for Greek ones, and : in Arabic ones
Answers will vary

Islam-Related Terms
Umayyad, Shi'a, Quaraysh, Muslims, Mecca, Islam, Hajj, Ka'ba, Bedouins, Abbasids, caliph, Hadith, Hijira, jihad, mulluh, Quran, sharia, Sunni, umma.

Chapter 10: The Worlds of Christendom

Cyrillic Alphabet

The Byzantines diffused Orthodox Christianity to Kievan Rus, including the architectural style of church building. The domes of St. Sophia in Constantinople became incorporated into St. Basil's cathedral in Moscow and other churches.

The Byzantine form of government was monarchical, with the emperor doubling as the head of the Orthodox Church, represented by the word caesaeropapism. Russia gleaned from the Byzantines the absolute monarchy that existed until 1917, and perhaps conditioned the people under the czars to look to a strong leader. This continued, it can be argued, in the Soviet period, and perhaps even today under Putin. On the spectrum between order and freedom, Russians in poll after poll are more toward order than Americans and other Europeans.

А а	Б б	В в	Г г	Ґ ґ	Д д	Е е	Є є	Ж ж	З з	И и
І і	Ї ї	Й й	К к	Л л	М м	Н н	О о	П п	Р р	С с
Т т	У у	Ф ф	Х х	Ц ц	Ч ч	Ш ш	Щ щ	Ь ь	Ю ю	Я я

Name in Cyrillic will be different, good day is Ґоод Дау. Dobry den is Добру Ден.
Left row cities: Moscow, Saint Petersburg, Novosibirsk, Yekaterinburg.
Right row people: Rurik, Igor, Olga, Vladimir.

Medieval Philosophy

Answers will vary, but most people will choose free will, either of their own free will or because they are predetermined to do that.

Answers will vary, but in the Age of Faith, the idea that the afterlife will be a heaven or a hell was a great driving force in the behavior of people on earth. The hope that the soul did go on, and transcend time, was very much a part of reality.

This funny question is like a psychologist asking, "what's your power animal, or safety animal…"

Anselm might be agreed with or disagreed with.

Most Muslims view Averroes with suspicion because Islamic doctrine says the Quran is literal truth, and that there is life for the soul after the body dies.

A student may agree that God is undefinable or they may not

Answers will vary.

Slavic Terms Used in English

Czar, sable, tundra, mammoth, pierogi, spruce, pavlovian, robot, parka, Boyar, dacha, taiga, matryoshka, slave, kremlin, paprika, vampire, troika, trapak, polka.

Central European Sights

Budapest	Prague	Krakow
Krakow	Budapest	Prague
Prague	Krakow	Budapest
Krakow	Budapest	Prague
Prague	Budapest	Krakow

Romanesque – B, gothic – D, renaissance – A, Neo-Gothic – C.
Answers will vary on which city would be number one for a tour.

Cathedral

d. Beaulieu

1. a. Romanesque, 2. a. Veil of Mary, 3. b. Years, 4. Bishop Gervais wanted his own stone to be used, so he could profit from it. It was of inferior quality, however, which led to the collapse. 5. It brought the people together in aid of a superordinate goal, one they could only accomplish together. 6. Gothic aspects are buttresses, vaulted ceilings, flying buttresses, rose windows and other stained glass, tall spires, ironwork on the doors, statues, etc. 7. The merchant was inspired to give up his possessions to the church, which then could be finished.

Vikings
There should be labeled lines going to all these places the Vikings journeyed.
"Hedging their bets" means in this context that the Vikings were honoring the Norse gods on one side and Christ on the other because they were making sure one of them was right, Valhalla or Heaven, so it was a kind of insurance policy.

Comparisons: Byzantine and Latin Christendom

Western	Byzantium
Kingdoms	empire
Small cities	grand imperial capital
Charlemagne	Justinian and Theodora
Canon law & decree	corpus iuris civilis
Papal supremacy	casaeropapism
Monasticism	iconoclasm
Missi Dominici	theme system
Feudal	Bezant
Vikings/Magyars/Mus.	Sassanians/Muslims

Surnames
Answers for this will vary depending on the student's ancestry.

Castle!
Wales, rebellious.
Defensive: the English, especially castle and town residents.
Offensive: the Welsh, natives of the land.
P, S, E.
Drawbridge, curtain wall (outer, inner), ward, well, murder holes, portcullis, arrow loops, towers, chapel, great hall, quarters, storerooms, etc.
Catapults (trebuchets), siege engines, arrows, flaming arrows, armor, swords (broad, short), chainmail, sapping (under the tower).
Yes, the castle withstood the siege
They declined because of better relations with the natives (Scots, Welsh), because of increased trade, economic factors, because the towns became more populated, and because the feudal order was transforming into a mercantilist one.
The town grew in importance, its port became of great import, and its rise mirrored the castle's decline.

Castles Grand
The castle is on the right, on the high hill, the palace is more luxurious.
They built castles as offensive weapons to hold the territory they conquered by attrition.
B.
B.
Not much, foliage, a few peasant hovels were elimintated.
The oldest stone building in Britain.
Aberwyvern (err, that was supposed to say Carnarvon).
B.
Conway.
Answers will vary.
Windsor is the seat of the royal family, the Tower of London.
Moat, he was angry because he was giving up some sovereignty to the nobles' Parliament.
Answers will vary, answers will vary.
French gardens are geometric, answers will vary.

Chapter 11: Pastoral Peoples on the Global Stage

Central Asian Terms in English
Coffee, Batman, Yogurt, Caffeine, Baklava, Cossack, Janissary, Khan, Kiosk, Ottoman, Pastrami, Pilaf, Shaman, Shish-kabob, Ataman, Pasha, Balkan, Altai, Yurt, Kumiss, Urdu.

Great Clips: Genghis Khan / Pax Mongolica
1) flat grassland, almost no trees, very little in the way of foliage, sometimes hilly.
2) ate meat and dairy, did not eat vegetables, fruits, or grains
3) khans would send messengers to the city to spread fear and try to compel surrender before the fight khan routinely slaughtered everyone in cities that resisted, and in one case feigned retreat
4) they ensured travel and trade, "gold plate on the head" etc. built inns each horse-day away, integrated the largest landmass

1) Great Khan will take silver from them and give them paper money instead.
2) Like Pony Express, allowed travel to be swift, information highway. Food and shelter too, news.
3) different things are sold at different gates, lots of foreign artisans, good doctors, tolerant, cosmopolitan.
4) A
5) They invited (or just brought) scholars and craftsman to Karakorum.

Great Clips: Yuan Dynasty China / Tamerlane's Empire
Out of the saddle of conquest, they become acclimated to the luxuries of the places they conquer.
Xanadu.
Marco Polo.
Legal restrictions were imposed on the Chinese by the Mongols.
Chinese expressed culture through the arts and language.
Kublai Khan was decadent in that he became soft, had many wives and servants, tons of food & leisure.
The ships sank in a storm, they became depressed, and he contemplative as well. "What does it all mean?"
By conquering the luxuriant country and ruling its population, he became less heroic as he became more enamored with that luxury.

Blue.
C.
B.
200,000, India, Persia.
Muslim.
His empire fell apart when he died.

Chapter 12: The Worlds of the 15th Century

Renaissance Literature
Dialogues and Poetry, A.
The Decameron, J.
The Courtier, A.
Ninety-Five Theses, F.
The Prince, M.
Institutes of the Christian Religion, K.
In Praise of Folly, L.
On the Revolutions of the Celestial Spheres, E.
Utopia, G.
The Spiritual Exercises, N.
Notebooks, B.
Gargantua and Pantagruel, I.
The Essays, C.
Laments, D.

Zheng He's Treasure Ships / Renaissance Fashions / Russian Empire
Arabs, Malabar and Coromandel Coast Indians, Swahili Coast Africans, Chinese, peoples of the Indies such as Funan, Shrijava and the Khmers, among others.
The Ming took power from the Yuan, who were seen as outsiders because they were Mongols.
A giraffe.
To demonstrate the undeniable power of China- it was a show of strength.
They were much larger than Columbus' ships.

Fashion is a form of status, it confers status anyway, it also is an object of interest, like the arts, for people with the leisure time to appreciate and delve into it.

Wealthy nobles patronized artists (this is not a slang term, they really paid them) to produce works that would justify the cost, increase their status and be beautiful objects. The commissioned paintings, sculptures, music, furniture, buildings, historical and literary works, and supported the whole Renaissance endeavor. Everything.

The Renaissance was a cultural surge that began in Italy and spread to Northern Europe. In all fields of the arts and sciences, but there was more cultural evolution than social evolution.

St. Basils commemorated the throwing off the Mongol Yoke.

Early cinema glorified the strength of certain czars, like Ivan the Terrible, and Russia's defeat over Germany in the Battle on the Ice in the movie Alexander Nevsky.

The Oprichnina was a state police force under the Ivans that started a trend that has had mixed results in Russian society- the trend of large security bureaucracies, including secret police. The later czarist Ochrona, the post-1917 communist Cheka, the WWII-era NKVD, the political officers who had power of life and death over enlisted men, the postwar KGB and the modern-day FSB, are all incarnations.

Great Clips: Mehmed II and the Ottomans / Akbar and the Mughals
1. Since 1071 when the Saljuk Turks fought the Byzantines at Manzikert – 400 years.
2. Climbed up the sewer.
3. B.
4. They spin themselves into a kind of ecstasy.
5. Coffee.

6. Islam.
7. They were not conservatively dressed and wore bright colors, and they danced in a vivacious way.
8. Plunder.
9. They would not submit to his rule, they revolted.
10. More.
11. 800, give or take.
12. Not very successful, because the representatives of the various faiths argued.
13. She was dissatisfied with Akbar's having been seduced by life in India, much like Kublai in China.

New Horizons Vocab Review
1. B, 2. F, 3. O, 4. L, 5. A, 6. H, 7. K, 8. R, 9. N, 10. P, 11. C, 12. E, 13. I, 14. G, 15. M, 16. J, 17. Q, 18. D.

Chapter 13: Political Transformations: Empires and Encounters

Explorers' Matrix

Explorer	Year	Country	Description
Dias	1488	portugal	rounded Cape of Good Hope
Da Gama	1498	portugal	reached India sailing around Africa, set up trade relations
Columbus	1492	spain	reached the Caribbean Islands, rounded Hispaniola and Cuba
Vespucci	1497	spain	realized Columbus had found a new world, now called after him
De Balboa	1513	spain	discovered Pacific Ocean by crossing Isthmus of Panama
De Leon	1513	spain	discovered Florida and named it
Magellan	1519	spain	sailed around the world, dying in Philippines but crew made it
Cabral	1500	portugal	located Brazil and claimed it for Portugal, used Volta do Mar
Albuquerque	1507	portugal	Red Sea, Persian Gulf, Straits of Malacca, admiral of Indies
Cabot	1497	england	discovered coast of North America, claimed for England
Cartier	1534	france	sailed into Gulf of St. Lawrence, down the river, claimed Canada
Cortes	1519	spain	conquistador of the Aztec Empire, established New Spain
Pizarro	1532	spain	conquistador of the Inca Empire, established New Castile
De Soto	1539	spain	explored Florida interior, Southeast USA
Coronado	1540	spain	explored Northern Mexico, Kansas,
Drake	1577	england	2nd to circle the world, upped English prestige, defeated armada
Hudson	1609	dutch	looking for NW Passage, landed at Manhattan, Hudson River
Raleigh	1587	england	helped start the Lost Colony of Roanoke, first in America
Smith	1607	england	started the Jamestown colony, first permanent ENG settlement
Bradford	1620	england	led Pilgrims to found the Massachusetts Bay colony
De Champlain	1608	france	father of New France, founded Quebec City, Lake Champlain
Marquette	1668	france	explored the Great Lakes, part of Mississippi River
De La Salle	1684	france	explored more Great Lakes, claimed all of Mississippi basin
Cook	1770	england	discovered Australia, New Zealand, Hawaii and other Pacific...
Tasman	1642	dutch	discovered Tasmania, Fiji, other places for the VOC

Bligh	1789	english	captain during the Mutiny on the Bounty, set adrift but lived
Bering	1728	russia	explored eastern Siberia and Alaska, found a new sea/strait
Barents	1597	dutch	arctic explorer, Barents Sea named after him, stranded a year
La Perouse	1786	france	explored Alaska, California, East Asia, Japan, Russia, Pacific
Lewis/Clark	1803	american	went from sea to shining sea and came back to report to USA
Parkman	1846	american	wrote a famous book about exploring the Oregon Trail
Bellingshausen	1820	russia	circumnavigated globe for Russia, discovered Antarctica
Peary	1909	american	discovered North Pole
Amundsen	1911	norwegian	discovered South Pole

First Around the World?
Magellan: captain who led the expedition of five ships around the world
Pigafetta: kept the diary record of the entire expedition, later published
Lapu-Lapu: tribal leader in the Philippine islands who fought Magellan in the battle where he died
Elcano: after Magellan died, Elcano led the remainder of the crew all the way back to Spain
Atlantic: storms mostly
South America: couldn't find passage through to the Pacific Ocean, continent was larger than believed
Pacific: world was larger than believed too, crew hit doldrums and it was very hot, scurvy, hunger
Philippines: did battle, lost Magellan
Spice Islands: finally arrived to destination, loaded ships up with spices, but were chased by Portuguese
Indian: kept trying to elude the Portuguese
Spain: barely got back, one ship out of five, with 18 men including Elcano and Pigafetta
Answers will vary. Answers will vary.

Crash Course World History #23: The Columbian Exchange
Top: There are many benefits and costs to the Columbian Exchange, students should get at least five of each from the episode.
Answers will vary as to whether it was a net gain or loss.
Animals old to new: cat, cattle, chicken, donkey, goat, bee, horse, rabbit, pig, sheep, water buffalo

Animals new to old: alpaca, guinea pig, llama, Muscovy (chicken) duck, turkey.

Plants from old to new: almond, apple, apricot, asparagus, banana, barley, basil, beet, broccoli, cabbage, cauliflower, collard greens, kale, carrot, celery citrus fruits, cucumber, cumin, eggplant, coffee, flax, fig, garlic, ginger, hemp, leek, lentil, lettuce, mango, oat, okra, olive, onion, opium, oregano, pea, peach, pear, pistachio, pomegranate, radish, rice, rye, sorghym, soybean, spinach, sugarcane, watermelon, wheat, yam.

Plants from new to old: agave, allspice, avocado, bell pepper, cashew, chili pepper, cocoa, bean, feijoa, guava, maize, manioc, papaya, passionfruit, peanut, pecan, pineapple, pitaya, potato, prickly pear, pumpkin, quinoa, sapodilla, squash, stevia, strawberry, sugar apple, sunflower, sweet potato, tobacco, tomato, vanilla, yucca, zucchini.

Diseases from old to new: plague, chicken pox, cholera, flu, leprosy, malaria, measles, scarlet fever, smallpox, typhoid, typhus, whooping cough, yellow fever.

Diseases from new to old: Chagas, syphilis.

Chapter 14: Economic Transformations: Commerce and Consequence

Great Clips: Jamestown / Brazilian Slavery and Sugarcane
King James.
Simple cloth garments.
Pests and disease because of the swampy conditions, lack of food and security.
The relationship had its ups and downs, a deal here and there for trade, but lack of security.
"He who shall not work, shall not eat."
Tobacco was the salvation of the colony.

A.
Lack of indigenous labor, overall labor shortage, cash crop potential, especially sugarcane.
There was a shortage of indigenous labor
Many stages of harvesting and production, boiler room conditions were difficult, cutting was difficult.
African dance, social hierarchies, architecture of housing, drums and music, syncretic holiday rituals.

Labor Systems
1. Mesopotamia, 2. Egypt, 3. Hebrews, 4. Helots, 5. Latifundia, 6. India, 7. China, 8. Swahili, 9. Serfs, 10. Aztec, 11. Mita, 12. Encomienda, 13. Africa, 14. Brazil, 15. American South.

16. Indenture, 17. Dutch East India, 18. Janissaries, 19. Slave, 20. Barbary Pirates, 21. Corvee, 22. Laissez-faire, 23. Asia, 24. Russia, 25. Zaibatsu, 26. Draft, 27. Axis camp, 28. Gulag, 29. Workers' Paradise, 30. Sex trafficking, 31. Sweatshop, 32. Tax farm.

Piracy on the Spanish Main
1. c. Columbus. 2. Buccaneers. 3. c. Hispaniola. 4. The bucs and the Spanish fought often and the Spanish killed all the animals the Bucs ate. 5. d. Henry Morgan. 6. c. Jamaica. 7. Privateer. 8. b. Grenade. 9. They pissed it away on prostitutes and drinking. 10. Answers will vary. 11. They were disappointed with their booty. 12. Not well. 13. The treaty (1713) ended the War of the Spanish Succession between England and France. The English had the upper hand in it, as the thrown of Spain and France almost were combined. The treaty stopped that.

How to Pirate Sources
1. L'Olonnais: 1660s, attacked Spanish ships and towns, cruel.
2. Roberts: Well dressed, captured 400 ships, was strict and for a pirate, rather moral
3. Morgan: Attacked Spanish cities and ships, captured a lot, became wealthy, died of alcoholism
4. England: 1720s, a privateer in the war of the Spanish Succession
5. Bonney: Two timed her husband, a pirate, with a second pirate, Calico Jack
6: Teach: Blackbeard, served England as a privateer before fighting in Queen Anne's War
7. Calico Jack: Wore calico clothes. Designed the Jolly Roger flag
8. Barbarossa: Muslim pirate who raided Christian villages in the Mediterranean, awarded by Suleiman
9. Read: Cross dressed as a man, joined the British military as "Mark Read"
10 Drake: Knighted for circumnavigating globe, fought Spanish ships, did slave trading in 1570s
Answers will vary depending on which pirate is chosen.
A source should be cited correctly for the extra info on the pirate.

Inca Gold (or Silver)
1. Finance is the system of lending that banks, companies, sharks and individuals do. 2. Labor. 3. To meet the Inca rulers and perhaps conquer them, extending the power and prestige of the Spanish Empire. 4. They found a mountain of silver, which is mined still today, 500 years later. 5. The Inca did not have a monetary system based on coins, metals, or paper. 6. Work a certain amount of time on what the colonial government told them to. 7. Inflation occurred due to the flooding of the world market with mita-mined silver. 8. B. 9. Americans trust the U.S. treasury and federal reserve bank will not print so any dollars that they will lose their value. 10. B. 11. Various.

Chapter 15: Cultural Transformations: Religion and Science

Christian Denominations
1. Answers will vary depending on what city you live in
2. 1054   3. 1517   4. 1534   5. 1536

Henry VIII: The Tyrant King?
1) People were generally happy and excited because his father, Henry VII, usurped the throne and now Henry provided a bit of stability to the crown- if he could produce an heir...
2) England had a rigid class status system, nobles, commoners and kings all took their titles very seriously. There was less social mobility.
3) His father was a usurper, and if he couldn't produce an heir, it might not work to leave the crown to a near relative or even a daughter, because there would be challengers to the throne.
4) Thomas Wolsey was favored by Henry at the beginning, he was Archbishop of York anyway so he was busy, but in London he became Lord Chancellor and a great advisor to the king. Trouble started for him when he failed to negotiate with the pope for the divorce of Henry with Catherine.
5) Answers will vary.
6) B
7) B
8) She was very anti-pope, believing that the pope was anti-Christ and counseled Henry to break from the church.
9) Cromwell well-played this by gaining the support of Parliament so it would seem to the people, who were not all ready for Reformation, to accept the break from the church. He likely avoided a massive revolution by doing this.
10) Injury came from a jousting accident.

11) Jane Seymour was his third wife, but bore him a sun, the future Edward VI, who would not reach maturity and whose 10-year reign was governed by regents.
12) Wars in Italy, Catherine Howard's (wife #5) execution
13) Actually, it does well- for all his bellyaching about a son, his daughter, Elizabeth I, was one of England's greatest monarchs.
14) Answers will vary.

A New Worldview
Eratosthenes, Ptolemy, Copernicus, Kepler, Galileo, Newton, Einstein, Lemaitre, Hubble, Hoyle, Gamow, Dicke, Penzias & Wilson.

Every 'heliocentric system' will be different, but if we are making a map of the heliocentric system with every world that is a sphere (the minimum diameter is about 500km, a bit bigger if it is made mostly of rock, a bit smaller if there is a large component of water ice), then we have a bigger job than we thought. First the Sun in the center. Then Mercury and Venus, no moons there. the Earth should have its Moon, while Mars is next (it has two moons but they are tiny and shaped like potatoes. Ceres is a sphere in the Asteroid Belt (and Vesta and Pallas almost are), then comes Jupiter and its four spherical moons: Ganymede, Callisto, Europa and Io. Next is Saturn, with Titan, Rhea, Iapetus, Dione, Tethys, Enceladus, and Mimas (the smallest spheroid in the Solar System). Next is Uranus, with Titania, Oberon, Umbriel, Ariel and Miranda. Next is Neptune with Triton (Proteus is almost a sphere but not quite, despite being bigger than Mimas). Pluto and its moon Charon are next, both spheres, then Eris, 2007OR10, the largest object in the Solar System without a name, Makemake, Haumea, Quaoar, and Sedna, Orcus and Salacia.

Newton's Discovery
Trying to solve how gravity works mathematically.
Gothic style at Cambridge.
C.
D.
A.
The inverse-square law, which became Newton's Law of Universal Gravitation.
Royal Geographic Society.
E.
Mathematical Principles of Natural Philosophy.
B.
Answers will vary depending on how old the students are.
Answers will vary.

The Age of Reason
Answers will vary, but anarchy might be part of a realistic one.
Leviathan.
Good people might have to be 'bad' to protect themselves from bad people, this is diffidence.
Answers will vary from national defense to a guaranteed income. Lots of room here.
Life, Liberty and Property.
The box should have the correct labels around, with a person inside it, arrows from the influences to the person and vice-versa, and the term "Human agent" or "Human agency" accompanying the outbound arrows.

Governing Strategies
Tradition: C
Force: B
Social Contract: A
Nationalism: D
Answers will vary as to what the names of the students' home places are.
Answers will vary as to which one informs the identity of the student the most.

Word Project Builder
The images should accurately represent the concepts of humanism, vernacular, 95 Theses, Council of Trent, heliocentric theory and Boyle's Law.

Chapter 16: Atlantic Revolutions, Global Echoes

Absolutely Awesome! and Enlightenment Story

	England	France	Austria	Russia
Dynasty	stuart	bourbon	habsburg	romanov
Monarchs	James ii	Charles I	Charles V	Catherine II
Capital	London	Paris	Vienna	St. Petersburg
Palace	Buckingham	Versailles	Schonbrunn	Zimni (Winter)

Gravity, Newton, Yes, Order, Life, Liberty, Property, Natural, Consent, Popular Sovereignty, Legislative, Executive, Judicial, Balances, Separation of Powers, Religion, Speech, Press, Assemble, Associate, Wealthier, Currency, Capitalism, Equality.

American History Diagnostic Test
1. Great Britain.
2. Celebrate Declaration of Independence.
3. 1776, but it's a trick question because Venture and Booth were not founders.
4. Celebrate Declaration of Independence.
5. Washington, Adams, Jefferson, Madison, Hamilton, Franklin, Jay, Hancock, Paine, Henry, etc.
6. 1776.
7. Wrong.
8. Answers will vary.
9. We did not win independence from China.
10. We did not win independence from the Axis of Evil.
11. The Fourth of July celebration of declaring to be a free and sovereign country.
12. 1776.
13. Washington, Adams, Jefferson, Madison, Hamilton, Franklin, Jay, S. Adams, etc.
14. *We, the People, in order to form a more perfect union, establish justice, ensure domestic tranquility, provide for the common defense, promote the general welfare, and secure the blessings of liberty to ourselves and our posterity, do ordain and establish this Constitution for the United States of America.*

In Congress, July 4, 1776
1. No, because the states were not, as yet, united by the Constitution.
2. All Mankind.
3. Life, Liberty and the Pursuit of Happiness.
4. When a long train of abuses and usurpations… reduce them under absolute despotism.
5. Students will circle all the "He" pronouns Jefferson uses in this section.
6. Yes.
7. refused, forbidden, neglected, called together, dissolved, caused, endeavored, obstructed, made, erected, sent, kept, affected, combined with others, quartering, cutting, imposing, depriving, transporting, abolishing, taking away, suspending, abdicated, plundered, transporting, constrained, excited, etc.
8. Petition for a redress of grievances.
9. No animosity toward the people.
10. Circle: *That these United Colonies are, and of Right ought to be Free and Independent States; that they are Absolved from all Allegiance to the British Crown, and that all political connection between them and the State of Great Britiain is and ought to be totally dissolved.*
11. Levy war, conclude peace, contract alliances, establish commerce, etc.
12. Their lives, their fortunes and their sacred honor.

Got Rights? Prove it!
1. 1st, 2. 3rd, 3. 4th, 4. 2nd, 5. 4th, 6. 9th, 7. 6th and 7th, 8. 6th, 9. 5th and 8th, 10. 10th.

Phases of the French Revolution
Ancien Regime, War debt, Enlightenment consciousness, Estates-General, Tennis court, National Assembly, Bastille, Great Fear, Declaration of the Rights of Man, Constitution, Olympe de Gouges, Flight to Varennes, Girondists, Jacobins, September Massacres, Committee of Public Safety, Levee en Masse, La Marsaillaise, Marie Antoinette, Thermidorian Reaction, Le Directoire, Coup of 18 Braumaire, Victories, Defeats, Elba, St. Helena.

Text Analysis: American Revolutionary Songs
1. Circle: tyrannous acts or in freedom we're born, live.
2. In freedom we're born, in freedom we'll live.
3. C.
4. American, Boston, Congress.
5. It is a call for unification in a time there were still many Loyalists, emphasizing reminders of what the cause was, and why it was being fought at such a huge sacrifice.
6. Five.
7. Sweet, where my fathers died, pilgrim's pride, noble free, rocks, rills, woods, templed hills.
8. The American flag.
9. Does the flag still fly over a land of free and brave people.
10. If we praise the power that hath made and preserved us a nation. Only then can we conquer when we must, and when out cause is just. Only then will the star-spangled banner in triumph wave over us.
11. Crown thy good with brotherhood; Confirm thy soul in self-control.
12. Answers will vary.

Text Analysis: European National Songs
1. The queen/king.
2. May she defend *our* laws (not *her's*) and ever *give us cause* to sing…
3. B.
4. Navy.
5. They are an island, impenetrable in the days before air bombing, with a powerful navy, and also they had a huge empire flung around the world, managed, defended and monitored by naval power.
6. B.

7. B.
8. It is a marching song, played to a marching beat, rousing and aggressive.
9. Size of the country (implied by from this to that and this to that), women, loyalty, wine, song.
10. They got rid of the first, because it put country ahead of everything in the world, and the second, because it bragged that all these things that were *German* were good and great. The third they kept, and it is the anthem of today, because it sings about the same rights and freedoms all countries can ask for under the rubric of the Enlightenment.

The Count of Monte Cristo
1. Napoleon was on Elba under guard so he couldn't escape. He did (The Hundred Days).
2. Marseilles.
3. Mr. Morrel, the owner of the *Farallon,* gave Edmond the captaincy because Edmond made the decision to try and save the sick captain's life on the voyage. Danglars was next in line for captain, but didn't act like it. He was jealous and angry, and felt slighted.
4. Edmond and Fernand had a few sources of animosity. One was Mercedes, who they both were interested in, but she loved Edmond and Fernand was jealous of that. Another source was Fernand's jealousy over Edmond being a commoner and he a nobleman, and yet Edmond seemed to enjoy life more than he did, finding joy in the little things (he loved his simple whistle more than you your fancy pony…). Another source was the fact that Edmond didn't reveal the existence of the letter from Napoleon to Fernand, because he gave his word to Napoleon he wouldn't tell anyone about it.

traits	motivation
5. Innocent, warm-hearted, and loyal.	Seeks revenge because his friends betrayed him, put him in jail.
6. Conniving, cold-hearted, skilled.	Betrays Edmond because he wants Mercedes and is jealous.
7. Loyal, loving, pragmatic.	Marries Fernand only because was told Edmond was dead.
8. Conniving, jealous, bad temper.	Conspires to put Edmond in jail so he can captain the *Farallon.*
9. Just, loyal, honest.	Gave Edmond the captaincy of the ship because he deserved it.
10. Conniving, selfish, opportunist.	Sentenced Edmond to prison and lied to family to protect himself.
11. Intelligent, experienced, moral.	Wanted Edmond to read, fight, and be a good man. And escape.
12. Loyal, pragmatic, humorous.	Wanted best for he and Edmond after Edmond pardoned his life.
13. Pragmatic, loyal, honorable thief.	Helped Edmond (for money) at key moments.

14. Answers will vary.
15. Answers will vary.
16. Symbols will vary.

Casta Culture
Haiti's social hierarchy triangle should have grand blancs at the top, petit blancs next, then gens de coloeur, and finally black slaves. The top three should be about 20 percent of the population, the slaves 80 percent.
Mexico's social hierarchy triangle should have peninsulares at the top, then criollos, mestizos and indigenous peoples at the bottom. The top two should be about ten percent, mestizos should be about 70 percent, and indigenous 20.
1. B.
2. Social status, desire for "European" Enlightenment rights coming out of the French Revolution.
3. A, due to the role of germs in making it happen.
4. The *criollos* wanted to keep their social status, which was under threat from Spain, and thus the Mexican Revolution was in a sense 'conservative' in a time when Enlightenment values were promoting more liberal concepts such as natural rights and, in the case of Jacobin France, an end to slavery and class statuses.
5. Maximilian I.

Crash Course World History #31: Revolutions in Latin America
1. Spanish crown, Catholic church, patriarchy
2. A.
3. A.
4. Brazil, Portugal.
5. Peninsulares
6. Hidalgo led a peasant uprising against the peninsulares, but they also attacked cirollos.
7. They wanted to hold on to their privileges after the 1820 liberal revolution in Spain.
8. Junta is a revolutionary army or paramilitary force, llaneros are cowboy types in Latin America.
9. Chile, Argentina.
10. Llanero, the kind of cowboy who helped Bolivar win the day in northern South America.
11. Simon Bolivar got the letter, and he tried to united a large part of South America as Gran Colombia, but it didn't work out.
12. F
13. The revolutions were AGAINST the Enlightenment principles and liberal reforms taking root in Europe and America.

Chapter 17: Revolutions of Industrialization

Mill!
1. They sought out investors and found Josiah Gresham.
2. Bobbin, flying shuttle, pedals, etc.
3. Water rights were big because the new Northgate Mill slowed the water's speed by backing it up, and this slowed down the mill wheel at the Huntington facility- the one case in history when being 'up' river was a negative thing...
4. A.
5. E.
6. P.
7. S.
8. G.
9. E.
10. He goes out to the Great West, and winds up as a '49er in San Francisco. He struck a little gold and is doing well. With the dearth of women out there, no wonder he sent his very nice letter all the way out east!
11. Answers will vary.

Industrial Manchester Game
Each student's city will be different-looking. However, they should all have the essential features.

Inventions Flowchart
Industrial age: locomotive, phonograph, stove/oven, steam engine
Machine age: internal combustion engine-carbureted, operator phone, room-sized computer, rotary phone, toaster
Space age: cassette tape, desktop computer, internal combustion engine-fuel injected, microwave, push- button phone, VHS
Digital age: cell phone, compact disc, digital video disc, hybrid electric engine, laptop computer, mp3, mp4, Internet.
Answers will vary about future speculation on technologies, but a good clip to watch to get a hint at some cool ones is Video Search: *Michio Kaku the World in 2030*.

Social Criticism in Art: Hogarth
Poverty, alcoholism, homelessness, prostitution, broken families.

1. Moll arrives in London, and is drafted into prostitution by the brothel-keeper.
2. Mistress of wealthy Jewish merchant, who treats her "well" giving her stuff and servants.
3. From 'kept woman' to full prostitute.
4. Arrested for being a harlot and in jail.
5. Sick with syphilis.
6. At her funeral wake, her friends fight over her stuff and steal what they can.

1. Son of a rich man, this rake (a debauchee) is ending it with his pregnant fiancée. Says he'll pay her off.
2. Gone to London to chill and hang out, the rake Tom is getting up with his new friends.
3. Wild, drunken party at a brothel- maybe it's Molls, who knows- where Tom is having a crazy night.
4. Having spent all his cash, Tom is being chased by the cops for his debts. Sarah his baby mama helps.
5. He is marrying an old woman who is rich to save himself, but is slyly checking out the chick to her left.
6. Newly rich again, he's gambling his wife's money away, while a fire breaks out- and he doesn't notice.
7. He's in debtor's prison on Fleet Street, with other down and out people. Sarah visits but can't help.
8. Insane and violent, he is sent to Bedlam, the infamous madhouse. Sarah visits but he's not interested.

Artists Take On Substance Abuse
1. a glass with friends.
2. a glass to keep the cold out.
3. a glass too much.
4. drunk and riotous.
5. the summit attained – jolly companions. A confirmed drunkard.
6. poverty and disease.
7. forsaken by friends.
8. desperation and crime.
9. death by suicide.

1. husband convinces his wife to just have a bottle.
2. discharged from his employment, pawn their clothes to supply their alcohol habit.
3. debtors collect their furniture (repo), they take a drink to 'comfort themselves'.
4. they lose their house now, and are in the street- all they can do is beg, and use the money for alcohol.
5. cold, misery and want kill their youngest child, they console themselves with a bottle.
6. they hit each other for all this, and drink while doing so.
7. enraged, one day in a fight the husband picks up the bottle and hits his wife, killing her.
8. the bottle has done its work- killing the kid and the mom, leaving the dad a hopeless maniac and two orphaned kids.

1-7 drunkard's neglected son given alcohol in a gin shop, dancing, gambles, arrested, on trial, sentenced, dies. 8. drunkard's neglected daughter jumps off a bridge.

Worship of Bacchus: we are in a cult-like trance of substance abuse, and Bacchus, the party god, is our cult leader. Conveyed by showing scantily clad people in a state of debauchery worshiping the idol Bacchus

Fruits: when we temper ourselves, and not abuse substances, it bears fruit in our lives by healing our family relationships, keeping us prosperous and whole. Conveyed by father bringing kids back home, nice house, everyone all smiles, there's even a white picket fence.

1) Misfortune, the wife has committed adultery. Children surprised, saddened, dad looks like death.
2) Prayer, the husband killed himself out of heartbreak. Daughter cries into the lap of the older one. Amazing how Egg painted a flat-screen computer to the right.
3) Despair, the wife is chilling out under a bridge in it. At the same moment her girls are crying at home. The wages of sin is death.

Awakening conscience: lots of different objects in the room. Should be an explanation for whatever was picked. Answers will vary.

Traditional or Modern?
Modern = Gesellshaft, industrial, exchange, fluid, bubble, calendar, exploitative, alarms, rational, electronics, openness, information, achievement, rule of law, state schools, professionalism.

Greco-Roman = Academy, Medieval = Apprenticeship, Modern = Government run schools
Answers will vary

Great Clips: Industrial Britain / Industrial Working Life
1. B.
2. F.
3. B.
4. B.
5. C.
6. Because there are 24 hours in a day.
7. Longer hours, polluted conditions, repetition, punishments at work, had to be on time, you go 'to work' as opposed to working at home on a farm or in a cottage industry or craftsmanship in the yard, etc.
8. Answers will vary but most will answer it was in some ways dehumanizing.
9. Bessemer Process refines the impurities out of iron to make steel.
10. Nations that industrialized could arm themselves or trade for arms, entered the population transition.
11. Any medical or sanitary invention, such as soap, cotton clothes, vaccinations would count, so would many other things.

The Political Compass
Student should have 18 dots with labels on the graph. Debate with the students if these dots are in the right place and where, for example, Cuba or China should be in relation to North Korea, or the Visegrad countries in relation to Scandinavia.

The Political Compass - Values
In the blanks, we have A1, C3, F5, E1, A3, D3, C4, B3, E3, C1, A5, C5, C2.

Spectre of the Gun
1. Answers will vary.
2. Answers will vary.
3. Buoy said "turn back, do not approach the planet."
4. Answers will vary.
5. The Melkotians obtained the memory engram from Kirk's brain and constructed it around that.
6. His girl took a liking to Claiborne.
7. He tries to fabricate a gas grenade to use in the gunfight, because they know they're going to lose.
8. B.
9. They realize by putting puzzle pieces together (Claiborne lived in real life, the gas grenade should have worked, etc.) that this is *not* the O.K. Corral, that their minds have been fooled into believing it is- and if they use their minds over the matter around them, if they truly believe in the truth of the situation, they cannot die.
10. the Cowboys
11. They see that Kirk and crew really do not hold any animosity or negative intentions, that they really are good people, and they agree to meet the Federation delegates as friends.

Chapter 18: Colonial Encounters in Asia, Africa and Oceania, 1750-1950

ABCs of Imperialism
Army, Battles, Colonies, Daring, Empire, Flag, Game, Hunting, India, Judges, Kings, Lion, Magnates, Navy, Ocean, Parliament, Queen, Roast beef, Scotland, Tub, Unicorn, Volunteers, Word, X = London police, Youngsters, Zeal.
Answers will vary.

Victoria's Empire
1. Britain.
2. Industry, commerce and navigation. HMS Warrior w armor plate, breech loading guns, steel. Also, telegraph, railway line, steamship, science of cartography.
3. C.
4. They were surveyor-spies in Northern India who were figuring out where British India ended, and spying on the Russians in Central Asia.
5. The queen protected her subjects. She sent the rapid-reaction force from India, and they, under Robert Napier, assaulted Magdala, and annihilated Theodore's army.
6. The world saw that Britain was in full control- only 11 years before had been the Sepoy Rebellion.

7. Female infanticide and the Sati ritual of widow burning.
8. C, D.
9. The British used a greasy extract from beef and pig as paste on the cartridges that had to be bitten off by the soldier when loading the ammo.
10. C.
11. Answers will vary.

The Darwin Controversy
1. A. 2. Natural selection. 3. B. 4. B. 5. B. 6. A. 7. 8. B. 9. A. 10. B. 11. B. 12. Imaging the double helix. 13. Discovered DNA as the master molecule of life.

Anna and the King of Siam
Before watching: c. 1. To communicate with the British. 2. Answers will vary. 3. There is cross-border trouble in Burma (a British colony). 4. She is disobedient. 5. Lots. 6. A. 7. B. 8. Answers will vary. 9. Places without independence. 10. Answers will vary.

Eugenics: All About the Seed
1. Answers will vary.
2. They are stronger, smarter, more devious, abler, but not more moral…
3. C.
4. They participated in a war on Earth where the superhumans fought the regular humans and had to be exiled.
5. They send gas through the ship's vents and knock everyone out.
6. Kirk leaves them on a planet called Ceti Alpha 5.
7. Answers will vary.
8. Answers will vary.
9. Answers will vary.

Chapter 19: Empires in Collision: Europe, the Middle East, and East Asia 1800-1900

Great Clips: Hideyoshi / Qing Isolationism
1. Isolationist.
2. The Bald Rat.
3. Toyokuni Shrine.
4. He loved tea ceremonies, bunraku puppet shows.
5. Koreans stopped the Japanese invasion by luck of storm and by turtle boats with flamethrowers on them.
6. Family issues included paranoia about his nephew, ordered seppuku suicide of many members, paranoia about Hideyori, his son, and ultimately, he was right. Regents weakened his rule, then he lost a civil battle against Tokugawa.
7. False.
8. George Washington is a good answer.

9. False, the Ming did.
10. They 'air mimic' the motions of the teacher, who has drawn the symbol on the board.
11. Science, "Dutch learning" / clocks, telescopes
12. The instruments remain there, in much the same state, in the museum.

Asia and the Islamic Empires Matrix

	Qing	Tokugawa	Ottoman	Safavid	Mughal
Place	china	japan	turkey	persia	india
Capital	peking	edo	istanbul	isfahan	fatehpur Sikri
Building	forbidden city	yoshiwara quarter	topkapi	ali qapu	taj mahal
Religion	neo-confucian	shinto	sunni	shi'a	divine faith
Rulers	hongwu	tokugawa	mehmed ii	abbas	akbar
	kangxi	hideyoshi	osman bey	ismail	aurangzeb
	qianlong		suleyman		babur
	yongle				jahan
Issue	E	A	B	D	C

Great Clips: Zenith of the Qing / Opium Trade

1. Population tripled to 300,000. Wealth reach record levels. Szechuan saw an influx of people from across the Qing Empire.
2. Manchus came from the north.
3. Kangxi relocated 1,000,000 people by force to Szechuan. Kangxi introduced New World crops like maize, potatoes and sweet potatoes.
4. Porcelain was found on the sunken ship.
5. Qianlong was skeptical because he knew China produced goods like tea that the British wanted but he led them established a trading house anyway.

6. British grew opium in India and traded it to China to get them hooked on a trade good and to obtain tea in exchange.
7. China
8. Sam Adams threw British tea overboard at the Boston Tea Party, and Lin Zexu had all the British opium thrown into the Pearl River.
9. Gladstone thought it was dishonorable.
10. Treaty of Nanking gave British Hong Kong, trading concessions, and influence in the Chinese court.
11. USA-China is more like Britain-China in the 18th century because there was a large balance of trade favoring China in both cases. In the 19th century the British-China trade was more "balanced".

To Be Industrialized, or Not To Be?

Ottoman --- territorial losses --- tanzimat
Romanovs --- Crimean war --- zemstvos
Qing --- opium war --- self-strengthening
Tokugawa --- rice prices --- maiji reforms
China
Japan
Russia
Turkey
Turkey
China
Russia
Japan
Japan
Russia
China

Chapter 33: The Great War

WWI Objectives
Austria,
Serbia,
Russia,
France,
Germany,
[Belgium...]
Britain,
Turkey,
[Netherlands...]
Italy, Polish, United States.

The Guns of August
Militarism: Dreadnaughts built to compete Britain vs. Germany in the seas, more money and resources spent on new weapons and stockpiling equipment.
Alliances: Entente powers swore to back each other, Alliance partners did as well.
Nationalism: War fever struck, many regular people were thrilled to fight for their country, and everyone was overconfident.
Imperialism: colonial competition, Germany wanted inroads into the colonial game, Britain wanted to block them.
Assassination: Archduke Ferdinand's murder sparked the powder keg, and all these other factors informed the decisions like "Attack Serbia for not fulfilling the last stipulation…"
Answers will vary.
Answers will vary.

WWI Clips: Trenches / Truce / Lusitania
Machine gun, poison gas (chlorine and mustard), zeppelins (blimps), aeroplane, tank, gas mask, trench fortifications, flamethrowers, U-boats, etc.

British and Germans. Called a cease-fire on Christmas Day, 1914, on the Western Front, because war is against the Christmas spirit. The Germans came across No Man's Land at zero hour, unarmed and singing carols, which the British reciprocated.

A passenger ship carrying over 1,000 people from America to Europe.
Its sinking helped turned American public opinion, previously neutral, against Germany.
It was sunk by a Germany U-boat torpedo.
Over 1,000 people.
The POV of the Winsor MacKay film was anti-German in the sense that it portrayed the sinking as the dastardliest of deeds using imagery mixed with statistics and case studies (lists of well-known people who were on the ship). It did not say there were also war materials on the ship, it also didn't say the Germans warned ships not to enter that warzone.
Sketches will vary.

WWI Comics
Each of the shapes will be different, with a weird little smile and some weapons or other gear.
Germany has an Iron Cross, a sword, and a helmet with a #1 on it, Russia has a bottle of alcohol, France has a funny moustache, England has a teacup.
Newspaper says "United States Declares War on Germany" on April 6, 1917.
Germany is portrayed as angry.
Wet, nasty trenches after it rained, nastiness of No Man's Land of barbed wire, tragedy of total wasteland when everything was quiet, despair in hospital wards. Battles of Ypres, Passchendaele, Nieuport, Fernes and Pervyse are fine.
Answers will vary as to which ones affect the students most, and why.

American WWI Posters
1. War bonds: People were encouraged because the government needed their contributions to fund the war. Everything was dependent on them, freedom in the world, not letting the Hun win, safety of the soldiers…

2. Enlistment: people were needed for the army and navy, air corps and marines, along with secondary services. They used some shaming, "Look everyone else is doing it…" "This woman wishes she were a man so she could join…" They appealed to patriotism and sense of duty, they made it seem like a great crusade, exciting and adventurous.

3. Women's Roles: Nurse and other medical support staff, secretaries, telephone, telegraph and communications operators, munitions makers.

4. Kids: Saving food, eating corn (specifically), starting school garden clubs, encouraging the soldiers with gift packages and books, etc.

5. Charity: The troops always needed care packages, hunger afflicted much of Europe, so food collection was asked for, the Red Cross needed supplies and volunteers.

6. Propaganda: Germans portrayed as bullies, in league with Satan, butchers of innocent people (Remember Belgium!) and as bent on world conquest.

Women's Roles in WWI
Answers will vary depending on which posters students pick, but they have to be about women.

Battles of WWI
1914: Liege, The Frontiers, Tannenberg, Heligoland Bight, Marne, Masurian Lakes.
1915: Sandfontein, Ypres, Isonzo, Gallipoli, Armenian Genocide, R.M.S. Lusitania.
1916: Great Retreat, Verdun, Jutland, Kut, Brusilov, Somme.
1917: Nivelle, Baghdad, Kerensky, Russian Revolution, Zimmerman, Balfour, Jerusalem, Cambrai, Passchendaele.
1918: Belleau Wood, Chateau-Thierry, Amiens, Vittorio Veneto, Friedensturm, St. Quintin, Argonne.

Trench War - Simulation
Answers will vary depending on what scenario and trench the student picks.

WWI Dead
Bars should reflect the data.
Allies: Portugal, British Indian, Australian, Canadian, Belgian, Port. African, Irish, Nepalese, New Zealand, Montenegrin, Estonian, British SA, Japanese, Rhodesian.
Central Powers: Bulgaria.
Neutral: Norway, Sweden, Denmark.
Allies: 9,901,000 lost, Central Powers: 4,365,000 lost, Other: 2,704,000 (Polish, Armenian, Jewish).

The Edge of Forever
1. Answers will vary on whether the Butterfly Effect is relevant in history or only "big things".
2. They enter a time portal called The Guardian.
3. Dr. McCoy has jumped through it and into the past, and did something there to change the future.
4. Cloths are plain, flannel, skirts and dresses, even in a time of poverty the modest clothes people have still look dignified in some way, compared to modern pop culture fashions, but answers may vary.
5. People tended to be more courteous, even in a time of depression and want, but answers may vary.
6. They find out Edith Keeler must die in order to restore the future, and this choice is especially difficult for Kirk because he has fallen in love with her.
7. She told them, "One day soon, man is going to be able to harness incredible energies, maybe even the atom... energies that could ultimately hurl us to other worlds in... in some sort of spaceship. And the men that reach out into space will be able to find ways to feed the hungry millions of the world and the cure their diseases. They will be able to find a way give each other hope and a common future. And those are the days worth living for."
8. She would have started a peace movement that would have supported American neutrality in WWII, and kept the U.S. out of the war. In the alternate timeline, Germany developed an atomic bomb and used it to win the war.
9. Answers will vary.

Germ Theory of Disease
1. Answers will vary.
2. Answers will vary.
3. Answers will vary.
4. Four assassinated: Lincoln, Garfield, McKinley, Kennedy. Four died in Office: W.H. Harrison, Z. Taylor, W.G. Harding, F.D. Roosevelt. Three were shot but lived: Jackson, T. Roosevelt, Reagan.
5. Assassinated.
6. Many things wrong. Didn't sterilize instruments, didn't wear gloves, masks or caps. Used ether, that's okay, but they had to turn out the lights. Had to work in the dim light. Gave him raw eggs, enemas and injections of strychnine.
7. **Bacteria**: anthrax, plague, cholera, dysentery, legionnaires, leprosy, lyme, meningitis, salmonella, sepsis, tetanus, tuberculosis, typhus. **Virus**: HIV/AIDS, cold, ebola, hepatitis, measles, stomach flu, pneumonia, rabies, smallpox, yellow fever, zika. **Nutrition deficiencies**: xerophthalmia (vitamin A), rickets (vitamin D), beriberi (thiamin), pellagra (niacin), scurvy (vitamin C), anemia (iron), goiter (iodine).
8. More simple.
9. They believed it was a hotbed for the spread of Bubonic Plague.
10. They wanted to stop the plague from spreading to America.
11. B.
12. A.
13. Answers will vary.
14. American South.
15. When he realized the connection between what people were eating and who was getting the disease, that it wasn't a germ, but a lack of something.

16. Didn't believe a disease could be caused by a lack of vitamins, and didn't like the idea that he might be anti-Southern culture.
17. In the experiment, he took away the vitamins from their diet by giving them mush, cornbread and some pork.
18. Answers will vary.
19. They got pellagra.
20. Answers will vary.

The Messages of Modernism
Uncertainty/insecurity, disillusionment, the subconscious, overt sexuality, violence and savagery.
1. Munch, the scream
2. Marc, animal destinies
3. Kandinsky, on white ii
4. Klimt, Judith i
5. Klimt, wrogie sily
6. Klimt, the Kiss
7. Klimt, danae
8. Matisse, carmelina
9. Matisse, open window
10. Braque, violin and candlestick
11. Braque, woman with a guitar
12. Braque, still life lejour
13. Picasso, les demoiselles d'avignon
14. Picasso, studio with plaster head
15. Picasso, woman with a flower
16. Klee, red and white domes
17. Klee, Sencio
18. Grosz, grey day
19. Grosz, daum marries
20. Grosz, the pillars of society
21. Hausmann, abcd
22. Duchamp, fountain
23. Duchamp, nude ascending a staircase
24. Dali, soft construction with boiled beans
25. Dali, persistence of memory
26. Dali, apparition of the face and fruit dish on a beach
27. Dali, geopoliticus child watching the birth of a new man

Gropius house will be drawn differently by each student
Chair will be draw differently by each.
Philosophy: 1) industry and mass production rather than individual craftsmanship, 2) teachers should be at the advance of the profession, 3) a new modern synthesis, 4) schools should employ both creative and practical artists side by side for the benefit of the student.
Answers will vary.

Tariffs: Tariffying or Tariffic?
Students should place dots in the right place for each of the 12 data items, and connect the dots to make a graph. A question mark should be at the far right.

The circular loan graph should have the US, Britain and Germany, with arrows from the US to Germany, from Germany to Britain, and from Britain back to the US.

Advantages of tariffs include lower unemployment in your country, more wealth recirculated within the domestic economy, a more diverse and self-sufficient economy, and a more favorable balance of trade.

Disadvantages include higher prices for consumer goods and the possibility of retaliation from abroad and a lessening of exports.

Rise of the Dictators
1. B.
2. Usually arrested, interrogated and shipped off to a Gulag.
3. A Gulag is a prison work camp with very tough conditions, often in bitter cold.
4. B.
5. A.
6. He demonstrated how to attract followers by cult of personality, various strong-arm techniques, including the gaining of power at a critical moment, how symbols can be used as unifying features of the party.
7. black shirts, military uniforms, the fasces itself, fashionable attire.
8. The telecast began with a birds eye overview of the Balkans and Central Europe, from Greece north through Yugoslavia, Hungary, Austria and finally to Germany, the path of the Olympic torch from Olympia to Berlin.
9. The Americans did not salute back to Hitler, but they were not disrespectful either (some countries did salute).
10. C.
11. A.
12. The camera pans to the Olympic torch as it reaches its destination, which is 'passing the fire' to light the Olympic flame in a huge goblet. But it pans in such a way that as the sun is setting on the horizon, the flame and the sun combine.

Rise of Japan
1. Yamato-Damashii is the Japanese conception of its own unique spirit. It has been around since the Heian period in the Middle Ages, and informed the Bushido code of the samurai. In the Meiji era, it got another boost, by the government which formulated the concept of wakon, yosai, a conscious borrowing and adaptation of Western methods, within the context of the overall Japanese spirit. It represented a new, modern synthesis.
2. Ziabatsu are large corporate conglomerates that fostered a familial relationship with their workers. They allied with the government to catch up with and in some areas surpass the West in industrial method. They influenced legislation.
3. A strict, orderly society, rather fanatical, dangerous.
4. The emperor, who in the past was a figurehead behind a shogun, was now very much the ceremonial head of state and a major influencing sovereign.
5. The vision was to rule East Asia as a colonial power.
6. Both Germany and Japan had similar beliefs about themselves as superior strains of people within their respective races. Both pursued living space because their countries are small and densely populated. Both are resource poor as far as fossil fuels go, so both needed to obtain them. Both believe they were the countries of destiny, and that the future belonged to them because they were united and strong.
7. Answers will vary.

The Nazi Olympics
1. Because the ancient Olympics were played in Greece. 2. 1916, 1940 and 1944. They were cancelled due to WWI and WWII. 3. London is the city, USA the country. 4. Tourism, money infusion, infrastructure, advertising, cleaning up. 5. Depends on the city in question. 6. The Nuremberg Laws applied to Jews but not to Africans, or African Americans, but there was a system of double standards as in the American South. 7. France seemed to but they were giving an Olympic salute. Italy did, Britain did not. British India did not. Japan did not. America did not. Canada did not. Germany did. 8. Hitler did salute the flag. 9. He was not supposed to congratulate German athletes but he did, so he was reprimanded and decided not to congratulate any athletes. 10. Four gold medals.

Cartoons Go To War
Answers are interpretive and will vary. But the messages overall are pro-American values, vilification of the fascist system, and an intent to justify the war.

New Alliances: Allies and Axis
Status quo: France, Great Britain, Greece, Poland, Yugoslavia.
Revisionism: Austria, Bulgaria, Czechoslovakia (even if against the will of most people), Germany, Hungary, Italy, Romania, Soviet Union.
Neutral: Baltic states, Belgium, Denmark, Norway, Netherlands, Finland, Ireland, Spain, Switzerland, Sweden.

Dear Professor...
1. Answers will vary.
2. The issue of portrayal of Japan during WWII and especially in the conquest and occupation of Manchuria, China. 'Comfort Women' (euphemism for forced prostitution) ran into the tens or even hundreds of thousands, servicing the Japanese occupying army. Most came from Korea and China. They, and the Rape of Nanjing, were the main bones of contention.
3. Ziegler seems to object to the message and the messenger. He defended academic freedom and resented the attempt to influence him from an official representative of the Japanese government.
4. Anna Fifield, her POV seems to agree with the professor.
5. Answers will vary, but it amounts to freedom to research and publish results no matter what they might be, so long as the methods were sound and the research was honest.
6. Answers will vary.
7. Answers will vary, but don't let students off the hook. Make them answer this difficult question of scruples.

Massacre of the Innocents: WWII Dead
Spanish, Russian, Italian, English, Japanese, German, Polish, French.
1. Allies: 52,678,000. Axis: 13,952,000. Neutral: 635,000.
2. Famine: 6,300,000.
3. Spain had just finished a terrible civil war in the late-1930s, in which 500,000 died.
4. American casualties were less than the other major belligerents.
5. Answers will vary.

Chapter 21: Revolution, Socialism and Global Conflict: Rise and Fall of Communism

20th Century Ideologies Simplified
Answers will vary.
Answers will vary.
Answers will vary.

Animal Farm
1. Manor Farm. 2. Humans. 3. The bourgeoisie. 4. He neglected them, and he was a drunk manager who was corrupt and decadent. He also shot Old Major. 5. He treated them like mincemeat and sent them to WWI to die in the millions. 6. The seven commandments: If it has two legs, it is an enemy. If it has four legs, or wings, it's a friend. Animals shall not wear clothes, sleep in a bed, drink alcohol, kill other animals. All animals are equal. 7. Napoleon uses persuasion, propaganda and finally force to take control, he uses pups as security guards and builds a security state apparatus. 8. Napoleon uses TV to propagandize the animals. 9. Napoleon and his apparatchiks get the mild and apples. 10. He says he saved the farm, that the animals are meeting their quotas, etc. 11. Boxer is worked and worked by Napoleon like peasants. He does this partly willingly out of a shared vision of the future, which represents patriotism. 12. Answers vary. 13. Napoleon eventually dies. 14. In 1989 the communist system began to fall in Eastern Europe.

AиIMAL FAяM
1. Kids in the car take pot-shots at the farm animals. 2. Old Major gives a rousing speech. 3. Farmer Jones tries to borrow money from Pilkington and Frederick. 4. The farmers have a decadent party where they cheat on each other and dangerous laison themselves. 5. The animals rally around Old Major's song and words. 6. Jones shoots stay shots into the barn. 7. Jones spends time away from the farm and neglects the animals. 8. The animals decide to overthrow the owner and take control of the means of production themselves. 9. The animals defeat the humans, who flee. 10. Pilkington and Frederick rip on Jones for what happened on his farm. 11. The animals change the name from Manor Farm to Animal Farm. 12. The animals bust into the farmhouse, and examine what the humans lived like. 13. The animals make a new symbol. 14. Napoleon sees the people's TV and figures out he can use it for his own gain. 15. The leaders debate what kind of rules to have. 16. Napoleon takes over the farm and created an enemy out of Snowball. 17. The rulers get the milk and apples. 18. They put Old Major's head on a pike. 19. Frederick tells Pilkington not to deal with the farm. 20. Napoleon has a new anthem made for the farm. 21. Any animal is now under threat of being against the revolution. The security state is deepened. 22. The horse, Boxer, is taken to the slaughter house. 23. A meeting is called. 24. Napoleon falls.

Totalitarian Government
1. F, C, D. 2. C, F, D. 3. D, F, C. 4. D, C, F. 5. F, D, C. 6. F, C, D. 7. D, F, C. 8. D, F, C. 9. F, C, D. 10. C, D, F. 11. D, F, C. The controversy surrounding Mein Kampf is whether it should be reissued to the public in Germany, which it was after the Bavarian government's hold on the copyright expired in 2017. Answers will vary.

Russian Security Terms
Agitprop, cosmonaut, duma, Bolshevik, apparatchik, cheka, commissar, FSB, KGB, kolkhoz, kulaks, NEP, NKVD, nomenklatura, okrhana, oprichnina, perestroika and glasnost, politburo, spetznaz, zemstvos, gulag, samizdat, gavlit.

Lyrics of the Communist Left
1. the internationale will be the human race, its vanguard are the communists of the present day.
2. there is no god, and freedom of religion is irrelevant.
3. group together, decree the common salvation, fan our forge ourselves, strike while the iron is hot.
4. people are cheering for the communists, the kulak who tries to have a private farm is portrayed as a bad guy, the people convincing the farmer to tie his land together into a kolkhoz are shown in a positive light, like they are helping their comrade, the private shop is shown as greedy, fleecing the people, whereas the cooperative shop is shown as a good place to borrow and use, replace and return.

Comparing Chinese & Soviet Communism
1. 1917 and 1949. 2. Guomindang and Whites. 3. Lenin and Mao. 4. Puyi and Nikolai II. 5. Collectivization and Great Leap Forward. 6. Holodomor and Great Chinese Famine. 7. Great Purge and Cultural Revolution. 8. Laogai and Gulag. 9. Solzhenitsyn and Wu. 10. Socialism with a Human Face and Socialism with Chinese Characteristics. 11. Perestroika and Glastnost, and Open Door Policy. 12. Tiananmen Square and Berlin Wall.

Decade by Decade
Boxes on the graph should reflect the data. 1940s.
Ukrainian Holodomor, Soviet Great Purge, Great Leap Forward.

Every Atomic Bomb
1. New Mexico.
2. Hiroshima and Nagasaki.
3. Pacific.
4. Soviet Union.
5. Great Britain.
6. Hydrogen bomb.
7. 300.
8. It was a French colony at the time. Not long after, however, West Africa became independent and France no longer tested there.
9. Tsar Bomba is the largest explosion ever caused by man.
10. There were no electronics within the radius of the EMP shower. Had it been done over a country, it may have affected the electrical grid.
11. China- closer to the USSR.
12. India.
13. Answers will vary but try to pause it right at January 1992.
14. Pakistan.
15. Israel has an estimated 200 nuclear weapons but doesn't officially acknowledge it. South Africa's apartheid government had atomic weapons but disassembled them rather than let the ANC/Mandela government, which entered into power in the 1990s, have them. Atomic racism? Ukraine was left with a lot of nuclear weapons after the fall of the Soviet Union in 1991, and they were paid to decommission them. North Korea has an unknown number, possibly around 10, and has claimed to have detonated a few tests. Iran is said to be working on building one, to the dismay of Israel and the U.S.

Presidents and Premiers of the Cold War
1. Truman. 2. Eisenhower. 3. Kennedy. 4. Johnson. 5. Nixon. 6. Ford. 7. Carter. 8. Reagan. 9. Bush 41
1. Stalin. 2. Khrushchev. 3. Brezhnev. 4. Andropov. 5. Chernenko. 6. Gorbachev.
7. Silly putty.
8. Stalin's treatment of his family was not very nice. He was a bad person all around.
9. The past seems far away… but it really isn't. In fact, the past may be in our future too.

Cold War Map
On the map on the back, there should be A-Z, all 26 letters labeled in the right spot.

Balance of Terror
1. Answers will vary.
2. C. The line of fortifications destroyed is kind of like destroying outposts over the Iron Curtain.
3. B.
4. They have a cloaking device to hide the ship, like American stealth technology of the 1980s.
5. B.
6. The Romulans put a nuclear bomb in some debris to fool the Enterprise crew into thinking they won.
7. Kirk played possum, pretending the ship was damaged beyond repair, then struck by surprise.
8. He is a good sportsman, congratulating Kirk for the victory of the Enterprise over his ship, even in the bitter end.

Who Won the Space Race?
SOV, SOV, USA, SOV, SOV, USA, SOV, USA, SOV, SOV, SOV, SOV, USA, USA, SOV, USA, SOV, USA, SOV, USA, USA, USA, SOV, SOV, USA, SOV, SOV, USA, USA, USA, USA, USA, BOTH. 1. Each has sixteen 'firsts,' so it is a tie. 2. Answers vary. 3a. Twelve objects flown by. 3b. Nine objects orbited: Moon, mars, venus, sun, Jupiter, asteroid, Saturn, mercury, ceres. 3c. Six objects landed on: Moon, Venus, Mars, asteroid, Titan, comet. 3d. Three objects roved upon: Moon, Mars and asteroid. 3e. Three sample returns: Moon, comet, asteroid. 3f. One object visited: Moon. 4. One check mark only- in the Optical-Visible. 5. UV. 6. Microwave. 7. Gamma rays. 8. Radio. 9. Answers will vary.

Worst Game of Chicken… Ever!
1. Tornado, hurricane, active shooter, elevated threat, bomb threat, fire, etc. Surely they can be found on a flip chart in each classroom. 2. Go under your desk and place your hands over your head. 3. It may be good advice, but hardly effective. 4. Fallout is the leftover clouds of radiation that come by. 5. They were calming in the sense that they told people they had a chance if only they followed the right procedures. 6. Answers vary. 7. Baltimore. 8. Arkhipov is unknown as a person, but he was the man in the Soviet sub who did *not* authorize a nuclear launch upon an American city. Two officers did, he refused, and averted nuclear war.

Tear Down This Wall!
1. Khrushchev sent in the tanks to retake Budapest from Nagy and his supporters, and prevented them from leaving the Warsaw Pact by putting down the uprising with force.
2. The German castle and the Austrian archduke's residence are symbols from the past of the fact that the Czechs have rarely in history governed themselves, having always been surrounded by more powerful neighbors. In the present, it is the Soviets who dominate.
3. T.
4. Answers will vary.
5. D.
6. Lech Walesa and the shipyard workers wanted more freedom, more travel rights, more pay, better conditions, and to have a trade union to represent them, *Solidarity.*
Marshall law is when the government deploys the military domestically, enforces curfews and travel restrictions within the country, to gain some social or political goal. In this case, they wanted to stop the popularity of *Solidarity.*
7. The pope, a beloved figure in Catholic Poland, brought a message of hope for the people. The authorities were worried that the communist president, Jaruzelski, was booed by the crowd when he stepped onto the stage to introduce the pope, who was wildly cheered. They even cut the TV feed so people who were not in Krakow wouldn't see what was going on.
8. B.
9. Secret service/cops: 1 and 2, 4.
Stuff in the background: 3 (in a window), 5 (window of limo).
Reagan: 6.
10. B.
11. He says to the crew that their mission is to engage the new technology- a stealth drive system- and sneak up to the coast of America, and fire a nuclear warhead at New York City.
12. Red stars, hammer and sickle, red banners, busts of the leaders, the Year 1917 banner, military equipment, etc.
13. D.
14. SDI's goal was to orbit a series of satellites with lasers on them to shoot down incoming Soviet missiles while they are over the ocean.
15. East Germans wanted to be rid of the wall because they saw it as a symbol of state oppression.
West Germans saw it as a barrier to German unity, and wanted their fellow countrymen to have the same democratic rights they had.
16. Answers will vary.

17. Gorbachev went on vacation to the Crimea, and while he was gone, Boris Yeltsin engineered a coup in Moscow. There was a power struggle, and Yeltsin's faction was stronger. On December 25, 1991, the Soviet Union's government dissolved itself. And the Cold War was over, just like that.

Chapter 22: The End of Empire: The Global South on the Global Stage

India's Political Order
1. Harappa and Mohenjo-Daro.
2. Vedic Age.
3. Mauryan.
4. Gupta.
5. Harsha and Chola.
6. Delhi and Vijayanagar.
7. Mughals.
8. East India rule.
9. Crown colony.
10. Independent India and Pakistan.

10	Bandung
9	Direct Action
4	India act 1937
3	stir for self-rule
7	mass migration
8	millions die
6	Vivisection
2	14 pts.
1	British bleed too
5	WWII

Decolonization in India & Africa
The deal was to split India into India and Pakistan- the Vivisection.
Riots happened on the day of freedom.
Millions. The exact number is unknown.

Nixon and MLK represented USA.
Transfer was peaceful.
This decade is the decade of African independence- he wanted a United States of Africa.
Flag should be three horizontal strips, red, orange and green, with a black star in the yellow band.

The Mau Mau goals were to get the British out of power in Kenya, and to get the European settlers out as well, so they terrorized the settler population.
The British dealt with the Mau Mau Uprising harshly, with direct military force. Not as harshly as Victoria dealt with Theodore of Ethiopia's forces, however. The will to domination is not as strong anymore.

He says apartheid is a policy of good neighborliness, accepting there are differences between people, but at the same time live together like good neighbors always do.

Smith: Independence. British: Get colony back; put under majority rule. African Rhodesians: Majority rule.

Postcolonial Conflicts
Answers will vary depending on which conflicts the student investigated.

Matching Political Leaders and Their Goals
1. D, 2. H, 3. K, 4. Q, 5. I, 6. B, 7. T, 8. C, 9. E, 10. A, 11. W, 12. X, 13. G, 14. F, 15. M, 16. U, 17. V, 18. O, 19. L, 20. J, 21. S, 22. N, 23. P, 24. R.

Regime Change
Answers will vary on objectives, but as for who the U.S. supported and installed, and by what method, we may say: Hawaii, Cuba, Puerto Rico and the Philippines were all direct occupations, Panama was occupied in order to build the canal, Honduras was Bonilla, Nicaragua, Haiti and Dominican Rep. were all occupations, in Russia failed support went to the White Army under Kornilov, Panama was Arango, Italy was Gasperi, Greece was Papandreou, Philippines was Osmena, Belgium was Pierlot, Netherlands was Beel and the Queen, Wilhelmina, France was deGaulle, in Germany Adenauer was installed, in Japan a democratic government was installed and the Meiji emperors kept on as figureheads, in China failed support was given to Chaing Kai-Shek who fled to Taiwan, Syria it was Za'im, Korea Syngman Rhee, Egypt Nasser, Iran Shah Mohammad Reza Pahlavi, Guatemala Armas, Congo Mobutu, Laos Nosavan, Dominican Bosch, Cuba was the failed Bay of Pigs, where the U.S. supported the anti-Castro rebels, Brazil Branco, Vietnam was first the Army of the Republic of South Vietnam, then (Vietnam 2) was the South, Dominican was Balaguer, Indonesia Suharto, Greece Papadopoulos, Bolivia Banzer, Iraq Kurdish rebels, Chile Pinochet, Afghanistan the Mujahideen (and bin Laden), El Salvador the Atlacatl Batallion, Nicaragua the Contras, Ecuador Larrea, Panama Aguilar, Granada Austin, Panama Endara, Iraq Kuwait (though, in an unusual situation, Saddam Hussein kept power in Iraq), Indonesia Habibie, Yugoslavia Kostunica, Afghanistan Karzai, Iraq al-Maliki (after a transitional government), Syria no one, as U.S. supported groups did not oust Assad, who has Iranian and Russian support, Palestine the Fatah faction, in Libya a temporary Government of National Accord still runs things, Yemen Hadi, Syria same as before, the U.S. supports rebels against Assad, who remains in power, Venezuela Guaido, and in Iran, the U.S. supports the nascent anti-governmental forces, though no military action has been taken.

Elaan of Troyius
1. Answers will vary.
2. He is to educate her in the culture and manners of the people of Troyius, the leader of which she will wed.
3. No.
4. B.
5. C.
6. She respects his strength, something Petri did not show. It is part of her culture.
7. She tears up and he touches the tear, which has a biochemical reaction on him.
8. Her necklace is made of crystals common in her star system, which are nice, like gold to the West Africans, and usable as jewelry, but to the outlanders, it is precious, like gold is to us (or oil). It is dilithium, which is the fuel that powers starships! That's also why the Klingons were interested in the star system.
9. She gives him her dagger, having learned that "on Troyius they have a different culture- they don't carry daggers around."
10. Answers will vary, of course, but it might be a good discussion to have here. Psychologists say some people marry for eros (attraction), ludus (playfulness), storge (companionate friendship), mania (obsession) agape (actual deep, selfless love) and/or pragma (rationality). Rationality? What does that have to do with love! Well, it has to do with why people get together. Sometimes 'love' isn't the reason. Elaan married for pragma.

Iranian Revolution
Safavids: Made Shi'a Islam the official religion in 1501
Qajars: gave the Shi'a clergy official power (hence the Ayatollah today)
A.
1906: Forced ruling Qajars to accept constitution, made parliament, protected minority rights. Failed.
Farsi (Persian).
1921: British supported Reza Shah who turned Persia into a modern secular state.
1935: Renamed Persia "Iran"
Both were secular leaders, both Westernized/modernized the country to an extent.
1941: Muhammad Reza Shah took over from his dad after dad abdicated.
1951: Wider latitude in elections and Muhammad Mossadeq, nationalized oil industry. No more democracy.
1963: British and CIA helped engineer a coup to remove Mossadeq, who quit, and Shah and Shi'a clergy supported that. Shah instituted a "White Revolution" that helped develop Iran's oil industry and infrastructure, and education.
1975: Shah abolished parties, except his own. Autocracy was in Iran to stay.
Khomeini did not like the White Revolution because reforms brought rights to women, like voting, but he said government was corrupt, neglected the poor, and sold oil to Israel. Also, the very idea of a king (shah) is, he said, un-Islamic (there were caliphs in the past, but that's different than a king).
1978: protesters were dissatisfied with repression, corruption, unemployment, especially in Tehran, and yes, some Shi'a fundamentalism. State newspaper criticized Khomeini, and protesters came out, and cops shot them. People didn't like American pop culture being "the goal of life".

1979: Shah thought prosperity he brought in White Revolution would be enough. It wasn't. He abdicated, and moved to America. Islamic revolution was successful, a real revolution. Islamic Republic of Iran under sharia law. Ayatollah was supreme ruler.
Democratic because it has elections for president and parliament. Women can vote. People voted in a fair election for the Islamic Republic.
Undemocratic because it isn't the will of the people but the will of Allah that is ultimate authority in the constitution. Khomeini created Hezbollah to defend the revolution against coup attempts. Created sharia courts. State-run media.

Chapter 23: Capitalism and Culture: The Acceleration of Globalization

Population Through Time
1. Europe, China and India
2. Mongol invasion, then the Bubonic Plague
3. Not many, answers will vary.
4. Industrialization, sanitation
5. Not very much changed
6. Continued rapid increase, perhaps past 8.5 billion.

Graph should be rather stable with slight dips in the mid-1200s to account for the Mongol invasions which killed ~16 million people in an age when populations were small, and the mid-1300s to account for the Black Death, which killed ~100 million people worldwide. It should rise very slightly after 1500 and then increase dramatically from 1800 on. The ~100 million dead in 20th century wars are about the same as the Black Death total, but the overall effect was much less, heartless as that might seem when thinking about it.

Earth: Cosmic Paradise or… Other?
Answers will vary a bit, but should all be succinct summaries of the sections.

Civs and Dynasties @ a Glance
This one is wide open as to grading. First time one in most categories? Should we brainstorm a list as a class?

The Geography of Disney

North America: Dumbo, Bambi, Song of the South, Ichabod Crane, Davy Crockett, Davy Crockett, Lady and the Tramp, Johnny Tremain, The Rescuers, Pete's Dragon, Fox and the Hound, Oliver & Company, Brave Little Toaster, Pocahontas, Toy Story, A Bug's Life, Wreck-it-Ralph, The Incredibles, Brother Bear, Teacher's Pet, Home on the Range, Chicken Little, The Wild, The Cars, Bolt, Princess and the Frog, Planes, Inside Out.
Europe: Snow White (Germany), Pinocchio (Italy), Fantasia (Austria), Peter and the Wolf (Russia), Cinderella (France), Alice in Wonderland (England), Robin Hood (England), Peter Pan (England), Sleeping Beauty (France), 101 Dalmatians (England), Sword in the Stone (England), Mary Poppins (England), The Aristocats (France), Winnie the Pooh (England), Great Mouse Detective (England), Black Cauldron (Wales), Beauty and the Beast (France), Hunchback of Notre Dame (France), Hercules (Greece), James and the Giant Peach (England), Return to Neverland (England), Tangled (Germany), Brave (Scotland), Frozen (Norway), Gigantic (England).
Latin America: Three Caballeros, Emperor's New Groove, Up
Middle East / North Africa: Aladdin, Duck Tales
Sub-Saharan Africa: The Lion King, Tarzan
South Asia: The Jungle Book, Arjun
East Asia: Mulan, Spirited Away, Ponyo, Big Hero Six
Southeast Asia: None
Oceania: The Rescuers Down Under, Lilo & Stitch, Moana
Out in or Under the Sea: Treasure Island, 20,000 Leagues Under the Sea, The Little Mermaid, Atlantis, Nemo
Prehistory / Future: Dinosaur, Wall-E
Other Worlds / Places Out There: Man in Space, Man and the Moon, Mars and Beyond, Monsters, Inc., Treasure Planet, Zootopia

Disputes: Fantasia is only partially in Vienna, but it's nice to know it's role in the world of classical music. Guilt by association. You can make a case that Treasure Island is partly in "Europe" (England). You can make a case that Peter Pan and Return to Neverland are in "Other Worlds" part of the time. You could make the case that the Little Mermaid is "Caribbean" i.e.: Latin America as well as 'Under the Sea'. You can make a case that Atlantis is an 'Other World'. Lilo & Stitch is a tough one, because is Hawaii part of Oceania or part of North America? Well, it's the northernmost island of Polynesia, which is a subdivision of Oceania. You could say Gigantic was part 'Other World.'

Musical Journey
This one is wide open. Students need only rate the composition according to whatever criteria you set, and say whether they've heard the piece before or not. It's the end of the year, and we're feeling fine!

Thank You!

If this resource book has no use for you, it has no value. We strive to make materials you can actually *use*. No waste, no filler, only usable resources with minimal marginalia aligned with the course for convenience. This is how *Tamm's Textbook Tools* works:

Coursepak A, the *Assignments* series has daily book-based guided readings for homework or in class. It has the vocab, people and chapter work covered, along with some application and subjective questions. Look for the Strayer 4th.

Coursepak B (this one), The *Bundle* series of bell-ringers, warm ups and openers, available on *Amazon* and elsewhere, has material to be used as grabbers at the beginning of an hour, along with reading comp., online activities if students have computer time, multimedia and video clip response forms, short answers, and tickets-out-the-door. Look for the AP World History *Bundle* coursepak as well.

Coursepak C, The *Competencies* and *Crossovers* series, is the part of the *Tamm's Textbook Tools* line that goes into more depth on the one hand (competency) and stretches out to connect the disciplines (crossover). If you teach World History, for example, and want a history of the great moments and big ideas in the development of human cultures, or if you want to get an integrated curriculum crossover going with English, Math, Science, Fine Arts, Foreign Languages, or another department of the school, a *Coursepak C: Competencies and Crossovers* might be what you're looking for.

Look for these and more in the *Tamm's Textbook Tools* series, a low-cost, timesaving way to find high quality, custom materials tailor made to textbooks in many different subjects. Contact the marketing department anytime with suggestions, corrections and any other correspondence at hudsonfla@gmail.com. Find *TTT* on Facebook as well. Please inform your colleagues of the existence of this series if you think it will benefit them. Thank you!

© 2019 David Tamm

Made in United States
North Haven, CT
18 March 2023

34267239R00135